Simply Nora
"High Heels and Diapers"

Based on true events

by

Theodore Marquez

A Club Lighthouse Publishing USA Book

ISBN: 978-1499648430

For information contact:
comments@clublighthousepublishing.com

A Club Lighthouse Biography Edition
Published in USA

"Rare Beauty"

*A single seed
From her majesty
The most rare
African Black Rose
Is
The offspring
Of its
Magnificent blossom*

*You too
Like this seed
Are
The origin
Of a very
Unique
And splendid flower*

*So rare
She
May be found
But once
In a lifetime*

*Yet
Will exist forever
Through
The blossoms
Of her seed
Then again
Through
Their seed*

*'Tis
The rarest
Of beauty.
Our Mother....*

Family. The source from which we draw strength.

In Memory of:

Mother: Nora Marquez
Father: Ed Marquez

Daughter: Flora Aragon
Son: Rudy Marquez
Son: Lawrence Marquez

Granddaughter: Peggy Aragon
Grandson: Larry Aragon
Granddaughter: Barbara Jean Le Blanc
Grandson: Ernest Jr. Gurley
Great-Grand-daughter: Desiree Francisco
Granddaughter: Becky Gurley
Great Granddaughter: Samantha (Samii) Marquez
Grandson: Jerry Aragon

And those who passed before.

I wish to thank those listed below for their contribution to this book. I couldn't have done this without you. You helped make this dream become a reality.

Pricilla Gurley.
Juanita Le Blanc.
Billy Marquez.
Charlotte Martinez.
Becky Duran.
Carole Francisco.
Cordie (Maria) Rubio.
Andrew Marquez.
Jimmy Marquez.

CHAPTER 1

1929. HERBERT HOOVER BEGINS his doomed presidency. The Great Depression looms. Legalized gamblers frolic in Las Vegas. Production of Ford Motor's venerable Model T is a thing of the past. The Dust Bowl leaves havoc in its path. Gasoline sits at a staggering ten cents a gallon.

* * * * *

IT IS MAY OF THAT year in South Fork, Colorado, far from the hustle, bustle and chaos of the times. Spring carpets the landscape with brilliant shades in bloom. Wildflowers blanket meadows in an explosion of color. Lilac bushes perfume the spring breeze with sweetness irresistible to hummingbirds and bees. Butterflies flutter in and out of blossoms in search of the lingering scent in the air teasing their instincts.

An eagle soars on currents overhead, its cry echoing in the mountains and cliffs. Ice yields to the warming sun. Rivers and creeks swell. Drops of morning dew sparkle like diamonds.

Taking it all in was Nora Prien, who sat up against a rock beside a creek near her home at the base of Beaver Mountain, an area known by the locals as *El Bosque,* or The Forest. The majestic cliffs soaring above it were once a lookout for Native Americans.

Today, May 24th was Nora's thirteenth birthday. Over the years of her young life, Nora had spent hours and hours at this creek where nature and thought were her only companions. At times, she had ice skated here with Christine, her older sister by a year plus. The thawing surface of the creek wore scars of their skating escapades.

But this was more than another birthday. This was a day of joy and apprehension. Soon she was to be a bride. Destiny had called her name. Next to her sat her favorite doll, its face worn and faded with time, its gaze seeming to hold secrets.

Suddenly, a single word broke the stillness.

"Nora!"

The stern voice of her mother, Rebecca, pierced nature herself. Even the wildlife stood still as that voice barged into the serenity Nora found here. But today nature sensed something more, that the path of destiny was about to unfold. It was though nature celebrated fate at its birth.

But Nora heard nothing. She was deep in thought of the new adventure life was about to bestow upon her. The morning sun glistened through her dark, curly hair, newly trimmed for the big day ahead. Her olive complexion spoke of the German-Native American heritage she wore proudly. A beauty mark on the right side of the chin gave Nora her undeniable uniqueness. At thirteen she had blossomed into a young woman prepared for the fate that awaited her.

"Nora!" the voice boomed again. This time she heard it, quickly arose, took her doll by the arm and started back home.

At the top of the trail sat their house. A chrome bucket next to the water pump reflected the sun into Nora's eyes when she walked by. The house was simple yet had an elegance all its own. A porch in front beckoned family and visitors. Hummingbirds feasted on succulent nectar of the blossoms found all around. There was a coop for chickens, a hutch for rabbits, a fenced enclosure for goats and lambs, a barn for horses. A wagon stood at the ready for logging.

Rudolf and Rebecca's home

The screen door creaked when she stepped into the kitchen that went the full length of the house. The aroma of ginger bread just out of the cast iron oven greeted her. Next to the ginger bread on the counter top sat trays of fresh cinnamon rolls.

"Child, where have you been? I've been screaming my fool head off!" Rebecca scolded.

"At the creek. I was just thinking."

"You think too much. It's time for breakfast. What's with you and that darned creek?"

"Sorry."

Many times Nora had questioned the anger, the resentment of Rebecca toward her. She could not understand it, nor ever would throughout her life. She could only question in silence.

At the breakfast table Nora sat with the family in prayer, another of Rebecca's rules in the household. Religion came before chores or anything else.

At the head of the table sat her father, Rudolf, presiding over Rebecca, the boys William, Charles, Henry, Ernest and Ted, and the girls Nora and Christine. Rudolf was a lumberjack, had been most of his life. Next to him sat Nora, his pride and glory, his world. Below the table top Nora was careful not to hit his stiffened leg caused by an injury suffered long ago. How she loved him.

Rudolf's heart ached as he glanced at her. He hated the mere thought of his baby girl married off at such an early age. To him, she was a child in a woman's body. Desperately he had fought against it only to find himself in confrontation with Rebecca's domineering, harsh disposition. There were only two choices: her way or else.

Still, he had vowed to stay at Nora's side no matter what. Some time ago Rebecca had promised Nora's hand to a man she knew and admired. The wedding was set for the following month, June 19th. Tears filled his eyes. An aching tormented his heart.

* * * * *

RUDOLF'S FATHER, HEINRICK PRIEN, was born in Holstein, Prussia (now Hamburg, Germany) in October 1850 and emigrated from there at the age of seventeen during a German-Russian war. He went with his brothers John and Fred and settled in New York. Later he settled in Wisconsin, then in Las Tusas, New Mexico, in the late 1800s. There he married Nicanora Martinez, born in February 1881. She was a New Mexico native. They had six children: Cristina, born 1884. Rudolph born 1886. Emma born 1889. Enes born 1892. Federico born 1893, and Emilia born 1898. They lived on a fifty two-acre farm.

Rebecca's parents were David and Tonia Allen. Tonia's maiden name was Roybal. Rebecca was their only child. Rebecca had three half brothers, Ted, Joe and Andrew, and one sister, Charlotte, from her father's second marriage and three half sisters, Genoveva, Cleofes and Carmel, from Tonia's second marriage. For reasons known only to David and Tonia, Rebecca was adopted and raised by a minister, Vicente Romero, and his wife in New Mexico.

She attended school in Tres Pierdas through the eighth grade and was then issued a teaching certificate after several days of testing in Santa Fe. She taught school in Santa Fe and in Taos. It was in Taos where she met Rudolf. Rebecca later taught English to the Native American children on a reservation. She knew five dialects of Indian, Spanish and English and had ties to her ancestors, the Sioux Indians of the Dakotas. Rebecca was born February 22, 1890.

* * * * *

NORA WAS BORN IN Las Tusas. From the moment she left the womb, Rudolf knew she was special – destiny's child. She was named after his mother.

Rudolf always recalled the countless times he held Nora in his arms gazing into her eyes, how he told her she was special, unique in every way. Tragically, it was this closeness, this bond that drove the wedge between Nora and Rebecca and disrupted their entire family.

The resentment became so great that at the tender age of two, Nora was placed in a boarding house, breaking Rudolf's heart. He despised Rebecca for her harsh decision to tear Nora away from him into the care of strangers.

In 1921, when Nora was five, the family moved to Colorado. For weeks upon weeks they traveled across the plains and prairies by covered wagon, with plans to rendezvous with Rebecca, who traveled by train into the San Luis Valley with infant Charlie. The other children, Nora, Christine, Henry, William and Ernest, had no choice but to rough it.

The days were long and dreary, sometimes hot and dusty. The nights were often chilly, uncomfortable and difficult on the children. Some nights the sky became a blanket of stars over the darkened prairie lands. The glow of the moon was their only guidance once the sun made its descent.

After what seemed like an eternity, Rudolf brought the wagon to a halt three months later in Wagon Wheel Gap, Colorado. There he and Rebecca planted roots and commenced to raise their family. Nora's eyes were filled with excitement. The mountains seemed enormous to her, like giants out of an enchanted story once read to her in the boarding home.

* * * * *

AFTER BREAKFAST, NORA SAT at her dresser gazing into the mirror. She found it hard to conceive the idea of marriage. She had no idea of what it could or would be all about, knew precious little about household responsibilities. Life had just begun for her.

Her thoughts were on Edumino, whom most called Ed, born May 16, 1907, nine years her senior. Rebecca and Ed's parents, Delfino and Atanasia Marquez, had arranged the marriage a few years before. As usual, Rudolf was allowed nothing to say about it. Ed, the youngest of six, had three brothers, Jose, Max and Rumaldo, and two sisters, Pauline and Cresalia. Over the years, Ed had watched Nora blossom. One day a mere child, she almost suddenly had become to him a young woman who captured his heart. He knew destiny called his name the very first time his eyes set on Nora.

By nature, Ed was a kind and compassionate man. He was of Spanish-Indian descent. His middle name was Barcelon. A proud man, he had little education but a will of iron. He was a carpenter by trade. A Navajo heritage gave him his sharp features, high cheekbones and a classic Indian nose and profile. Esquibel, not Marquez, was his real last name. His ancestors were slaves and took the name of their master.

Like Nora, Ed had a hunger for life. A love of music was something the two of them shared. Nora enjoyed nothing more in life than music and dancing. To get Nora on the dance floor was to see her come to life. She literally danced with destiny.

Ed played with the local band during Saturday night dances. He peered from behind his fiddle, admiring Nora whenever she stepped into the dance hall with her sister as chaperone. It seemed everybody knew or had heard of the Prien sisters. Christine had hair the color of new copper. Where there was a camera you could also find her. She photographed well. She and Nora were extremely close in growing up. Christine's photo sat on Nora's dresser. Many times she took Nora under her wing to shield her from the harshness of Rebecca's resentment. She, too, had felt its scorn. Her salvation came from a gentleman known to all as Uncle Tom, who took an instant liking to Christine and grew to love her as he would his own daughter. He was a wealthy man, provided well for her.

* * * * *

A KNOCK AT THE door broke into Nora's thoughts. It was Rudolf. She ran a brush through her hair and opened the door for him. He looked concerned, as always. As the wedding day grew nearer, the broken heart ached more and more.

"You were quiet at breakfast," he said. "Are you all right?"

"I was just thinking."

"Your mother tells me you think too much."

"I can't help it, Daddy. There's a lot to think about."

"Your mother's hard to understand. She really doesn't mean the things she says and does sometimes. She really has a good heart. Sometimes I don't understand her myself. I don't know why she does the things she does. But ..."

Both of them knew his words were lies.

Nora tried to comfort her beloved father. "You don't have to worry about me. Really."

"If that man hurts you in any way ..."

She laughed, taking his hand in hers.

"Don't worry. I'll tell you if anything happens. He's not going to hurt me."

"I have something for you," he said, holding out a small box wrapped in blue, Nora's favorite color.

Inside were purple, handmade, mesh earrings in the form of roses.

"They're beautiful. Why do you always give me jewelry?" she asked, holding up the earrings.

"Because you wear it the way it should be worn. The way it was meant to be worn. Happy Birthday."

For a moment he embraced her. Words were not needed. The bond between them would never perish, would last for eternity. The sweetness of her hair filled his head with each heavy breath he took in. His Nora – his world. Whatever was he to do without her? What would he do without her to awaken for each day? He would miss having her presence in the house, the scent of her perfume that reminded him of his purpose for living.

A kiss on the forehead and then he walked out of the room with his head held low.

Nora listened as his footsteps faded. Moments later she heard Rebecca's voice in conflict with her father's. Quietly she stepped into the hallway to listen more closely. Her heart ached while she listened to her father's pleas.

"Rebecca, she's too young for God's sake! She's just a child! Why are you doing this to her? To me? I beg of you, Rebecca, please reconsider. The times are too hard for young folks."

"This depression has no effect on us. We are accustomed to struggling as Nora is. It's the wealthy who are hit the hardest. That hardly includes us. My decision is made! There's no more to discuss. You know what will happen if you try to stop it."

"How can I forget? You remind me of it constantly. You've given me a choice between this and my family. What is it about her, Rebecca? What has she ever done to you besides being born? It seems there's nothing that poor child can do to please you but leave. You are a wicked woman. The things you have put that child through are inexcusable. Unforgivable."

Nora could only suffer inside as Rudolf stomped out of the house, slamming the door behind him. The fear of losing his family left him unable to do anything but observe and tolerate.

Nora sat back at her dresser. It seemed nothing was to prevent her unity with Ed; forces beyond anyone's control were at work. Some things were just meant to be.

Next to her bedroom was the living room. Rebecca played the piano, the notes from her favorite gospel hymn, *"That Old Rugged Cross,"* filling the house and blending with the rich aromas from the kitchen. Nora found herself humming along. Today, the notes held a distinct sadness.

For an hour Rebecca's music filled the house. The piano was an escape when the anger was too heavy a burden even for her. In her heart she felt Nora's fate was no longer in her hands. She believed the path Nora was to walk had long since been set. Not even she could alter its course. She, too, had always felt Nora had been born "destiny's child." It frustrated her to think fate had more control over her child than she did. The other children were unlike Nora. They all had their individuality, but Nora's was unique. She had destiny on her side. Perhaps the conflict was not resentment, but frustration.

When the music stopped, Nora knew it was time to go. Many chores awaited. And much needed to be done before June 19th so much to learn with so little time. Rebecca's discipline was a cruel teacher.

That afternoon, Rudolf beckoned Nora to the front porch where he had a camera set. He prepared her for a snapshot sitting in his favorite dress of copper and blue tones. This photo he would carry to his grave.

Rebecca stood in the background observing. He noticed the look of resentment in her eyes when he glanced up at her. A look he struggled with daily. Through the lens he admired Nora in bloom. It seemed like only yesterday he held her in his arms as a baby. The lens now revealed the young woman she had become almost overnight. He sighed and took the picture. Tears filled his eyes.

Nora

CHAPTER 2

JUNE 19TH ARRIVED. NORA'S heart burned with anticipation, excitement. She rose early, sitting in solitude gazing out of her open bedroom window. The glow of the descending full moon cast soft shadows against her face. Stars filled the sky. An occasional falling star shot across the heavens. She closed her eyes and made a wish.

From a spruce tree beyond the bedroom window an owl's call carried through the silence. The glow of the moon reflected in its eyes as they peered through branches. A lost cloud roaming across the vast sky cast its shadow over the land when it passed before the moon. Nature was at peace.

A tear found its way down her face when certain, special memories filled her mind. In many ways the thought of marriage frightened her. The thought of being away from the security of her father brought her fear of its own. She couldn't help but wonder what awaited her. What would it be like without her father and siblings?

A soft breeze swept through, causing a stir within the silence of the room. Next to her, moonlight crept in and out of the fine stitches and fibers of her wedding dress hanging against the wall. Moonbeams reflected off the white satin below the lace in delicate pink and lavender hues. They, too, seemed to whisper secrets of their own.

New melodies filled the air as time slipped away. Birds with their morning concertos sang from the treetops. Night creatures retreated into their dwellings. From the chicken coop a rooster's crow greeted the dawn. A new day was born, a special day, an unforgettable day for young Nora.

She sat at her dresser. The mirror cast the room in reflection. She would miss this bedroom that had been her escape from the sometimes cruel realities of life. She thought of her sister, of how she'd missed her since the day Christine had left the household for good. To this day she still questioned why. Behind her sat boxes and boxes of packed belongings almost eager for this day to arrive.

Noises came from the kitchen as Rebecca prepared for this day. Much had to be done. After the wedding, dinner was to be served at the reception. Many would come together for this occasion. Following the reception there would be a dance in honor of the newlyweds. Once more Nora heard her father's voice in conflict with Rebecca's, only to fade all too quickly when the tone hardened.

Nora heard a knock at her bedroom door. She opened it to find Rudolf, his eyes sorrowful, on the verge of tears.

"I wanted to see you before they took you away."

"You look troubled, Daddy. I wish you wouldn't take this so hard."

"I know. I'm trying to be happy for you. I just can't. Something in my heart won't let me."

"I think too much, and you worry too much. That's what Mama says."

"Yes, she does say that. I wish she would worry sometimes herself. I will never understand today. A day of sadness."

Rebecca's booming voice beckoned Rudolf. He sighed deeply, taking Nora in his arms as though never to let go.

While dressing she could hear Rudolf and Rebecca. Even in these final moments he pleaded with Rebecca to reconsider. She would do nothing of the sort. Relief touched Nora's heart when another knock at the door brought Christine into the room. Filled with emotion, she'd promised to help Nora get ready. Deep sighs betrayed her sadness.

"It never ends, does it?" she said. "Bet you're happy to be getting out of all this mess. I brought these for you." She handed Nora a bag containing silk and rayon dresses. Christine had a flair for fashion.

In the background they heard Rudolf slam the door and leave the house in disappointment.

Nora pulled out several garments. "They're beautiful. Thank you. I love silk and rayon." She paused. "I'll miss Daddy."

"You'll do fine – so will he. You just have to get through this day first. Look at me. I'm a mess! And you're the one getting married."

"Yes I am, aren't I?" Nora said, pausing in front of the mirror. "I still can't believe it. It just doesn't seem possible."

"With Mom, anything is possible. Haven't you learned that by now? You'll be glad to get out of here. Believe me."

"I just don't know if I'm ready for this."

"You'd better be, because it's here."

"It's like I didn't even have a choice."

"Did we ever? You know what Mom says goes. We never had much choice with anything. Not even this. I don't understand and guess I never will."

"Understand what, Christine?"

"Why Mom does the things she's done to us. I mean, look at you. You're still a kid. You still play with dolls, which you know will have to stop. Here she is marrying you off. Do you love this man? He's almost ten years older than you."

"I guess. Yes, I suppose I do. He's good to me. And you know how he cares for me. I couldn't ask for somebody who cares for me more than he. He's kind. He makes me laugh. Besides, he promised to take me dancing every Saturday night."

"Yes, but there's more to marriage than dancing on Saturday nights. Did you ever think of that? Did Mom ever talk to you about what's involved in marriage?"

"A little. She said most I would have to learn on my own. I guess it's like with anything in life."

"What if he wants kids? Are you ready for that?"

"I don't like to think about that. I don't know."

"You have to think about these things, Nora. Didn't Mom discuss anything with you?"

"Now you're beginning to sound like her. And no, she didn't."

"What about Ed? What does he have to say about all this? You hardly know him."

"No, I don't. But Mom says I could get to know him. Besides, she said we were promised to each other. He says he cares for me."

"Well, I'll be there when you need me. You know that. Now let's get you ready. You're going to look beautiful."

"I want to wear these," Nora said, handing Christine the new earrings. "Aren't they beautiful? Daddy gave them to me."

"Yes they are, but I don't think they're going to match with what you'll be wearing."

"I don't care. I want to wear them anyway. I'll never get rid of them."

A half hour later they both stood back admiring her reflection. Nora truly was beautiful. And Christine was right. Her strand of pearls did clash with the earrings. But Nora didn't care. Her hair was full in masses of curls and waves. Christine had fixed her makeup to perfection. Her dress fell in layers of lace above the knee. Her ankle-strapped heels went well with the garment. No bride could have been more beautiful than Nora was on this day. Tears of joy filled Christine's eyes just to look at her sister.

* * * * *

RUDOLF LOST HIS BREATH when Nora stepped out of the house into the bright, sun-filled morning. Dark blues and purples glistened in her hair. Her dress swayed with every delicate move she made. Never had he seen her look more beautiful.

Rebecca stood in the background with almost a glare at Nora, observing her every move as she stepped into Rudolf's arms.

"Enough slobbering," she finally pronounced. "Atanasia and Delfino are here for a photograph." Ed's parents were equally eager for this day.

Rebecca stepped off the porch with them at her side, proceeding to position the couples for the photo shoot.

Nora and Ed were in the center. To Nora's left stood Atanasia, then Delfino. Ed admired Nora through eyes of awe. To merely gaze upon his young bride set his heart in flames. Next to Ed Rebecca and Rudolf stood. Rudolf wore a broken heart, and even Rebecca looked in the opposite direction with certain sadness.

Rudolf and Rebecca   Ed and Nora   Atanasia and Delfino

Atanasia was proud of her son, more so that he'd found himself such a bride. But she and Delfino were also concerned that Nora was so young. Even they had little say when it came to Rebecca's domineering personality. Atanasia had taken Nora under her wing to help in what awaited the young bride. They knew their son loved Nora beyond a doubt. This was the strength from which they drew.

Later that day Nora stood dazed before the preacher. It seemed like a dream. It was hard to believe that from this day forth she would not return to her home. That she would no longer hear her father's voice each morning awakening her at daybreak. Thoughts were heavy. Vows spoken seemed like echoes.

She glanced around the chapel at the many faces of friends and relatives. In many ways when she said "I do" it was a farewell to the life she knew and felt secure in. To the life she once cherished—a life soon to become a memory—perhaps a long, lasting craving.

Rudolf sighed when the vows were over. Tears filled his eyes. A lump swelled in his throat. In silence he prayed for her happiness, her well being. Through blurred vision he glanced at Rebecca, then at Ed. In his heart he knew from this day his life with Rebecca would never be the same. The pain Rebecca had placed in his heart would never find peace. His broken heart would never mend.

Instinctively, Nora's eyes met his when she and Ed walked by on their way out of the chapel. She smiled and whispered "I love you" into his ear. Rebecca turned her face, finding it difficult to look her in the eyes.

The sun was bright. A cool spring breeze swept over the mountain range. Standing with her husband for more photos, Nora basked in the moment as a new bride. Her fears and worries gave way to eyes of joy. Ed had promised to dance through life with her, to help make her dreams come true. She was ready to take on the world with whatever challenges were before her. She was content, in many ways happy. At last she had broken away from the harshness of Rebecca's web of resentment.

Ed looked at her with ever so much pride. One of his dreams had come true. In his heart he knew Nora was the one for him. He knew it from the moment he set eyes on her. His heart was on fire at the mere sight of his bride. She was ever so beautiful standing in the sun's glow. With admiration she gazed back at him.

One person observed in the background with a gleam in her eye. For reasons known only to her, she resented Nora, even more so now that Ed had married her. She had cautioned Ed from the beginning, planting seeds of doubt in his mind. Nevertheless, not even she could destroy the love he had for Nora.

The breeze whispered through the spruce, pine and aspen down into the valleys and meadows. Gently it swept through Nora's hair, shifting the curls and swaying the layers of lace on her dress. The pearls around her neck reflected the sun in glorious hues. The earrings from Rudolf stood out proudly against the pearls.

* * * * *

THAT NIGHT, NORA DANCED with destiny, with life. Her laughter came from the heart. How she wished the night would last forever, the music a lifetime. With the music she and Ed would glide across the floor. Love was theirs.

Rudolf sat at Rebecca's side observing Nora and Ed through the night. An injured leg kept him from the dance floor. It made him uneasy to see Ed's possessiveness of Nora. He wondered to what extent it would go. Many young men were attracted to Nora. It was her passion for life that made her different, separating her from all others. She had an unmistakable flare, the quality that kept Ed on his toes. In his heart Rudolf knew she was never to come home again. He worried desperately for her. Her youth made her naive to so much in life.

Rudolf snapped to when Rebecca pulled on his coat sleeve. He peered at her through tear-filled eyes and walked away. He was angry, hurt, blaming her for whatever misfortune Nora might encounter in life.

* * * * *

THAT NIGHT RUDOLF LAY in bed staring at the ceiling. The room spun from the whiskey he'd drunk in his attempt to cope with the sadness that Nora now belonged to someone else. The house seemed different. Already the loneliness had set in. Memories echoed through the silence, seeming to dwell within the halls and walls. The scent of Nora's perfume lingered, tormenting him.

Rebecca slept next to him. Her mind and soul were restless. Her face twitched. She mumbled things Rudolf could not understand. She spoke in languages unknown to him. She uttered "Nora" more than once. Through the night he drifted in and out of restless sleep. Visions of Nora haunted him. It was though he'd relived his entire life with her in one very long night. Memories were vivid, so clear in detail. He tossed and turned, struggling to find peace. There was none. The night lasted an eternity.

CHAPTER 3

MARRIED LIFE TURNED OUT to be difficult. Nora's youth and lack of experience brought obstacles into their lives. All she knew was what Rebecca, and then Atanasia for a brief time, had taught in her short life. She knew little cooking, even less in the up keeping of a household. She looked forward to Fridays and Saturdays when Ed would play with the local band at the dances. On the dance floor her troubles vanished.

Most of her days were spent at the homestead, where she could be with Rudolf. It was he who guided her through life, through the ups and downs of marriage. It was he who held her while she wept in doubt and confusion. He was her strength when there was nowhere else to turn – no one to understand the youth in her innocent eyes.

Little by little she learned the basic necessities of maintaining a household. But marriage was far more complicated for her. It didn't take long to become familiar with Ed's moods. She'd come to recognize them the second he stepped through the door after a hard day's work of building homes. She knew not to have her favorite doll in her arms when he came home.

Days turned into weeks. Sometimes she and Christine took to the river to their favorite swimming spot. There she could hold her head back and be herself, and laugh – really laugh. She and Christine shared their deepest secrets. For hours they tossed their troubles to the wind, and enjoyed life to its fullest.

It was on one of these days that Nora became ill. Many times Ed awakened in the wee hours of the morning to find her vomiting. It frightened him to be so helpless in caring for his young bride when she needed him so badly. Neither understood these sudden morning attacks of nausea and discomfort.

Finally, desperate to end her tormented mornings, she consulted Rebecca. Her mother laughed, shaking her head in amazement.

"Child, don't you know your own body? You really don't know what's wrong with you?"

"No. I feel like this nearly every morning. I've tried everything. I just can't stop it," Nora said, finding her mother's humor confusing.

"You're pregnant. That's all that's wrong with you. You're going to be a mother. We both are."

"What? That's not possible! How could this happen? You too?"

"If you don't know by now, you'll never know. You'd better let your father know. He'll be delighted with both our news."

"Are you sure about this? I'm scared."

"I've had enough children to know. Believe me, there is nothing to be afraid of. That's what getting married is all about. Having babies and raising a family."

Nora drew a deep breath and walked away, totally confounded. The thought of her having a baby and being a mother just didn't seem real. It was more like a dream. It didn't seem so long ago that she and Christine joked about her becoming a mother. Today the joke was on her.

Rebecca

Rudolf SUSPECTED SOMETHING WHEN Nora walked up. There was a peculiar look on her face. She was pale, in a daze. He'd not seen her like this before.

"What is it?" he asked, helping her sit next to him.

"I'm okay, Daddy. Mamma just told me something, that's all."

"That explains it. What is she doing this time? What can that woman be up to now?"

"Nothing. She hasn't done anything."

"So what's wrong then?"

"I'm not so sure that it's wrong, Daddy."

"You look like the weight of the world is on your shoulders. Do you want to talk about it?"

"Mamma says I'm pregnant. She said you'd be happy for me."

He didn't respond. His heart sank. He feared this day would come only didn't expect it this soon. He resented Rebecca even more now. He stood.

"I was afraid of that. Are you okay?"

"I guess I am. I don't know. I'm not sure. It doesn't seem possible."

"No, it doesn't. But it's here, and we have to deal with it. You'll do fine."

"I believe that. I really believe that, Daddy. Are you happy?"

"Are you?" he replied reluctantly.

"I think so."

"Then I'm happy for you. I will love your child as I love you."

"I need that, Daddy. I love you," she said, embracing him.

Tears filled his eyes when he watched her walk away, a child having a child. Her introduction to marriage and now motherhood were just all too abrupt to him. All he could do was be at her side whenever she needed him, no matter how often. He felt in his heart that the difficult path she was destined to walk had now begun. The stars had control.

* * * * *

Nora SWELLED A LITTLE more with each week. The thought of having something in her life she could call her own made the discomfort tolerable. It seemed she was constantly in front of the mirror in amazement of the changes her body was going through. Friends and neighbors supplied her and the unborn child with enough of everything to see them through. They showed their true colors.

Older wives in the area came to Nora during the day with their knowledge and experience. What Rebecca failed to teach Nora they were more than willing to. Many were fond of this young mother in bloom. Their hearts filled with compassion for they knew only too well of what she was in store for. They took Nora under their wings, caring for her as though she were one of their own.

She felt the subtle movement of life stirring within her. Ed was happy, seeing to her needs as best he could. The child she carried was an extension of their wedding vows. He was excited about the arrival of his first born. The entire community waited with anticipation and celebration.

Soon the multi-colors of autumn speckled the landscape and mountains. The aspen were ablaze with deep red, yellow and gold shades of fall. Maples were rich with auburn tones. Geese formed designs across the heavens in their migration southbound for the incoming winter.

Days grew shorter. Autumn's chill was in the night air. In the wee hours of the mornings, frost sparkled on the golden leaves and petals of trees and shrubs. Fog crept from mountain tops into the valleys and meadows. Leaves fell and flew, riding the unpredictable winds.

Golden sunlight filled the afternoons. Once more, squirrels and chipmunks gathered nuts and acorns for their long winter storage. Other wildlife sought dens for their annual hibernation. Snowbirds gradually made their appearance, while songs from the chick-a-dee began to fill the crisp morning hours. Streams of smoke from chimneys hidden among the spruce and pine veined the sky, filling it with country aromas.

Gradually, the spirit of Christmas sprouted everywhere. Carols echoed through the stillness of the countryside. Nora glowed with the spirit. Christmas was her favorite holiday. Within her the movement of life brought a happiness she'd never known. Each day that went by she counted with anticipation. Ed wanted a son. To her it didn't matter. A son would be named after her father. A daughter she would call Pricilla.

It turned out that Rebecca gave birth first. He was a boy, born twelve weeks prematurely. He was fragile and tiny. They named him Luther. All were concerned with little Luther. Rebecca and Rudolf did all they could in assisting to his needs, but the entire family was thrust into a state of shock when the baby passed away after just one month. He was laid to rest in the Del Norte Cemetery. Nora's heart was broken. She'd never seen a baby die, and for it to be her brother made it even more devastating. Nora, Rebecca and Christine wept for days on end.

CHAPTER 4

1930. THE COST OF gas is ten cents a gallon, while the average rent for a home is fifteen dollars a month. A loaf of bread costs nine cents, a pound of hamburger thirteen cents a pound. Following the Wall Street Crash, 1,350 banks in the United States fail. The unemployment rate is 8.9%. The government embarks to regenerate the economy, which includes the building of Hoover Dam. The Dust Bowl worsens. The nation can only watch as it sweeps across the heartland, ripping the livelihoods from thousands of families. Between the Wall Street Crash and the Dust Bowl, the country is in peril.

"All Quiet on the Western Front" is on screens across America. *"Three Little Words"* by Duke Ellington is very popular. Television gains momentum for those fortunate enough to afford one. Others gather around radios to keep up with national and world events.

* * * * *

THE NEW YEAR OF 1930 was one of great anticipation for Nora. She grew eager as each day brought her closer to the birth of her first child.

April brought calmness to the mountains. Nora was now in her eighth month. She was big, uncomfortable. Rudolf and Rebecca kept a close eye on her. Ed was concerned about his young wife's health. The midwife made her daily call.

It was early May when signs of birth began to emerge. The child within her seemed restless, eager to face the world. Seldom was Nora left alone. Local wives attended to her personal and household needs—cooking, baking and keeping tabs on the movement within her.

Finally it began. The pain of giving birth was about to plunge Nora into womanhood, motherhood. A world she scarcely even thought about in her young life. The midwife stayed at her side as the labor pains grew more intense. Nora was engulfed with pain so incredible she swore this child would be the first and last. Little did she know. She resented Ed for each spasm of pain that tore through her body. She hated him for not having to share the agony with her.

Just when she felt she could take no more, relief unlike she'd ever known swept through her. Nora collapsed back in the bed, her hair drenched from sweat. Like music to her ears she lifted her head at the sound of the first cry. Nora gave birth to a beautiful girl weighing in at slightly over nine pounds. She had a light complexion with signs of reddish hair.

Pricilla was born on May 8th.

All the while, in the next room, Ed and Rudolf paced the floor. Rebecca sat calmly knitting necessities for the newborn. Also in the room were Atanasia and Delfino. They arrived quickly upon receiving the news of Nora's labor. Their nervousness turned to joy when the midwife stepped out of the bedroom with the infant in her arms announcing it was a girl. All gathered around the child in awe.

But not everyone was happy. Doubtful eyes took in the infant, observed her with a suspicious eye for a moment, then left. This woman hadn't cared for Nora from day one. Yet she never had the courage to say why. She left the house without informing anybody of her departure. Most people called her Hueso, due to her bony stature. In the front yard, Hueso stood in secret conference with other wives of the community, no doubt spreading her gossip. Sixteen days later, on May 24th Nora turned fourteen.

May quickly became June, and just as suddenly summer and fall came and went. Nora and Ed made their home near the sawmill where he worked in addition to helping build homes. Their lives were filled with a new joy since the baby's arrival. All seemed well, almost too good to be true. It was all Nora had hoped married life and motherhood would be. When she was able, on Saturday nights Ed would take her to the local dance hall where he played his fiddle.

It was on one of those joyous Saturday occasions when an event caused a chain reaction of incidents that would occur throughout Nora's life. It was something she had not prepared for but was hardly unexpected.

It started when Nora rose from where she sat with Christine and others and made her way through the crowded dance floor and out the front entrance.

Hueso followed, an aggressive walk in her strut as she shoved her way through.

Nora went to the outhouse behind the dance hall. Hueso stood waiting for her to step out. She glared at Nora and made it obvious something was on her mind. She seemed angry, disturbed. She didn't say anything and waited anxiously for the other ladies to either go into the outhouse or back into the dance hall. Once they were alone she stepped up to Nora.

Nora ignored her and tried to step around, not saying a word. She and Hueso from day one could not get along. Hueso was older than she. There was nothing, in Nora's opinion that she and Hueso shared in common. She was just another face to Nora.

Hueso finally spoke.

"Looks like you're having a good time."

"I always have a good time," Nora replied.

Hueso snickered, glancing down while adjusting her clothing. Her attitude spoke clearly for itself. "That's something you don't have to tell me. I already know that."

"Then I guess there's something else you want to know?"

"As a matter of fact there is. I don't know if this is the time and place for it though."

"Then why did you follow me out here?"

"I didn't follow you. I needed the bathroom if that's all right with you."

"So what's this about then? If you've got something to say, say it and get it off your chest. Or do your business here. It really doesn't matter to me either way."

Hueso wouldn't respond. Her face grew red as Nora turned and walked away.

"You know where I live when you're ready," Nora said.

"Where's your baby?" Hueso asked, immediately getting Nora's attention.

"With her grandmother. Why? What does my baby have to do with this or with you for that matter?"

"Nothing, really."

"Good! Then I guess we're finished with whatever you're trying to prove." Nora started walking away.

"Not when she isn't Ed's," Hueso blurted.

Nora stopped in her tracks. "What did you say?"

"You heard."

"I thought I did, but I want you to repeat it."

"I said, not when she isn't Ed's."

"And how would you know?"

"You may have him blinded but not me."

"This is not even worth listening to," Nora said, walking away again.

"Why not? What are you hiding? Some things we can't hide."

"What are you talking about?"

"That child isn't his."

"If anybody should know that it's me. You don't know what you're talking about."

"That baby is white. A blind man can see that."

"Only a damned fool like you could possibly think something like that! She takes after my side of the family. Are you really that stupid? Yes, you are."

"It's Ed who's the fool. It's him who is blind. Not me. If you don't tell him the truth I will."

"What did you say?"

"You heard."

"You do that. But let me warn you, Hueso. I'll come after you if you hurt my child or home in any way. I'll drag you from one side of this valley to the other. You realize that before you open your big mouth," Nora snapped, shoving her against the outhouse, walking away in frustration.

Christine noticed the anger in Nora when she returned. She knew instantly something had happened. Nora's face was red. Her hands trembled. Christine took Nora by the hand, leading her out onto the dance floor.

Nora told Christine what happened. Luck was on Hueso's side when Nora finally convinced Christine it wasn't worth her trouble to thrash Hueso within an inch of her life. Christine never did care for Hueso to begin with. To her Hueso was a snake in the grass.

Hueso glared at them from where she sat with her husband. She sneered when she saw Nora hold Christine back from getting to her. Hueso's husband was unaware of what was going on. He had no clue. Hueso's snickering and mocking laughter brought Christine's blood to a boil.

Aggressively, Christine fought to break away from Nora's grip. Her face was red with rage. The more Hueso laughed the harder she fought to get at her. They began to draw attention from those around them and from the stage where the band played.

Modesto, Christine's fiancé, went to Christine's side, pulling her back to her seat where he eventually calmed her. Their usual Saturday night out came to an end when he took her and Nora home.

* * * * *

THREE A.M., AFTER THE dance was over, Ed stormed into the house, awaking Nora in the bedroom where she lay with Pricilla in her arms within the glow of the kerosene lamps. Pricilla began to cry. Instantly, Nora knew Hueso was behind it. She had spread her venom.

"Get out of bed!" Ed ordered harshly. "You've got a lot of explaining to do."

"What's the use? It's obvious you already believe what that snake has told you."

"Is it true?" Ed shouted, causing the baby to cry harder.

"You really can't be that stupid. This child is yours. I ought to know, and so should you."

Ed glanced at the baby. "That's why her hair is that color, isn't it?" he yelled.

"I can't believe this. She's a redhead like my sister. She takes after my side of the family. Are you that blind? Or has that snake poisoned your mind that bad?"

"I don't believe it. She doesn't look like me or my family," Ed said.

"Give her time, for Christ's sake. She's just an infant. She can't look like anybody now. Use your damned common sense!"

Nora put Pricilla back on the bed and covered her with blankets.

"I want you to keep that damned woman out of our business. If I have to do it she's going to be sorry. You know damned well she has never liked me. She's been against us since the beginning. Or can't you see that either?"

"It's you who has never liked her."

"You're right, I don't! I can't stand that woman and never will. She's not a damned thing to me nor my child. I don't have to put up with her. And I'll be damned if I will. I don't ever want that woman in my home. Ever!"

"This is my home! She'll come in here any time she feels like it."

"Just let her try. If you don't want her hurt you'll keep her out of here."

Ed's face grew redder. His temples throbbed with anger. He threw Nora on the bed.

"You're going to hurt the baby!" Nora shouted.

Pricilla cried harder when the thrust of Nora hitting the bed bounced her.

"Look what you've done!" Nora yelled.

She rose from the bed in an attempt to lead him away from the child. Abruptly she fell back when Ed slapped her across the face with incredible force. Her nose and mouth bled. Nora lay dazed, unable to comprehend what happened. She started to cry. Instinctively she reached for the baby to shield her from his anger.

Blind with rage, Ed slammed the door on his way out of the room. He threw things against the wall, shattering whatever he got his hands on.

When Nora heard the front door slam she waited a few minutes, then ran out of the house with Pricilla in her arms.

Thirty minutes later, the glow of lamps went on at Rebecca and Rudolf's home. Nora was at the front door. When she told Rudolf what happened he got dressed and rushed out of the house, a man on fire. He'd sworn to kill the first man who dared hurt any of his daughters, especially Nora.

Rebecca tried to reason with him, to no avail. Neither she nor her dominating disposition was able to hold him back. He left her standing in the doorway calling out his name. Her threats echoed through the silence of the wee morning hours into the mountains.

Rudolf found Ed pacing at home and cursing up a storm, whiskey still strong on his breath. Rudolf was on Ed immediately, dragged him outside and thrashed him around the front yard.

"If you dare touch my daughter again I will kill you with my bare hands!" Rudolf screamed over Ed as he lay on the ground.

To Rudolf, for any man to strike a woman was totally inexcusable. That it was one of his daughters, and Nora at that, made it that much worse. The rage in Rudolf's eyes warned Ed of what might happen should he even attempt to challenge him.

Rudolf grabbed Ed off the ground, threw him against the house and slugged him over and over. The vision of Nora standing at the front door bleeding from the nose and mouth would never leave his memory. It tore at his heart. He didn't even care when Ed tried desperately to explain. Nothing would or could justify what he did to Nora.

After Rudolf could no longer continue, he left Ed slumped and coiled in pain, beaten within an inch of his life. Rudolf's main concern was getting to Nora and the baby's side. He left Ed with a final warning should it ever happen again.

Rebecca sat with Nora when Rudolf walked into the house. Nora wiped the blood from her face. Pricilla was in Rebecca's arms, innocent and unaware. He took Nora in his arms, caressing her.

"I'll kill him if he ever hurts you again," he promised.

"That was a foolish thing to do," Rebecca said.

"You are to blame for this," Rudolf snapped back. "It would be wise for you to keep your comments to yourself. You have already done enough damage to this child. To this family! Now shut up! I don't want to hear it!"

In amazement Nora glanced up at him. Never had she heard him talk back to Rebecca in such a manner. Deep in her heart she felt joy. How tired she was of seeing him dominated and manipulated by Rebecca's harshness. She had just witnessed a whole new side to her father. A side she had known would surface one day.

Rebecca sat at a loss for words. She was stunned that he got up the nerve to stand up to her and question her disposition.

"You will stay here tonight and tomorrow if you want. You can stay forever if you'd like. You and your child will always be welcome in my home. This is still and will always be your home. Don't ever forget that. I will always regret the day you married that man. You were too young. You were just a baby yourself," Rudolf told Nora.

"I'll be alright, Daddy. I just need some rest. I'm going to my room," she answered.

"Yes. Both you and the child need rest."

He kissed both Nora and Pricilla and helped them to her bedroom. Moments later he returned to find Rebecca still seated where he left her. Her glare was enough to scare the devil himself.

"You will never speak to me in that manner again!" she barked.

"You have caused enough heartache in my family. I will not tolerate it anymore. Is this the life you wanted for your daughter? Is this why you got rid of her the first chance you got? Doesn't it bother you that she's been beaten?"

"She's a married woman now. She'll have to deal with her own problems."

"She's hardly a woman! She's still a child. It really doesn't bother you, does it? You really don't care. In fact, I believe you find pleasure in seeing her go through this. You are a wicked one."

"Don't be ridiculous. She's my daughter. Of course I care."

"You have a hell of a way of showing it. You have a hell of a way of showing it to any of our children. Someday you will be sorry for all you've done to them, to Nora. Someday."

* * * * *

THE WAVES HUESO SENT through Nora's home brought turmoil for months to follow. Her words lingered in the back of Ed's mind when he thought of or looked at Pricilla. He argued with Nora constantly. When he drank, Hueso's words were like an arrow piercing him. His heart told him it wasn't true, but his mind and Hueso's words told him differently.

Rudolf kept a close eye on Nora. Daily he would visit and inquire of her well being. Not even he had raised a hand to his daughters, and to think of someone else doing it kept him on fire and on edge. His heart would not accept it. The friction between him and Rebecca seemed to never cease. They, too, continuously argued over the matter. He blamed Rebecca in so many ways for Nora's misfortune. For Nora's fate he held under Rebecca's hand, reminding her of it constantly.

Rudolf adored Pricilla. Just knowing she belonged to Nora made her even more special. Pricilla was an extension of what had always meant the world to him. Many times he wandered off in solitude to cry over what his young daughter was going through. Many nights he lay awake focused on the ceiling in deep thought. If only he had stood his ground in spite of the consequences. Seeing Nora go through this was surely far worse than the alternative Rebecca had presented him with.

The sadness in Nora's eyes hurt him each time he spoke to her. Although her smile and laughter were just as radiant as always, he sensed she was not the same inside. The spark had grown dim. She glowed in her motherhood, but the unhappiness was ever so obvious to him. Often he held her in reassurance of his love and support. He wanted so much to take her home and care for her as he always, but the reality of her belonging to someone else reminded him of his limits. The pain in his heart grew heavier with each day that went by.

CHAPTER 5

As FALL SET IN, NORA'S new role as a mother became more and more challenging. If it weren't for the local wives such as Julia and Angelica, she'd have been totally lost. They spent time with her every day teaching the art of motherhood and being a wife. They groomed Nora for the future that awaited, playing an important role in the destiny Nora was about to walk.

Nora's hair grew down to her shoulders in a cascade of waves and curls. She began to learn the art of using make-up, transforming herself into the young, beautiful woman she was becoming noted for. She accentuated the beauty mark on the side of her chin. She turned heads wherever she went. Her beauty kept Ed on his toes, feeding the insecurities Hueso had embedded in him.

Tension was ever so present in Nora's home. The venom Hueso had injected into their lives ate at Ed. He wanted so much to believe in Nora, but Hueso would not let it rest. Frequently she worked on him, driving doubt deeper into his heart. Although his love and passion for Nora remained as strong as ever, doubt was there. This love and passion was obvious to Hueso and those who knew them, thus it made her more determined to drive the wedge she was so certain of into their marriage and home. Nora did her best to diffuse the doubt Hueso had brought into their lives, but the damage was done.

The season's colors blanketed the valley, the landscape ablaze with reds, gold's, browns and yellows. The chill in the air was a premonition of what was on its way.

Ed piled up wood and coal for the harsh weather ahead. South Fork was notorious for its winters, and living in un-insulated homes made the cold feel even colder. Coming home from his daily work of building homes in the area along Church Road kept him busy for months at a time. One by one the homes were erected. He was an artist at his craft. Along with those homes, he kept busy with cabins on Chinook Lane. They were built in the early 1900s. He added to and updated them as he'd done since he was younger before he and Nora married. His passion for carpentry was obvious in whatever he built.

Thanksgiving came and went at Nora and Ed's home. With help from Julia, Angelica and Rebecca, Nora put on her first major dinner. What she'd been taught began to serve its purpose. Little by little, through trial and error, she learned about cooking, cleaning and all the household duties expected of her. At times Nora had Pricilla on one arm, and her favorite doll on the other. A child at heart she still was.

Rebecca was now pregnant with her eighth child. It appeared Pricilla would have a playmate soon. The news swept the valley as most news did. The Priens were more than happy to welcome a newborn into the family.

Nora felt familiar changes in her body during this time as well, so one day when Rebecca was visiting she asked her about it. Rebecca looked at her in astonishment. To see the innocence in Nora amazed her.

"Child, you are pregnant again. We are both expecting, just like the last time."

"I don't understand how this could have happened again," Nora said, putting Rebecca in a state of sheer laughter.

"If I have to explain it to you I will, but I think you already know the answer."

"What am I going to do? What am I going to tell Daddy?"

"Shush. He will be fine, and you will do whatever is necessary. We, of course, will help you all we can. Does Ed know?"

"No. I haven't told him how I've been feeling."

"Well, don't you think you ought to? He needs to know."

"I'll tell him tonight."

Rebecca left Nora's house with a heavy heart. Rudolf's words echoed in her memory. Even she had begun to see the immaturity in Nora, the innocence. The reality that Nora was still merely a child in so many, many ways hit her. Rebecca thought it best to inform Rudolf herself. She worried of what he would say and how he would react if Nora did it.

That night at the dinner table Rudolf glared at her through eyes of resentment when she told him. What he feared for Nora had become a reality. He worried for her even more now. He was concerned what Ed's reaction to the news would be, even more so after the incident with Pricilla. Would this be a repeat of that?

Ed was stunned, yet excited when Nora told him. In spite of what Hueso did, his love for Nora was ever so strong. For him there was no other. He embraced her for in his heart he was certain this child was his.

"We will do fine," he told her.

"I hope so. Does this mean you won't listen to any more gossip?" Nora questioned. She shivered to think of what Hueso might do this time.

"What is done is done," Ed said.

"Nothing has been done. You have a daughter with another child on its way. That is the truth. What you do with that truth is up to you."

Nora could see the gratification in Ed's eyes. She knew without him saying another word that he was pleased, and how he felt.

Outside, winter's first blizzard settled over the valley. Streams of smoke reached from chimneys throughout the land. The scent of burning wood filled the mountain air. In Nora's home a fire blazed in the potbellied stove, providing warmth and cooking the food. The aroma of her food seeped out into the coldness and carried through the neighborhood.

Christmas was a major event for South Fork residents. As always, households were busy with preparations for the upcoming holidays. Julia and Angelica kept Nora filled with necessities needed for the events. They were determined not to let hardship fall upon her and arrived at her home with bags of goods and homemade foods, and more lessons to be taught.

It wasn't long before Ed dragged in a Christmas tree he had cut down in the mountains. He and Nora discussed possible names for the child she carried. He was eager for the arrival. Once again he felt close to Nora, showing his affection constantly.

Rebecca brought over her usual bucket of candy and ornaments ordered from the Montgomery Ward catalog. She joined in sewing together popcorn and cranberry garland to decorate the tree and hung homemade taffy canes she put much love into. Multi-colored construction paper and chain trimmings were added, along with wax candles placed in candle holders neatly attached to the branches, the candles to be carefully lit on Christmas night. Icicles were placed neatly upon the branches, and angel hair completed the tree's dressing. Pricilla gazed at the tree in awe through eyes of innocence. The vivid colors of the tree captivated her.

Nora's pregnancy matured, as did Rebecca's. She couldn't imagine what it was going to be like having two children to care for. Never in her wildest dreams had she anticipated this. When Ed asked her to marry him, she envisioned a life of dancing and laughter. There was nothing she enjoyed more than putting on the beautiful dresses Christine passed down to her, then stepping onto the dance floor in her favorite high heels. She was known for her fashion, a trademark she would carry throughout her life. She turned heads wherever she went.

On Christmas Eve, Pricilla was left with Rebecca and Rudolf. Julia and her husband, Roberto, Angelica and her husband, Naccór, along with members of Ed's band gathered in Nora's home. It was to be an evening of celebration and joy.

Together they made their way from household to household in the cold, stinging air singing Christmas carols both in Spanish and English. This was a tradition carried on from one generation to the next. As they moved from each dwelling, members of the home joined in their caroling. Children were invited along the way with their Christmas bags being filled with goodies from each household visited. The bags brimmed with cookies, candies, apples, oranges and whatever else could be thought of. This was one of the holiday highlights for children. Caroling rang throughout South Fork as the group traveled from house to house.

By midnight they visited nearly every home in the region, finally settling at Roberto and Julia's for the evening event for the adults. Children went home. Guitars and Ed's fiddle began to play. Nora danced to her heart's content. She felt at peace with her surroundings and in knowing Pricilla was safe with Rudolf and Rebecca. She was worry free once again.

Christine and Modesto were also present, along with Hueso and her husband. She glared at Nora dancing with whoever asked her. This fed her bitterness even more. Her thoughts were obvious to Nora when she finally noticed her glare. Nora's laughter told Hueso the energy of her feud was a waste of time. Nothing was about to spoil her evening, especially Hueso.

She'd done enough damage. Christine kept a close eye on Hueso, studying her every move. She didn't trust her.

As the night matured, so did Nora's laughter and Hueso's animosity. In her eyes Nora was making a fool of Ed, knowing nothing of the trust and agreement Nora and Ed had between them. Ed was fine with Nora dancing with whoever asked. He had no reason to mistrust her other than the poison Hueso had driven into his head. His admiration of her was overwhelming to him at times. To him Nora grew more beautiful each passing day.

Christine got onto the dance floor when she noticed Hueso making her way toward Nora. What she feared and expected was coming true. When Hueso took Nora's arm she knew it would not end well. Christine rushed between them. She glared into Hueso's eyes.

"What venom are you about to spread now?" she demanded.

"None of your business," Hueso replied.

"Everything I do is her business," Nora told Hueso. "If you've got something to say, spit it out like you do all your poison."

"Maybe you can make Ed a fool, but you can't me. I know what is going on," Hueso sneered.

"And what is that?" Nora asked sarcastically.

"You still have him fooled, don't you?"

"I've had enough of you," Nora growled and reached back to strike the first blow.

But the next move was Christine's. She slapped Hueso so hard everyone in the room heard it. Hueso tried to fight back, to no avail. Christine had her from one end of the room to the other until others parted them.

Ed finally arrived at the scene. "Get your coat. We're getting out of here," he told Nora.

"It wasn't her fault," Christine told him. "She started everything as usual." She pointed to Hueso.

Ed took Nora by the arm, leading her out of the house. He was both concerned and furious at what happened. He worried for Nora in her condition, and wondered why Hueso would even do such a thing in knowing Nora was pregnant.

Christine faced Hueso as Ed and Nora left. "This isn't over," she warned. "We will cross paths again."

Hueso's snicker made Christine want to slap her around all over again.

Nora heard the music resume as they walked away. Julia stood in the doorway with a concerned look in her eyes. She worried for Nora as she was well aware of Hueso's vendetta. She couldn't imagine Ed harming Nora in her current condition. Still, she knew Hueso would not let this go. She wondered what her anger toward Nora was to begin with. Other than jealously she could see no other reason for her actions

CHAPTER 6

1931. THE EMPIRE STATE Building opens its doors in New York City as the tallest building in the world. Gangster Al Capone is sentenced to prison for tax evasion. Pearl Buck publishes *"The Good Earth."* The Great Depression grips America. Troubling events overseas seem too far away to worry about.

* * * * *

NEARING HER FIRST BIRTHDAY, Pricilla took her first steps in the world. She grew so quickly that Nora scarcely had time for her favorite doll. The attention Pricilla required and demanded was overwhelming at times for this young mother. Rebecca and Rudolf spent more and more time with the little girl. Rudolf wanted her with him as much as possible. He worried for what Hueso had injected into the Nora and Ed's life and marriage and didn't want Pricilla being a target in any shape or form. What few times Hueso took it upon herself to enter their home, Nora immediately took Pricilla outside, out of sight. Although she resented Hueso just entering her home, to avoid a scandal and scene she would allow Ed his space to visit with her. She wasn't about to put Pricilla in such a delicate position. Nora made up her mind the time and place would come when she and Hueso settled their differences, but never would she allow it in the presence of her baby daughter.

Ed had a second job at the sawmill. He was gone from sunrise to sunset, many times later. He worked hard, was determined to give Nora the life he felt she deserved. His excitement of the child on its way had his heart on fire. He was more than sure it was his. Hueso was not about to poison his happiness this time around.

Nora was kept busy with washing diapers, housecleaning and cooking. Watching Pricilla grow before her very eyes was amazing. Her hair turned to a deep copper red. She was a happy, beautiful child. Adults around her marveled, were mesmerized by her innocence and beauty. It seemed everyone wanted to run their fingers through her hair upon sight. At the local general store she was gawked at the moment they stepped in. Wherever Nora took her people were drawn to her. This fed Hueso's resentment even more.

Rebecca constantly brought Pricilla baked cookies, candies and other goods, keeping Nora well stocked with whatever the precious granddaughter desired. The bond she formed with the child grew stronger with each day that passed. At times she insisted that Nora let Pricilla spend the night while she and Ed went out on the town or visited with friends. Gatherings at friends' homes were a constant happening in Nora's life. The friendship of the local wives was a lifeline to her. She relied on them more than ever.

Simply Nora

Julia, Angelica and now Soléma became best of friends. They were with Nora every day, either at Nora's home or one of theirs.

Ed continued on the Chinook Cabins while working his shift at the sawmill. His craftsmanship was obvious, as was the hard, exhausting work at the sawmill, but he did it without complaint.

On warm days, Rebecca took Nora and Pricilla to gather chokecherries for jam and syrup. They gathered wild spinach, dandelions and other edible vegetation. She taught Nora what to do with each one, creating delicious dishes for lunch out of what they gathered. Nora had learned more in the past year than in her entire life.

Although Christine lived with Uncle Tom, she still made time to spend with Nora. Christine looked up to her with admiration. She, too, kept a close eye on Nora being cautious with what Hueso had done. She and Nora would find humor in the beating Christine administered to Hueso. Nora relished the day she would be able to do the same.

Ed was once again as close to Nora as ever. He loved her with an intensity even he found hard to understand. The affection toward his wife drove Hueso into a state of distraction that Nora simply could not understand. She never did anything derogatory to her, but knew that their mutual hatred would never end.

Pricilla celebrated her first birthday at home on May 8th with Rebecca and Rudolf, Christine, her brothers, Angelica and Naccór, Julia and Roberto, Soléma and her husband, Peté. Between them all they had a celebration dinner fit for a queen. Although Pricilla was far too young to understand, she was in awe with the cake candle and wrapped gifts surrounding her.

The local wives each had their own prediction of whether Nora would give birth to a son or another daughter. To Nora it didn't matter as long as the child was healthy and strong. Anticipation in Ed grew with each passing day as he anxiously awaited the arrival of his child. Nora turned fifteen on May 24th.

In June, Rebecca gave birth to her ninth child, a fair-haired, blue-eyed son they named Luther, after the boy they'd lost. A very pregnant Nora was present at his birth, as were many friends and family members. She couldn't help but think of what was in store for both her and Rebecca with infants to care for. But having a new baby brother was a joy for her.

In early August, Nora felt the faint pangs of birth. Everyone kept a close watch. The heat was unbearable. Finding coolness in the mountain shades was her only relief, while Rebecca and the wives tended to chores. Nora could hardly maneuver toward the third week of August. She was just too large.

On August 18th it all began. The pain and glory of giving birth commenced. For hours upon hours Nora was in labor until the blessed baby arrived, another daughter she and Ed named Flora. The first sight of Flora's dark hair brought a smile to Ed's face. Tears filled his eyes. He knew without a doubt this child was his. Not even Hueso could convince him of

30

anything otherwise. Flora was a beautiful child, favoring Nora in so many ways. Her olive complexion and dark, curly hair were a reflection of her mother. Pricilla gaped at the newborn sister as mom and dad held her wrapped snuggly after bathing. In the background Rudolf sighed.

As Nora spent time in recovery, her loved ones tended to her every need. Rebecca took care of Pricilla, while Julia, Angelica and Soléma washed and hung out diapers and laundry, cooked and canned goods and kept the house tidy and cleaned. They took turns going to the general store for goods they could not furnish themselves. Each took their turn in watching over Flora and her demands, which were plentiful around the clock. When Flora wasn't sleeping or crying, she looked about the room. Flora's bright eyes showed she was a happy, contented soul.

Ed saw to it that enough wood and coal were available for heating and cooking. He was not about to let Nora struggle or want for anything if it were up to him. Between all of them Nora was free to heal and recover as she needed.

Christine graduated from Del Norte High School that year, making all in the family proud. Her graduation pose was nothing less than what was expected of her. She looked beautiful, her hair in a cascade of waves down to her shoulders. Her fiancé, Modesto, was in the group photo, along with many others from the surrounding areas who graduated. She transitioned to working part-time to full-time at the post office sorting mail.

Christine's graduation

For Nora and Christine, this would also be a special year because "The King of Swing" Benny Goodman swept the nation and fed their delight on the dance floor.

Christine made her daily visits as well. She found it amazing that at fifteen Nora had two children already. On this day they sat alone in Nora's bedroom while the others busied themselves around the house.

"A mother again?" Christine said with a smile.

"I'm just as surprised," Nora replied. "Did you see the baby?"

"She's beautiful. She looks just like you."

"You think so?"

"How's Daddy taking all this?"

"He doesn't say much. You know him. He only says he'll be there when I need him. I don't know what I'd do without him. I rely on him in so many ways."

"And Mom?"

"You know her. She says it's my duty. Whatever that means."

"I think we both know what it means. Anyway, you'll be up on your feet before you know it. You'll be dancing across that dance floor in no time."

"I could sure use it. It's been so long since I've been out for a good time," Nora said, pausing to look out the window. "It looks beautiful out there."

"It is. Do you feel strong enough to go out for a few minutes? I'll make sure nothing happens to you."

"That would probably do me good. Just help me get something on to look decent. Can you put a little make-up on me?"

"Of course," Christine said, reaching into her purse. Like an artist she put Nora together, then helped her out onto the front porch to sit in the breeze.

"You're right. I needed this badly. It's very beautiful out. The fresh air feels good. How have you been?"

"I've been real good. You know me. I make the best case out of anything. Uncle Tom is very good to me."

"He always has been. He loves you like you were his own."

"He sent you this," Christine said, handing Nora an envelope.

"What's this?"

"I don't know. He just wanted you to have it. He said it would help."

Nora opened the envelope and was surprised to find several hundred dollar bills. A note was inside: *Dear Nora. Please accept this gift from your friend, Uncle Tom.*

"I don't know what to say," she said.

"I had no idea that was in there," Christine said. "But take it. It will come in handy. You know Uncle Tom. He's always there to lend a helping hand."

"This is so much money," Nora said. "I feel guilty taking it."

"Don't. That would insult him. He did it because he cares for you. You know that. He always tells me to make sure I'm there when you need me."

"You are."

"I need to be here more often now. You're going to need all the help you can get."

"The ladies in there help me a lot. They are very good to me."

"Yes, they are very good people. And they are very good to you. They are true friends."

"I hope I have them as friends forever," Nora said, gazing about the yard and mountainside. She noticed hummingbirds, chipmunks and squirrels and smelled the sweetness of the lilac bushes. The beauty surrounding them captivated her in every way. Laughter came from inside the house.

"Sounds like they're having a good time," Christine said.

"That would be Soléma. You know her, always laughing and joyful. She has got to be the happiest woman I've ever known. Such a joyful spirit and soul."

"It's good to surround yourself with those kinds of people. We both know what the opposite kind can do. Has she been around?" Christine asked.

"She has, but stays her distance. Before Flora was born I'd leave the house to get Pricilla away from her. I don't want her near that Hueso. I don't want any of my children near her, ever. She's wicked and up to no good. Have you run into her after that incident?"

"No," Christine laughed. "I'd love to, though. In fact I'd like to finish what she started. Someday."

"I'm sure she and I will have our day too," Nora said. "I shiver to think what will happen then."

Christine knew it was time to change the subject.

"So, is Flora it? Or will there be more?"

"More?" Nora exclaimed, shocked at the very thought. "I could barely handle one, now two. I don't think there'll be any more. I can't imagine what it's going to be like taking care of two babies at once. I know I could never handle more than two."

"Never say never. You are unique, you know that? Daddy sees it in you too. Do you talk to Ed about it?"

"I talk to him, but he believes what is meant to be will be. I'm just me. Nothing special. Just me."

For an hour they sat on the porch talking until Nora felt the need to lie down again. Carefully, Christine helped her back into the house to the bedroom, where Nora soon dozed off. Her heart was content.

* * * * *

WITHIN THE NEXT TWO days Nora was nearly recovered and back to her daily routine. With the help from Julia, Angelica and Soléma the household was running smoothly. Having a second child to care for was indeed proving a challenge. The demand for clean diapers was unending. Luckily her three friends seldom arrived at her doorstep without something in hand, whether it be baked or cooked goods or simply more diapers to add to her collection.

With the help of a monthly government book of ration stamps given to family members and children, food always managed to be on the table when mealtime came. A government relief truck also made its rounds to each household delivering boxes of fruits, vegetables and other food.

Rebecca taught Nora what types of wild vegetation to pick and how to prepare them. Local wives had the same knowledge and brought bagsful to Nora. Delicious aromas carried from Nora's kitchen during the day. When Ed came home a meal awaited him every evening. Her cooking skills matured nicely. Fried potatoes, pinto beans and homemade tortillas were among his favorite. Gradually, Nora learned his likes and dislikes.

Summer was long and hot. A fire going in the stove for cooking made it even more unbearable. Still, it was the way of the land. Nora did what she had to. Being a mother had plunged her abruptly into the realities of adulthood. Yet she loved being a mother, and to gaze into the eyes of her daughters humbled her in ways she never thought possible.

Pricilla loved flipping through the children's books Rebecca brought for her. And at Grandma's home there also were plenty of other treats to keep her occupied. But the disciplinarian in Rebecca would not go away. Already she had Pricilla on a rigid schedule when she was at her home.

Rudolf adored the child. He saw Nora in her in so many ways. His time spent with her was worth its weight in gold. To have Pricilla cradled in his arms while she slept only reminded him of the times he once held Nora in the same manner. He loved Flora equally. Her coal black hair and dark eyes were a reflection of Nora. He, too, wondered if these two children would be her last. His concern was they wouldn't be. He still kept a close watch on Nora. He had lost trust in Ed, as any father would.

CHAPTER 7

1932. THE BUZZ ABOUT the presidential election is everywhere. Democrat Franklin D. Roosevelt runs a strong campaign against Hoover. Many in South Fork expect and hope Roosevelt wins office. In Germany, Adolf Hitler and his Nazi movement continue to rise, becoming stronger and more venomous. History is unfolding before the eyes of the world. Americans, pinning their hopes on Roosevelt, sigh in relief when word gets out that he is leading in the polls. The country has never witnessed such an incredible situation as this Depression. Unemployment reaches nearly twenty five percent. Shantytowns spring up.

Bing Crosby's hit *"Brother Can You Spare a Dime?"* captures the mood of the nation. The bad news never seems to end even beyond the pocketbook. Charles Lindbergh's baby is kidnapped and found dead. Going to the movies and watching Hollywood's stars like Clark Gable and Bette Davis is one of the few sources of relief for a shattered people. Radio City Music Hall opens in New York.

* * * * *

IN SOUTH FORK, ED had all he could handle between the sawmill and home building. For the women, there was the daily routine of cooking and caring for children, along with gardens being harvested, vegetables and fruits canned for the coming winter. Every household in South Fork stocked up for the season. If one family was short, the others made up for it. Each looked after the next. It was the way of the land and its people.

Joy could be found amid the misgivings and hardships. Pricilla and Flora kept Nora and those around her on their toes, and Christine continued to bring Nora many of her most beautiful garments whenever she acquired new ones. Christine taught Nora her sense of dress and brought out Nora's own flare for it. The Prien sisters were noted for their looks and fashion. While millions of men around the country were out of work, Ed was constantly on the go. Long hours kept him away from sunrise to sunset, and many times beyond. He and Nora seldom had time for each other. Days off were foreign to him. There was virtually no time for rest. The dancing he promised Nora dwindled, replaced with diapers and more diapers, sleepless nights and responsibilities of raising a family. But Ed was content in every way imaginable. His love for Nora matured with each passing day. For him she was even more beautiful when she was pregnant.

What few hours Nora and Ed shared were spent discussing their growing family responsibilities. At night they lay together contemplating their journey, its trials and tribulations – and its bliss. At times while both children were napping Nora would dance to her heart's content. Although there was no music in the room, the rhythm was in her head, in her heart. Her dream and desire to be a dancer was strong. She longed for it, found more freedom and peace on the dance floor than anywhere else. Nora had always and would always love music. Throughout the day she hummed or sang her favorite tunes, in Spanish or English, while washing dishes or scrubbing diapers, it didn't matter. There was joy in her soul and spirit in spite of the hardships she endured.

A day didn't go by without Rudolf at Nora's doorstep. To find him standing there when she opened the door delighted her. She adored him more than anything or anyone besides her children. Anyone who knew Rudolf knew Nora was his pride and glory – his little girl. Rudolf struggled to find peace with Rebecca, but it would not come. Although the happiness was obvious in Nora and he was ever so grateful for his grandchildren, the struggles and challenges she endured lay heavily on his heart. For this he could not find forgiveness. The distance between him and Rebecca seemed to grow daily. Conversation between them diminished as days went by. To see the stress and hardship on Nora only made him resent Rebecca more.

Celebration and togetherness offered solace from the times. None had more than the other. And what each possessed was shared with a neighbor and friend.

Winter brought smoke from chimneys rising into the sky, the air crisp and chilly. Children sledded down the hillsides. For them in their innocence, there was always something to do regardless of the time of year. For them, life was a playground.

With Pricilla walking and Flora getting there, Nora was constantly on the move. They were inquisitive and curious, rambunctious as any children their age. Household chores became more challenging, yet a necessity. Fires in the pot belly heater and stove were kept going throughout the day keeping the house warm and cozy for the children. At night Ed stocked up the heater with large chunks of coal to assure warmth through the night. He was grateful he had stored enough for the hard season they were headed into. At night with Nora in his arms and the children sleeping soundly, his heart was ever so content. He could ask for nothing else.

When Christmas arrived, so did Nora's news that she was pregnant with her third child. She didn't need Rebecca to tell her what it was this time. Ed was delighted when she told him of her suspicions. Rebecca sighed deeply when she told her. Rudolf embraced her with compassion. There was nothing else he could do. The thought of having three small children was daunting to Nora. She could not comprehend the reality of it, although those around her had no problem in understanding the tremendous responsibilities that came along with it. Still, those close to her vowed to remain at her side and see to her needs, whatever they might be.

Nora joined in the yearly festivities of celebration from home to home singing Christmas carols. Nora didn't smoke and seldom indulged in alcoholic beverages, never when she was pregnant. The more she was exposed to alcohol and its impact on families, the more she loathed it. She witnessed homes and families torn apart by it. She saw wives abused even more so than she was. It seemed like a never ending trend among many households. From weekend to weekend one never knew what wife was to be abused and to what extent. On a rare occasion it was the husband abused.

She would never come to understand or accept this malice. She resented it more each time she saw another wife with signs of abuse.

CHAPTER 8

1933. PRESIDENT ROOSEVELT TAKES office after surviving an assassination attempt. Americans cling to hope as he tells them "The only thing we have to fear is fear itself" in his inaugural address. The beginnings of his New Deal are enacted in an effort to pull the nation of the Depression. *"King Kong"* makes its Hollywood debut. The World's Fair is held in Chicago. Hitler spreads his evil reign against the Jewish community in Germany.

*   *   *   *   *

PREDICTIONS WERE FOR A harsh winter and the predictions were right. The nights were long and cold. Many times people had to dig themselves out of their homes from feet of snow piled high against doors and windows. Nora's brothers were always there to lend a helping hand when neighbors were unable to assist due to their own burdens. Rebecca sewed blankets and clothing for Nora and the children, making sure they were kept warm even on the coldest of nights. Her blankets were art pieces of patch work and stitches, each magnificent and colorful.

As winter matured, Nora yearned for the warmth of spring and summer. In the midst of the hard, cold nights she worried for the loved ones around her. All were aware of what each family endured during these frigid times. Pieces of rags stuffed under doorways and windows helped ward off the bitter sting of the freezing weather. Fires going in the heater and stove kept the house tolerable most of the time. Still, there were times when not even they were enough. Nora wrapped the children snugly in blankets and sat them in front of the heater as she told stories to keep their minds occupied. Hot chocolate was always a treat. For them it was all a game.

Local wives continued their rounds, making sure she had everything needed, even though they themselves endured hardships. They always arrived with bags of goods in hand. Nora's cooking and baking skills improved to the point she could offer the same in return. Ed was out building cabins and homes, but at times the cold was too treacherous even for him. Then he would work at the sawmill or whatever else he could do to provide for his family. Calluses on his hands were testimony of the hard work he did.

On weekends to escape the hardship, friends gathered with guitars and fiddles for entertainment. Children were seldom allowed, although at times their bright eyes peered from doorways. They watched and listened in wonder.

Regardless of the harsh conditions and elements, Highway 160 through South Fork was busy with cars filled with families in search of a better life. Some chose to settle in the valley, while most took their chances going over Wolf Creek Pass hopefully to a better existence. Winter settling over the state meant difficult times for all who lived in it or ventured through. Nature had no mercy. Locals watched as the vehicles vanished into the elements of uncertainty. They worried for those peering through the car windows in desperation – their gaze seared into the minds and hearts of those who observed.

After the treacherous winter, signs of spring finally emerged. Robins made their appearance. The spring runoff began engorging creeks and rivers. Scars from children's ice skates embedded on river surfaces slowly melted away, as did the snow that provided a popular winter game called Pie. A circle made in the snow was cut into pie sections, and the object was not getting tagged before reaching the center.

* * * * *

A PREGNANT NORA GAZED at the reflection of herself in the mirror. Being pregnant was becoming a norm for her. As she felt over her bulge she could only wonder whether it'd be another daughter or a son she'd welcome into the world. To her it didn't matter just so they were healthy. The love she had for her children was unrivaled. She worried for the state the nation was in. Concerned of what kind of life she would be able to provide considering the struggles, trials and tribulations all were going through.

One consolation was her first RCA radio so she was able to listen to music as she pleased. She marveled at the latest technology, the clarity of the musical notes leaving the radio. She had it going constantly.

Louie Armstrong, Duke Ellington, Guy Lombardo and Bing Crosby dominated the airwaves with some of her favorites. Mae West singing *"I Like A Guy What Takes His Time"* and Ethel Waters with *"Stormy Weather"* fascinated her, as did the Oscar ceremonies in Hollywood. Nora loved hearing what was happening in a fragment of life that was merely a fantasy for most.

Nora yearned for the day her favorite Spanish tunes would be heard on the radio, but that was merely a far-fetched dream of many. Discrimination was rampant against those of color – the driving force behind the social network in South Fork.

* * * * *

ONE DAY, PRICILLA WAS with Rebecca and Flora had her afternoon nap. Nora smiled at the knock at the door. Christine walked in.

"You get bigger each time I see you," Christine said. "I can't believe you're having another baby."

"Imagine how I feel," Nora answered quickly. "I'm probably more surprised than anyone."

"Is this one it?"

"I'm afraid to say yes. Who knows?"

"How can you do it? I mean there will be so many to care for. What does Ed have to say? And Mom?"

"You do what you have to," Nora said. "Besides, they're my babies. I love them. He doesn't say much, and Mom says it's my duty. You know her."

"I know. We love the kids too. We just worry about you. Daddy is beside himself, you know? I see it in him. He and Mom seem so distant all the time."

"They'll work it out. I worry for him, too, but what can I do? It is what it is. Mom will never change. You know that. The boys come from time to time and chop wood for us. They're a great help."

"You're right. They'll work it out. I'm glad the boys come by. They're good brothers. Look, I have a new camera. Let's take pictures. I also brought these for you." She pulled out more beautiful garments of silk and rayon for Nora.

"You always bring me such wonderful clothes. Don't you want them anymore? Some you haven't even worn."

"Those I bought specifically for you. The rest, they'll look better on you whenever you can get into them."

"Ain't that the truth? Hopefully this fall I can wear them after the baby is born. I could sure use some dancing. Right now all I can wear is this old thing," Nora said, addressing her maternity frock. It was by far not easy on the eye, and a major challenge for fashion. Nora detested wearing it, but in her condition comfort was a priority.

They ventured out to the lilac bushes where Christine posed for the camera. The lens was easy on her. She photographed very well. Many felt she could have modeled for the fancy magazines and catalogs, but that, too, was a mere fantasy. Still, she stood proudly posed in the sunlight as though the world belonged to her. Her long, wavy, auburn hair glistened in the rays. Fashion was her obvious obsession. She looked her best no matter where she went. Nora took pleasure in photographing her but refused a photo in her condition. Their laughter filled the air.

Christine left when it was feeding time for Flora. Flora's cries carried through the house until her feeding commenced. Breast feeding was common for Nora, although she had heard of alternatives. Rebecca had instilled in her the necessity for a mother's breast milk for a child because of the bonding. It made total sense to Nora. It seemed remarkable to her having one child within her with another suckling. The irony was mind boggling. When feeding was over, she placed Flora back in her crib and continued with her household chores, many of which she mastered although her hands were sore and raw. With people coming and going from her home, she relished her time alone.

When Nora turned seventeen that May, her birthday was a joyous occasion spent with family and friends. Gifts were plentiful. Among them were sets of jewelry to add to the ever-growing collection she took so much pride in. She was grateful to be surrounded by those she loved most. She had grown into a young woman seemingly overnight. Her laughter carried as though she didn't have a care in the world. In many ways she didn't. All she had was right there with her – family and friends.

In summer, she was heavy with child. Still, she continued to do what had to be done. Having two small children to care for was an unending task. The thought of another on its way weighed heavily on her mind. She wondered if she could do it. Both Pricilla and Flora kept her constantly on the go from the moment they awakened to the second they dozed off for the night. The love she had for her children and family gave her courage to face the day, the strength to be a mother, a wife.

It was on those rare occasions when both children were napping that Nora did some of her heavy household duties. Baking enough bread for the week was one. She also made dozens of tortillas for Ed's lunches as they were his preference. She made sure he had all he needed when he left for work, rising at dawn to prepare whatever he desired for his daily lunch. He was young and strong and required a large meal. Meat was also on his menu.

During hunting season what was caught by one was shared by all. Meat was always available for them. Deer, elk, rabbit and fish were of abundance. On her better days Nora would sit at the river fishing when there was time. Often she would walk the river and meadows in search of vegetation for their meals. All the local wives did. Many times they gathered and made a day of it. It was a necessity for survival. The majority of what they had was taken from the land. That, too, was a way of life for the residents of South Fork. Most made their own butter, cheese, jams and jellies. Milk, eggs and slabs of bacon were delivered from local farmers, who had a strong relationship with the community. Many times they included vegetables and fruits. It was the residents who kept them afloat as well. They relied on one other.

As Nora became too large to do much of anything, she did what she could. As usual, many were there to help. The weather was hot, and there was no escaping it. Even with all the windows and doors open the intensity was almost too much for her. Children found refuge swimming in the shallowness of the river and log ponds used by the sawmill for cleansing newly cut timber. For hours upon hours they would splash and play to their heart's content. At most, Nora would place her feet into the coolness, finding temporary comfort in the currents massaging the soreness from her feet and legs. On occasion the baby inside her would kick in reminder that it wouldn't be long before he or she entered the world.

Fans going in the house merely blew hot air around the room. Still, when circumstances allowed, Nora would sit in front of them to escape the high temperatures of what seemed like a very long summer. At times like these she yearned for the cold of winter. For the children she would place a tub outside partially filled with cool river water. That would keep them busy for hours and shield them from the extreme heat as well. As usual, she and Ed celebrated their anniversary in private.

Days were long, filled with responsibility. Locals arrived with more diapers in preparation of the newborn on its way. There was excitement for everyone. At times when Nora gazed out of the kitchen window to see rows of diapers on the cloth line, she couldn't help but envision another row soon to be filled. Although her heart was bursting with joy, she wondered how many more children were to come. She never gave it a second thought as to how many she wanted. To have three children seemed daunting to her. Where had her own childhood gone?

June was nowhere near what July presented. The doors and windows wide open during the nights at least made for comfortable sleeping, but Nora was huge with discomfort. She counted the days as they crept by, waiting for the newborn to arrive. In spite of her dismay, she took pleasure in the beauty surrounding her. Summer time in South Fork was unrivaled. Children were outdoors from sunrise to sunset playing Hide and Seek, Hop-Scotch, Red Rover-Red Rover, London Bridges, Annie-Annie Over, Tug of War and Crack the Whip. Their echoes carried everywhere.

Sometimes Nora would sit on the front porch observing all that was happening around her while contemplating life. Solitude was foreign to her since the birth of her children. She was constantly reminded that her carefree days were long gone, a memory. Usually, no sooner did she sit for a moment's recollection but was on her feet again tending to something or someone. Still, with the radio going in the background, there was always a song in her heart. That would never go away.

Married life for her and Ed was turbulent at times. He was not himself when alcohol was injected into any situation. Like clockwork, they would end up quarreling. The personal doubt Hueso had put into his heart lay heavily on him and fed upon his insecurities. By now, he was certain Pricilla was his but damned himself time and time again for thinking otherwise. He couldn't understand why Hueso would say such a thing. The cruelty behind it made no sense to him. Still, what this person had told him had its influence on his lack of confidence.

Unbeknownst to Rudolf, and fortunately for Ed, he struck Nora on more than one occasion after drinking. Nora learned to pick up anything within her reach to protect herself. There was no limit to what she resorted to. She was young and frightened, frustrated with living under the constant fear of when it would happen, never knowing what mood Ed would be in when he stepped in after work or playing at a dance.

These situations Nora kept to herself to avoid another confrontation between Rudolf and Ed. She knew what Rudolf would do should he ever be aware of what transpired. Beyond a doubt he would thrash Ed time and time again just like he swore to do should it ever happen again.

It was only partly about Pricilla that set Ed off. It also was Nora's blossoming into a beautiful young woman. Heads turned wherever she went. Ed's love and jealousy for Nora combined with Hueso's venom was no match for him. Subconsciously it took its toll, surfacing when he drank. Alcohol and abuse worked hand in hand, not just for Nora but for many wives in South Fork. Often the wives would gather and discuss their misfortune, which sadly became a cultural fact of life.

When Rudolf questioned her, Nora explained away the bruises with excuse and reason, telling him one of the children had struck her while playing or feeding. She didn't want him hurt or involved. Also, she had gradually learned to protect herself and fight back and was getting good at it. Growing up with six brothers taught her this. Rudolf usually walked away with doubt in his mind and his heart.

By August 17th just as Nora felt she'd explode, pangs of labor began. For hours she lay in bed with the midwife and Ed at her side. Family members and friends awaited the verdict in the front room, each guessing whether it'd be a son or another daughter to enter the world.

Rudolf paced the floor nervously while Rebecca sat sewing clothing for the newborn. Each glance he took at Rebecca was a reminder of his resentment. Ed's parents Delfino and Atanasia sat patiently. They, too, were eager for the arrival of their next grandchild. Even Hueso was there, sitting in silence. Thoughts spoke clearly for themselves.

Finally a child's cry sounded from the bedroom. Nora gave birth to another daughter. She and Ed named her Juanita. Like Flora, her dark, curly hair and eyes brought a smile to Ed. Nora gazed upon her with love and admiration. Her olive complexion was from Nora, who saw herself in Juanita, just as she did her other daughters. She was so proud of each of them. Ed lifted the child, holding her close. His love for her was obvious, just like with his other children. For them he always had affection.

As usual, the guests peered into the bedroom taking their first admiring glance at the newborn. Nora was exhausted. Juanita twisted and squirmed in the cradle, her tiny hands grasping at life around her. She, like Pricilla and Flora, was well received into the world and family. Rudolf, too, saw traces of Nora in this new little one. He knew he would love this child as he would all of Nora's children, however many there would be.

Hueso looked into the cradle, then up at Nora, who glared at her in warning. The look in Nora's eyes always set the boundaries between Hueso and the children. Hueso knew not to utter a word as she walked out of the room. The joy she saw in Ed made her cringe. She knew it was a joy not even she would be able to penetrate, and dared not even try.

For the following days, Rebecca and local wives took care of the children while Nora recovered. Rebecca saw to it that she had all that would be needed when she finally rose from the bed. The house was cleaned, all the baking done, and Ed's meals prepared for the week. Nora was grateful as she sat in the front room with Juanita in her lap looking around. Nora had only one job for now – to care for the children. She was completely content.

Ed found himself gone for up to two weeks at a time building cabins at Pearl Lakes, near Creede. This gave Nora time alone with the children and herself as well as a break from the drama alcohol brought into their lives. She loathed alcohol more with each passing day. The moment she smelled traces of it on him she anticipated trouble, as did most wives in South Fork when they smelled it on their husbands. Although there was love for Ed, the resentment for alcohol was gradually overpowering it. She pleaded with him to leave it, but to no avail. The addiction was far too strong, its grip on him too great. His love for Nora and his children was evident – but his jealousy was crippling.

The mere thought of another man even glancing at Nora enraged him. Even though Nora did her best to ignore it, her beauty combined with her hunger for life was an attraction few men could resist. Each time Ed left, he walked away with a heavy heart knowing this. He struggled to come to terms with it. Added to that, the lingering memory of Hueso's words gave him no peace. He resented her for having brought this doubt and insecurity into his life.

Nora now had her hands full with three young ones around the house. Rebecca had made suggestions of keeping Pricilla on a more permanent basis to help out, but that was something both Nora and Ed were not quite ready for. On warm days Rebecca set a place out in the front yard and gathered the children to tell them stories. They listened to her tales in awe and wonderment.

Days and weeks went by and so did Juanita's demands. The chill of fall was in the air with another winter just around the corner. Already Ed had chopped and stacked enough wood and coal for the season. As usual a rough winter was expected for the region. South Fork would not be itself without its treacherous winters. Nora was back to her old self, wearing her favorite dresses Christine had given. When able she was out dancing while Ed played in the band. Rebecca watched the children. For Nora to take her children on a walk through the array of color was enchanting for all of them. She loved the countryside and all its beauty and serenity. While the two older children played among the flowers, she would sit with Juanita on her lap taking it all in. The chaos in her life with Ed was the opposite of the beauty surrounding her at times like this. She was at peace.

As Nora's skills as a housewife and mother grew, the help she needed from others waned. Still, the local wives, her friends, were there at her doorstep every day with something in their hands. They simply would not allow that to diminish or perish. Nora had sealed a friendship with them that she hoped would last a lifetime. Many of them were like sisters. She relied on them in so many ways. They were her support system through the good and the bad, always there when she needed them.

On occasion Nora would take a ride with her friends into Del Norte, about fourteen miles from South Fork due east on Highway 160. There they would shop and get items unavailable to them in South Fork. Del Norte was a busy town in comparison, but Nora was accustomed to the beauty and solitude of mountain living. She had even gone to school in Del Norte. Christine was still in high school there and was determined to graduate.

On these trips Nora also visited relatives and friends. Then, after a day of shopping and visiting, she and her friends from South Fork headed back home. In those days that was a long drive, but being with friends made it enjoyable. From time to time they pulled over to the side of the road and let the overheated engine cool. That, too, was a way of life. Highway 160 was always busy, either with locals or families traveling in hopes of finding a better life. For Nora, just having her children was all she needed. They made her truly happy.

CHAPTER 9

1934. COLE PORTER IS popular on the airwaves. A six year old girl named Shirley Temple appears in the film *"Stand Up and Cheer."* Alcatraz opens as a federal prison. DuPont introduces products made of nylon. The misery of the Dust Bowl forces thousands of farmers into bankruptcy. The jobless rate is twenty two percent. Bread lines are everywhere. Hitler reigns as *Der Fuehrer*.

* * * * *

THREE SMALL CHILDREN TO care for was the personal challenge for Nora. Although Rebecca did what she could to help, she had demands at home of her own. Nora's salvation, as usual, came from her friends, the local wives of South Fork. They continued to be there come rain or shine.

Ed was still gone a lot up in Pearl Lakes. Nora would not allow liquor inside their home, but she knew that whenever he was around, a bottle of Port or Tokay brought trouble. Ed's gatherings with his friends usually meant a night of music and drinking.

Along with spring came weekends at Louie's bar, a local tavern where husbands gathered after a hard week's work. Brawls were notorious. Jealously and liquor did not mix well. Black eyes were a common sight come Saturday or Sunday morning. The wives, too, became accustomed to what Louie's brought into their lives and homes. Children were subjected to the chaos on many occasions. Huddled in bedrooms, they cried, hoping the night and turmoil passed as their mother's cries during a beating carried throughout the house.

Nora was one of those wives whose home had been disrupted by the weekends at Louie's. She knew just what to expect whenever Ed stepped through the door after a night at the tavern. Like clockwork her expectations came to be. Carefully she placed the children in their separate bedroom, closing the door behind her to deal with the ordeal. She fought back when needed. Other times she resorted to going to Rebecca and Rudolf's with the children until morning when Ed sobered up. Still, the concern remained as she was aware of his bottle kept in a secret hiding place outdoors. Ed drank more as time went by. Rudolf was always at the ready should there be even a hint that he had hit Nora.

Although those times at Louie's brought chaos into homes, there were many occasions where a night out dancing was uninterrupted and enjoyed. Nora's heart was content as she glided across the dance floor dressed in her best. Many befriended her, both men and women. Her dance card was never empty when she stepped into the hall. The understanding that she and Ed had from day one diminished as the years went by and Ed drank more. His jealousy grew.

On May 24th Nora turned eighteen; a milestone in her eyes for it symbolized her maturity as a woman even though she'd been thrust into it as a child. As usual Rudolf gave her jewelry. Christine gave her more beautiful clothing made of rayon and silk. Rebecca gave things needed for the house and for her daily household chores.

Nora

By summer their home seemed happy and content once more. In August came signs of Nora's fourth pregnancy. The symptoms were vastly familiar to her by now. Like before, Rudolf was concerned, and Ed was thrilled.

Nora turned to the Catholic Church for counsel and guidance in having children one after another like this. The priest merely told her to "Keep having children until God says it's enough." Those words would haunt and echo in her mind forever. She simply could not understand the logic behind them. They didn't make sense, nor would they ever. This was the beginning of Nora's spiritual awakening, and her digression from the Catholic Church and religion altogether.

Common sense played more of a major role in her life than religion. Her strength and spirituality came from within even though she'd been brought up with Rebecca's strict religious views. She felt a person didn't have to be in a temple, hall or church to abide by the rules of life. For her the Higher Power was everywhere and limitless. And she wasn't about to turn control of her life over to any organization to dictate her every move, telling her what she could and could not do and what to believe in. The extreme contradiction and hypocrisy associated with religion was not for Nora, who always knew only she could determine what was best for herself. She didn't need or require validation from anyone. In her opinion this was what common sense was for. She learned this at a very early age. She turned to the Catholic Church upon Rebecca's recommendation, only to be extremely disappointed.

On occasion Nora attended church gatherings, but never sensed the comfort sought or felt by others. This indifference and resilient sense of self always kept her strong willed and confident. But she never imposed these beliefs on her children, instead allowing self-discovery for them. However, she did try to implant common sense, knowing they would need it throughout life just as she did. As with any parent, she could only hope that what she taught her children would serve its purpose and they would use it well and wisely and have a sense of reality.

Nora at times accompanied Ed to Pearl Lakes, where she and the children lived in a tent with hardly the comforts of home, but tolerable.

Ed, when he had time, fished. Rainbow trout were in abundance. He brought the large, succulent fish to the campground for Nora to prepare over the campfire along with fried potatoes and chili, foods both she and Ed were fond of. She made dozens of tortillas and biscuits in advance for their stay, enough to last for the time they were up there. Shepherd's bread was another of their favorites. Coffee was made with clean, clear mountain water from the river to go with their eggs in the morning. After meals Nora tended to the dishes at the river where she also did their laundry, hanging the clothes and diapers on lines Ed set up. The fresh air was wonderful.

The country serenity did Nora good, and the children were enchanted with their surroundings. And Ed had no time to drink. At the end of the day he barely had enough energy to eat supper and crawl into the bedding Nora had prepared for him. He was content with life, although the stresses of a growing family were mounting. Pricilla gradually made the transition and was now living with Rebecca and Rudolf on a semi-permanent basis.

At Pearl Lakes the beauty was breathtaking. Nora spent hours with the children basking in it. The night sky, majestic in its calm, featured a million stars. Occasionally a shooting star streaked across the heavens, and the children made wishes for anything from dolls to pretty dresses. Nora always took note of them for the Christmas holidays. The children had no clue. When Nora pointed out the man in the moon, they looked up with eyes filled with wonder. And when she tucked them in bed, they looked at their mom with eyes filled with adoration.

CHAPTER 10

CHRISTMAS WAS AROUND THE corner. Nora was five months pregnant. Ed was back working on the cabins at Chinook, while keeping the boilers going at the sawmill during evenings and nights – sometimes during the graveyard shift as well. For him there was virtually no rest. The demands and needs for his growing family were constant. His days off were spent doing chores around the house making sure Nora and the children had all they needed. What little free time he captured was spent with his fiddle and drinking with his friends.

To get necessities, shopping trips into Del Norte lasting the entire day were frequent. Penney's, Malauf's, Cash and Carry, Montgomery Ward and Gambles usually had what Nora needed. On occasion they traveled to Alamosa, a larger community thirty miles east of Del Norte.

The mineral well in the center of downtown Del Norte was a focal point for all. It was a gathering place for kids and teenagers during warm weather. There they kept tuned with all that was happening in the town. After school, kids congregated at the well for hours doing what kids do best. But it wasn't just for kids. Locals and visitors also went there to enjoy the unique, tasty mineral water. It was a meeting place for many throughout the years—the town buzzing with activity.

Nora knew the time would come when her children would be bused to the schools in Del Norte, as many children from South Fork were. At times she was in awe as to how fast they grew before her very eyes. Although there was a void with Pricilla's absence in the household she knew it was for the best. She wanted the best for her children, and if it meant having Rebecca and Rudolf raising Pricilla so be it. She still saw Pricilla every day. Decisions for her life were made strictly between Nora and Ed.

This Christmas was a joyous occasion as there was much to be grateful for. The children were healthy, there was food on the table, Ed had work, and Nora's pregnancy was going well. Christmas dinner was held at Nora's surrounded by family and friends. Rebecca worked hard during the year on gifts for the holiday, making beautiful dresses for the girls. The dolls they wished for while gazing up to the falling star streaking across the night sky in Pearl Lakes were placed neatly wrapped beneath the tree. The children's laughter and excitement filled the house.

But once Christmas passed, harsh reality set in. Winter was very difficult this year for the residents of South Fork. Snow accumulated by the foot, piling high against doorways and walkways. They had to dig themselves out of their homes once again. Streams of smoke rose from chimneys 24/7 to ward off the harsh, bitter cold. Ed stacked piles of wood and coal next to the heater and stove making it easier on Nora in her condition. During the night both she and he took turns keeping tabs on the fire in the pot belly heater making sure it kept going. The cold was brutal. Flora and Juanita were kept wrapped snugly in layers of the handmade blankets Rebecca worked on lovingly. Multi-colored patchwork spoke of the time and energy put into them. She made them for each of the children as well as for Nora and Ed. At times frost formed on the inside of windows, reminding all of nature's severe unpredictability.

Although Nora banned liquor from her home, Ed was consistent with his drinking. The smell of Tokay or Port on his breath nauseated her. Many times she slept with one of the children when the odor became too much for her. His abuse was also consistent with his drinking. The only way to keep peace in the home was to ignore his outbursts, remove herself from his presence. From one day to the next she never knew whether he'd step through the door free from the stench or not. Their battles grew increasingly violent. Her main concern was shielding the children from the madness.

To keep peace she kept the abuse to herself, other than those wives who were quite familiar with the symptoms of it. Rebecca and Rudolf were somewhat oblivious although Rudolf had very strong suspicions. He cornered Ed on several occasions warning him of the dire consequences should he become aware of him hurting Nora. In her defense Nora picked up the nearest thing available to fend him off. She fought back with anything from cast iron frying pans to pieces of firewood.

One Friday evening she smelled the familiar odor on Ed's breath when he stepped into the house. It was later than usual. Nora was grateful Flora and Juanita had been put to bed and were sleeping. She didn't like for them to be in his presence when he was in this condition even though he was never abusive toward the children. Tonight she would undoubtedly be sleeping with them. She long since refused sleeping with Ed while he'd been drinking. She rose the second she became aware and headed for the children's bedroom.

"That's it. Walk away like you always do," Ed sneered.

"I told you, I don't like to be around you when you're in this shape."

"We need to talk!" he barked.

"No we don't," she answered back and started toward the bedroom.

"There's talk."

"What's new? Who this time, or is it Hueso again?"

"No, it isn't her."

"Then who?"

"Does it matter?"

"To me it does. I'd like to know who said what."

"I heard things."

"You always hear things. The wrong things!"

He stepped up to her. Anger was in his eyes. His breath reeked of whiskey and wine. "You think I'm a fool, don't you?"

Ignoring him, she reached for the bedroom doorknob.

Ed took Nora by the arm and tossed her back into the living room.

"What is wrong with you? You'll wake the girls," she whispered.

"I said, we need to talk!" he shouted.

"What's there to talk about? More gossip? Haven't you heard enough?"

"Maybe what they say is true."

"Use your common sense. When do I have time for anything else but taking care of these kids and you?"

"When I'm at work."

"That is nonsense. I'm going to sleep with the kids tonight." She started to walk away again.

"The hell you are! I've got things to say." This time he grabbed her arm harder.

"Quit it! You're hurting me," Nora told him, trying to pry his hand from her body. "Damn it! Let me go. Leave me alone!"

He hurled her against the wall, knocking pictures to the floor, reaching for her again as she hurried into the kitchen.

"What have you been up to?" he screamed.

"I'm not even going to answer that. You know what I've been doing. What I do every day. Now, either go to bed, or get out of here!"

"This is my house!" he shouted.

"Stop! You'll wake the girls and scare them."

"I don't give a damn!"

"Forget it. I'll just go to Mom and Dad's and take them with me."

"The hell you will!" He slapped Nora across the face, drawing blood from her lip.

"Stop it!" she demanded, to no avail.

He lifted his fist to strike her again, but she dodged his swing and hurried behind the kitchen table. He staggered to her, hitting her on the side of the head with another blow. She fell against the table, knocking plates and bowls to the floor. Her head spun.

As Nora reached for a cast iron skillet, he grabbed a handful of her hair and dragged her to the front room. She whacked him on the elbow with the skillet, breaking his grip, and then backed away ready for defense.

"You hit me again!" she shouted. "Hit me again and see what happens!"

Inside the bedroom Flora and Juanita were awake, sitting up in the darkness in fear. They dared not move. They heard Ed's voice carry throughout the house, heard things being tossed and banged.

On the other side of the door Nora fought fiercely to defend herself. She was not about to let him abuse her. She struck him again and again with the skillet until he backed away from her. She bled from the lip and nose. He bled from the side of the head. Blood streaked down his neck. Ed was infuriated that she took a stand against him like this.

"Get out of my sight!" she yelled. "You come near me again I'll beat you within an inch of your miserable life! I'm getting the girls and leaving. You try stopping me and you'll find this skillet on your head again."

Dazed, he staggered into their bedroom and fell across the bed. Blood discolored the blankets. Quickly, she dressed, taking the girls and left. Rudolf was furious when he opened the door to find his pregnant daughter bleeding, skillet in one hand and the children in tow. He reached for his coat, ready to deal with Ed.

"Daddy, it's okay. I hit him with this. He's out," she said.

"I don't care. I'll beat him whether he's awake or not!" Rudolf answered.

Just then Rebecca stepped in. "What happened?"

"He's drinking again," Nora said. "You know what happens when he does that."

"He's been doing this all along?" Rudolf asked. "Why haven't I been told?"

"Never mind that," Rebecca said. "Let's take care of that later." She led Nora in, going for damp cloths to wipe her wounds.

Rudolf paced angrily, furious to find it'd been happening and he wasn't aware. Nora always seemed to have explanations. He realized she was lying all along.

"Enough is enough!" he said. "You and the kids come and stay here. You don't need to put up with that any longer."

Rebecca tried to calm him. "Let's put the children to bed. They're frightened. Talk to them. They can sleep with Pricilla."

Rudolf walked away with Flora at his side and Juanita in his arms, his heart pounding.

"Daddy's so angry," Nora told Rebecca. "I've never seen him like this."

"He'll deal with it," Rebecca said. "Are you hurt anywhere else?"

"No. Just banged up a bit."

"Things will be better in the morning when you go home. He's just under so much stress and pressure."

"That's no excuse."

"You have a family and wifely duties to contend with. Part of those duties is putting up with this. It's the way God meant it."

"Do you put up with these things?

Rebecca was stunned, speechless. Nora had never questioned her like this. "This is not about me."

"If you don't, why should I?"

"Because it is God's will."

"I don't understand. How can this be his will?"

"You will understand as you get older. Now go get some rest with those girls. Calm them down if you can."

In the bedroom Nora cuddled the children until they fell asleep again. Her heart sank when she thought of what they went through time and time again. Rebecca's words echoed in her head. She couldn't bring herself to believe it was "God's will" to live as she was. Those words resonated a sour taste in her heart and soul. She wondered what tomorrow would bring.

CHAPTER 11

1935. BRUNO HAUPTMANN STANDS trial for the kidnapping and murder of the Lindbergh baby, and is found guilty of first-degree murder in February and sentenced to death. *"Your Hit Parade"* is a smash on the airwaves. Millions tune in on their radios. People everywhere are ecstatic with this escape from the economic turmoil. They gather in homes to listen to the latest hits, practicing the newest dance moves. They are energized, ready to take on the world. They find a renewed hope within the notes and

* * * * *

IN LATE JANUARY, A HARSH, bitter winter had South Fork in its grip. Temperatures plummeted. Families struggled to keep their homes warm and children safe from the elements. Kids were bundled in layers of winter wear before being sent out to wait for the school bus in the arctic blast. Feet of snow covered the valley, with deer and elk hooves leaving their signatures in the whiteness. Mountain life descended to lower elevations in search of food and nourishment. It was a struggle for all.

By March, Nora, in her eighth month, could barely move. Still, she did what had to be done to care for Ed and the children. After the big Friday blowup, there was occasional arguing followed by spurts of peace. Whenever he took to drinking there was sure to be an argument of some sort or another. He didn't assault her again, but Nora knew beyond a doubt the time would come. It was a love-hate relationship for her. She detested his drinking habits, jealousy and insecurities, but loved him in ways she found difficult to understand at her young age.

In early April she felt signs of birth being near. The active child within let her know it wouldn't be much longer. All anticipated the arrival of the new baby, eager to know whether it'd be another daughter or son brought into the world. After three girls, Ed's heart was on a boy. Still, if it were a daughter he'd love her just the same.

Spring was everywhere. All were grateful the long, harsh, winter was behind them. Snowcapped mountains were remnants of the bitterness that had enveloped the valley. Bears came out of hibernation taking to the banks and shallows of the creeks and rivers in search of fish, their cubs tagging behind them. On occasion a family of bears was sighted, but rarely did they come close to human contact.

On April 16th the sharp pangs of birth had Nora bedridden, the local mid-wife at her side. Her labor was long and hard, and finally she gave birth to their first son. They named him Rudy. He, like Flora and Juanita, had dark, curly hair much like Nora. Ed was delighted with the news, as were Rebecca and Rudolf, Delfino and Atanasia. At eighteen, Nora now had four children, a mind boggling reality for her.

Within days Nora was on her feet again, although limited to what she was able to do. Obligations pulled at her as the household needs never ceased. Meals had to be prepared and cooked; clothes and diapers washed and hung out to dry, duties that had no end. She thanked the stars for the good weather, as winter had been far too difficult on them. The needs of an infant and two toddlers kept her on the go at all hours of the day and night. If Pricilla weren't staying with her parents, Nora didn't know how she would have managed. It was she who usually tended to Rudy's needs in the middle of the night as she knew Ed needed his rest. Still, on occasion he took care of the baby's needs and let her get the sleep she desperately needed.Having a son was different for Nora. Although she was raised with many brothers, it wasn't the same as raising a boy of your own. She learned quickly his needs differed from those of her daughters. What she didn't know she acquired

Nora turned nineteen on May 24th.

Ed was drawn to Rudy from the moment of his birth, as most fathers would to their first-born son. He had longed for a son in his life. And yet, he gave attention equally among his four children. He never showed favoritism toward any one in particular. More diapers and boy's clothing poured into the house. Nora was always in need of diapers no matter how many she had. Laundry was done daily, hung out to dry regardless of the elements. Those who went by Nora's home marveled at the rows of diapers on the clotheslines waving in the breeze like flags of testimony. All could but

Ed

MORE WEEKS WERE SPENT up at Pearl Lakes while Ed and others built cabins. It seemed Nora spent more time in a tent up there than she did at home. Tent living became a norm for her during warm weather, and she quickly learned how to cope with the obligations of the lifestyle.

Nights were cool and quiet. For the children it was all an adventure every time they went up there. Nora took them on berry hunts and gathered various types to snack on along with other vegetation to add to their meals. Wild spinach was one. Although it took a vast amount for a meal, the end result was well worth it. The scents simmering over the fire were smelled at palates of the people and wildlife around them. Ed always had a full appetite when he finally got home from work.

Although Ed's drinking was at its minimum at Pearl Lakes, whenever Nora came across the secret hiding place for his liquor bottles she shattered them against the rocks, ridding them from their lives. For Ed to rebel would mean admitting he had them in the first place. She never went on a quest to search for them, but on occasion she came across one or two hidden in the shrubbery, sometimes in the coolness of the river banks. She went to any extreme to eliminate the burden liquor brought into her life.

What she couldn't rid herself of was the venom Hueso injected into their marriage and lives. Hueso was consistent in that. Nora had recently discovered Hueso set up dates for Ed with women in the privacy her home. Hueso's determination to destroy Nora's marriage was now an obsession. She went to any extreme, regardless of what it took and whom she hurt. Being at Pearl Lakes gave Nora peace from those elementary games Hueso insisted on playing. Nora knew the feud Hueso created with her would never end. What her jealousy and envy was toward her she doubted she'd ever know. At this point in her life she no longer even cared. The extremes Hueso would take to destroy her home were the same extremes to which Nora would go to defend it. That was made clear to Hueso time and time again.

One night, Nora got wind of a secret date and felt the time for confrontation with Hueso had come. She ventured to Hueso's home once Ed left. His car was parked out front. Fiddles and guitars played inside Hueso's home. Nora heard laughter above the music. She felt the vibration of it beneath her feet as she stood and knocked. She was through with Hueso humiliating her. Hueso was stunned to find her standing at the front door.

"What do you want here?" Hueso demanded.

"You know what I want. Now get him to this door," Nora demanded in return.

"He's busy."

"Fine. I'll get him myself." Nora shoved Hueso aside. She found Ed seated with a woman on his lap, a bottle of Tokay shared between them.

When he looked up and saw Nora standing there his face went pale. Quickly he moved the woman away and stood to face his wife.

"What are you doing here?" he asked in a harsh voice.

"The question is what are you doing?" Nora snapped back, glancing at the woman she knew upon sight.

"Get home!" Ed demanded.

"I intend to. Don't dare show your face around the house after this," Nora answered.

"You have to leave," Hueso shrilled. "Now!"

"Get out of my face," Nora warned. "That will be the biggest mistake you'll ever make if you don't. You've done enough harm to my family, my kids."

Everyone knew something was about to happen. Some who knew Nora stood in her defense, while others who were friends to Hueso stood in hers.

"Get out of my house before I throw you out!" Hueso ordered. She approached Nora with ill intent.

Everything Hueso had ever done to Nora surfaced at that instant. Nora despised her more than ever, wanted nothing more than to beat her within an inch of her life. The second Hueso's hand reached for her arm, Nora's hand went across her face with a slap that stunned everyone, especially Hueso. Nora didn't stop at that. She dragged Hueso by the hair out of the house to the front yard, thrashing her from one side to the other. Those who tried to intercept were kept at a distance by others. Those who knew Nora had a high respect for her and would not allow any harm to come to her from anyone. Once they saw Nora had the upper hand on Hueso they kept others away letting Nora have her say and her way.

Nora slapped Hueso repeatedly, drawing blood from her mouth and nose. All the beatings Ed had given her she was now giving to Hueso. The abuse that she had brought into her life was now being given back. On the ground in a cloud of dust Nora thrashed Hueso until she could no more. With that she stood, leaving Hueso on the ground bleeding and breathless.

"You ever do anything to me again, the next thrashing I give you will be worse!" Nora warned. "You leave me and my family alone! I won't say it again!" She turned to Ed. "You can stay here with her. I don't want you near our home and kids after this. I warn you, if you come near that house you will regret it."

Ed couldn't believe his eyes and ears. He'd never seen this side of Nora before, not even in the midst of his abuse. She made it clear not only to Hueso, but him as well, that she had her fill of it all, had taken a stand against the gossip and abuse. At that moment, Ed realized Nora was no longer the little girl he had married. She had now become a woman able to defend herself to the fullest extreme. He stood and watched as Nora walked away, brushing her clothing of the dirt and dust. Her erect posture spoke of the pride, dignity and integrity she had regained.

Ed didn't come home for several days. He stayed at Hueso's as Nora ordered. He wasn't sure what he'd find when he returned. He knew one thing for certain, that he wouldn't find the same woman, the same wife he had left. The new Nora perplexed him. He wasn't quite sure how to handle her, or if he should even try. His heart beat hard against his chest as he drove up to their home. The kids played out in the front yard. He didn't know whether he should knock, walk in or leave. So, instead, he stood at the entry and called.

"Nora! Nora?"

She came to the door. "I don't want you here I told you," Nora said quietly. "Now please leave."

"I don't want to."

"It's not a question of what you want. It's what I want. Now leave. I've had enough of your damned drinking. You can have your women. Let them feed and take care of you. I sure as hell am not."

"I won't drink anymore," Ed pleaded. He wanted his family back.

"How many times have I heard that? A hundred? A thousand? How many?"

"I mean it this time. I want to come home. I miss you and my family."

"You weren't missing us that night. Why now? Now that you've had your fun and fill you miss us and want to come home? I'm not the fool I was."

"I know."

"If you know then you should leave."

"I can't. I love you. I love all of you."

"This is how you show it? Other women? Beatings? I don't need your kind of love. Go back to whoever you were with that night."

"I'll quit. I promise."

"I've heard that before too."

"I mean it this time."

Nora paused, then spoke softly. "I need more time. Now leave."

"I'll come back. Maybe you'll change your mind?"

"We'll see. Right now I don't even want to look at you. What you have done to me and your kids is inexcusable."

Nora stood at the door and watched as he walked to his car and drove away in a cloud of dust. She was firm in her decision. She was not about to tolerate any more abuse or look away at his drinking. Of this there was no doubt – or debate. She had made up her mind, and there was no going back.

* * * * *

A FEW WEEKS LATER, Nora decided to let Ed return but made it known things would never be the same. Ed found a very different person when he came home. Nora was not the meek, fragile individual she once was. She was confident and sure of herself, and this in itself made him aware of her new boundaries. She was unyielding on them. Hueso was forbidden from their home for good. That was another thing Nora was uncompromising on. Although Nora sensed remorse in Ed, the trust and faith she once had was gone. It had perished along with hopes of a good marriage and life with him. She knew within herself the damage was done for good.

Despite this, Nora did what needed to be done for her family. Ed tried to make up for his mistakes but to no avail. The hurt and humiliation he caused Nora, and allowed Hueso to do to her, could never be undone. He sensed indifference in his young bride. She was distant, withdrawn and impatient with him. Although they shared the same bed there was coldness there.

What was once a place for peace and solitude was now empty and meaningless.

This indifference followed Nora for some time. She did what she needed and wanted regardless of how Ed felt. Rebecca and Rudolf also sensed the change in her. Rudolf was as proud as any father could be to see his daughter finally taking a stand. Rebecca's attitude was unchanging as she believed in "wifely duties." That was something Nora had long since lost faith and belief in. The tide had shifted. She wasn't about to go backward.

Although Ed tried his best to set aside his drinking, the attraction was far greater than his will. He slipped out of the house to his secret hiding place where he could be with his addiction. Nora knew the second he stepped through the door what he'd been up to. Whereas before she would silently accept it and him, now she made sure her disgust and disappointment were obvious. He kept his distance from her when both presented themselves. At times he slept elsewhere as she would not allow him in the same bed with her. The stench nauseated her. Still, his loving nature beyond the liquor brought the closeness when needed. The nature she had learned to love long ago.

Those times when tension between them was low, Ed took Nora dancing as he knew it was what she loved. It was an escape from the routine at home. His insecurities were still constantly challenged when they stepped into a dance hall. Nora drew attention wherever she went, always at her best. While Ed played his fiddle her dance card was always filled. One after another men approached her, really only wanting to be near her. At nineteen years old she was the beauty she would always be known for. Her flair for fashion complemented her. She walked proudly in her high heels. Her laughter was intoxicating.

Hueso kept her distance, although her gossip never ceased. If Nora ran into her in South Fork or Del Norte, Hueso immediately went the opposite direction or crossed the street in avoidance. The warning Nora had instilled in her was effective. She had nothing to say to Hueso, and if she ever did again it wouldn't be pretty just as she warned. Nora was well versed in Hueso's venom, well acquainted with its symptoms. She knew instinctively when Hueso was at work.

* * * * *

THE WORLD TURNED. SNOW enveloped the valley. Winter arrived. Children were once again in awe with the variety of games available for them out in the elements. Sleds and toboggans filled the hillsides. Snowmen, snow angels and snowball fights were common. The scent of burning pine was thick in the air.

Among the crowd this year singing Christmas carols were Pricilla, Flora and Juanita. Rudy was in Nora's arms all bundled up. At this joyous time, Nora forgot all they'd been through and saw the holidays through her children's eyes. She focused on them having a good time, enjoying the festivities and gifts they were showered with.

CHAPTER 12

1936. THE UNEMPLOYMENT RATE drops to 16.9 percent, but the Depression is nowhere near ending. Roosevelt is in a heated presidential election battle with Republican Alf Landon. Hitler's Germany continues to show the world it is not afraid of anyone. For two years it has intervened in the Spanish civil war, bombing cities with impunity.

Unemployed Americans by the thousands travel to California in search of work but are stopped at the main entrance points by local police blocking the "undesirables," a practice later found to be illegal and stopped. Record temperatures are forecast to bake the country.

The book *"Gone With the Wind"* is published, and the movie *"Follow the Fleet"* with Fred Astaire and Ginger Rogers is a hit.

* * * * *

JANUARY WAS CRUEL IN South Fork. Icicles hung to the ground in an arctic mist. Blizzard winds blew snowdrifts against doors and windows, making it a challenge for those to venture out to gather wood and coal. Still, what had to be done was done. Children wore bundles in layers upon layers of clothing before being sent out to the school bus. For them it was another adventure.

Rudolf made his usual rounds to Nora's house making sure she had all she needed, bringing goods Rebecca prepared during the fall. In Rebecca's kitchen there was always something in the oven. She made sure her loved ones were never without.

Christine and Modesto lived nearby in South Fork. Often she visited Nora not only to help but also just to check in and see how she was doing. She resented Ed for the pain and suffering his alcohol and abuse brought into Nora's life. Her instinct was to protect Nora, as she had throughout their lives. To hurt Nora was to hurt Christine. She took up work as a seamstress, creating beautiful clothing shared with Nora and others she loved. She also did it to supplement her income. Many in town called upon her services from the simplest garment to a complete bridal gown and bridesmaids' dresses.

With spring came good weather, which meant Nora and the children going up to Pearl Lakes once again on occasion while Ed worked. It also brought realization of another pregnancy for Nora.

She looked at herself in the mirror. The thought of having five children amazed her. She couldn't help but ponder the life and path she was destined to walk. A deep sigh was testimony of the heaviness of her thoughts. Yet there was a familiar joy within her as well. She would welcome and love this child as she did her others. Of that there was never a doubt. She worried about breaking the news to Rudolf as she knew he would be concerned over the tremendous pressure another child would put her under. She knew he, too, would be there in support regardless, and he would love the child as he did her other children. His gentle, compassionate nature would allow for nothing less.

Ed was delighted with the news, although he, too, was well aware of the pressure both she and he would be under with another child. His growing family gave him incentive to work harder for their needs. Sadly, along with hard work came the stress, which in turn led him to his drinking binges. The grip of his addiction was far greater than Nora's desperate pleas for him to stop. He simply could not, like many in his situation. Alcohol had its grip on many husbands of South Fork and beyond.

Once Nora's friends became aware of her pregnancy, items of need commenced to pour in. Homemade diapers of flannel for cold winter months were provided, and diapers of Birdseye material for other seasons were brought in. At times Nora would gaze out her kitchen window and marvel at the rows of diapers on the clothesline. Now more would be added. She couldn't imagine it. Her hands were already red and sore from those she had to scrub and hang out in the bitter elements. It had become a fact of life to which she had no other choice but to surrender. The reality of diapers and daily laundry as a major part of her life had long since set in. She had two buckets, one in which she cleaned off the soiled diapers, the other for soaking before washing. Blocks of lye soap and a scrub board were fixtures in Nora's home as they were in many of her friends' homes. Nora's friends were bearing children along with her. Their pregnancies coincided at times.

She celebrated her twentieth birthday on May 24th.

Having a young son and two young daughters to care for, and sometimes three if Pricilla went along, made Nora's stays in Pearl Lakes even more challenging. As her pregnancy matured into the late summer months, her trips became less frequent. The challenges of tent living were far too great. Thus, she would stay home while Ed went up for a week or sometimes two. This also gave her a break from the drama his revisit with

By now, Nora had mastered the art of motherhood and being a wife. And music continued to entertain her through the long days. While Rebecca played gospel music, Nora listened to the radio and enjoyed the dance, swing and Hit Parade along with her favorite Spanish tunes. Many of her favorite songs she knew by heart, singing them to her infant son while changing him.

Halloween brought out children in droves moving from household to household in their traditional trick-or-treat hunt. They celebrated with overflowing bags of treats. Baked goods and homemade candy were handed out among the store-bought goodies. Fudge, peanut brittle, divinity and cookies were favorites of many, along with various fruits. Outhouses were overturned, a humorous tradition held by teenagers and adults that was not so funny for those who had to lift them into position once again.

On November 27th Nora gave birth to another son, named Lawrence. Much like Flora, Juanita and Rudy, Lawrence had dark, curly hair. All were delighted with his arrival. Those present arrived with necessities for the newborn. Nora's meals were prepared for the following week while she recovered, along with baked bread, pies and cakes. Nora lay in bed holding

Lawrence cradled in her arms in heavy thought of her life and children. How many more would there be, she could only wonder. This was a question on many minds, especially Rudolf's.

As winter settled in Juanita became ill with a cold. Rebecca stepped in, taking her to her home for recovery. It was then decided that Juanita, too, would make permanent residence with Rebecca and Rudolf. Still, having three small children to tend for was very challenging for Nora. Two were in diapers. Pricilla and Juanita would frequently be home with Nora when permitted as Flora needed playmates. Also the girls were very attached to each other and would miss one another when too much distance was there.

Ed and Nora moved for a time to Baxterville, a community slightly west of South Fork. Even though Pricilla and Juanita were usually with their grandparents, the girls still needed their own bedroom, and now the two boys also needed theirs. Baxterville was closer to some of Nora's friends as they lived along the back road leading into Agua Ramon, where Nora's friends farmed, supplying many with goat cheese, eggs, bacon and meat. Potatoes were brought in from various parts of the valley. Sharing among neighbors and friends was a common tradition. None went without.

Before the year was out, the family moved back to South Fork. Both Ed and Nora felt it was best for their family. It was far more convenient for them in many ways. For one thing Ed's work at the sawmill was a mere ten-minute walk from the house. Plus the house in South Fork was slightly larger, and with a growing family more space was needed. Both the girls and boys needed their own bedrooms.

Christmas dinner for family and friends was held at Rebecca and Rudolf's that year. As usual, food was plentiful. Ginger bread, pumpkin, apple and strawberry/rhubarb pies, cakes and cinnamon rolls were there for all to enjoy. Fudge, peanut brittle and divinity also fed the sweet tooth's. A traditional turkey and ham dinner was set out. A fresh tree decorated with all the familiar trimmings stood proudly in the corner of the living room; wrapped gifts below it piled high. The children stood around the tree wondering which gifts were theirs, eager for the time to open them. Rebecca played the piano singing her favorite gospel songs. All were grateful for what the packages revealed.

Yet each winter seemed more difficult than the last. The need for driving into Del Norte for goods became more of a necessity with Nora's expanding family. Nora always enjoyed shopping at the thrift stores, which became a major part of her life as time went on. Nora by now was proficient at making clothing for the children on her sewing machine, but with her growing family she couldn't possibly keep up. So she would happily spend hours rummaging through the stacks at the thrift stores. It seemed within weeks the kids outgrew what they had anyway. Her friends in Del Norte often made a day of thrift hunting uring her visits. This was something Nora always looked forward to.

CHAPTER 13

1937. DRAMA IS EVERYWHERE. As the New Deal takes hold, the unemployment rate, while still high, falls to 14.3 percent. The Golden Gate Bridge in San Francisco opens, giving Californians a new sense of pride. People scramble to get the first edition of *"Look"* magazine. Howard Hughes sets a record for transcontinental air flight, making the trip from Los Angeles to New York City in seven hours, twenty eight minutes.

The soap opera *"Guiding Light"* débuts on NBC radio. Millions tune in. Disney releases *"Snow White and the Seven Dwarfs."* Hollywood has a new actor, named Ronald Reagan. *"Death on the Nile"* by Agatha Christie is published. Amelia Earhart and Fred Noonan are lost attempting a round the world trip.

* * * * *

SPRING SPROUTED IN SOUTH Fork and the valley. Children took to the outdoors for their favorite games from sunrise to sunset, adults warning them of the *"La Llorona"* superstition that a spirit swept up little ones from the creeks and rivers where she notoriously roamed. In reality, parents were keeping them safe from the overflow of the thaw. The sweet scent of lilac bushes and wildflowers saturated the air in invitation to humming birds and bees. Windows and curtains opened in celebration of the new season.

Warmer temperatures meant more outdoor building for Ed. Whether he was in South Fork, Pearl Lakes or other areas, he was kept busy as cabins and homes were in constant demand. Nora was kept busy around the clock seeing to the children's needs. Rows upon rows of diapers flapped in the breeze at their home. It was a common sight. Flannel diapers from the winter were stored away once they were washed and folded. Spring clothing for all came down from shelves and out of storage. Nora and Ed's household, and South Fork, were abuzz with activity once more.

To no one's surprise by now, Nora became pregnant again in late spring. This child would be their sixth and Nora not yet twenty two years old.

With so many children in their lives and yet another on the way, dancing became less and less frequent, down to an occasional event. Ed still played with the band on some weekends even if Nora's obligations to the children and her growing pregnancy kept her at home. The arguments persisted as he would enter the house with the smell of Tokay and whiskey on his breath. Her intolerance of intoxicated people reached the point where she simply couldn't be around them. It nauseated her just to be in their presence. Although their arguments sometimes escalated in degree, Ed kept his distance and treaded lightly with her.

Peace came to Nora when Ed was up at Pearl Lakes or in other areas of the valley for a week or more. She relished her time without the drama. At times she wondered how much more of it she could take. Talking with Rebecca only brought disappointment. She loathed the words, "It's your wifely duties." When Ed was gone on these trips her stress levels were down to near nothing, but the second he stepped through the door they rose. The comparison was becoming obvious to her. Although she loved him, her sanity and that of her children was more important. She went to any extreme to shield them from the ugliness of the world. It was her motherly instinct.

Christmas was no time for caroling that year with the baby just a couple of months away. The joy of having a life within overwhelmed all the difficulty she had to go through. Come what may with her childbearing, she told herself she would love them all equally and unconditionally. Every time this new baby kicked it brought a smile to her face, filled her with joy. She loved being a mother.

CHAPTER 14

1938. Following modest success with the economy, the hard times get harder and the unemployment rate is back to 19 percent. In Los Angeles massive mudslides and flooding cause over two hundred deaths leaving a nation in mourning. Hurricane winds of a hundred eighty three miles per hour batter New England claiming over six hundred lives. Germany annexes Austria, bringing the world ever closer to war and 183,000 more Jews closer to the brink.

* * * * *

A NEW BABY WAS just around the corner, but the arguing between Nora and Ed was constant. No matter how she tried to avoid it, she was constantly confronted with the chaos. His love for her mushroomed into a jealousy he could not control. The poison Hueso had injected into their lives would not let go, her goal accomplished. In those heated confrontations, Nora was able to fend him off to only an argument. Still, she was well aware of the violence he was capable of. Peace and happiness were a rarity in their home.

In spite of the cold January weather, friends and family were there to see to her needs. She did what she could and what her condition allowed. Many days she simply stayed in bed, unable to tend to her duties. Although the sawmill was at a standstill during the winter months, Ed was kept busy keeping the boilers going. Many times he worked the graveyard shift. When she was bound to the bed, Rebecca and others were always there.

On February 28th a daughter named Lucy was born. She was very small and immediately nicknamed Ardilla, Spanish for squirrel, by Rebecca. Lucy slept in a box near the stove for warmth, also wrapped cozily in blankets Rebecca had lovingly made. All who handled the infant did so with extra care because of her tiny size. Nora was ever so grateful to put another pregnancy behind her. At age twenty one, she now had six children, and who knew how many still to come. It amazed many around her.

Ed celebrated as he had all the births, drinking with friends and family. He was proud of all his children, of Nora and her ability to bear him the children he wanted. He loved her and his children immensely. At times like these when liquor wasn't involved, Ed was a totally different person. He was gentle and caring. Then, as soon as he had a bottle in hand, there was a drastic change. His insecurities and jealousies surfaced, causing the dark, violent side of him to present itself. It happened like clockwork.

On March 30th Ed's father passed away. Ed took the news very hard. For days following Delfino's death, Ed drank his sorrows away, trying desperately to escape the pain. Still, there was no escaping the reality and loss of his father. The realization that he still had his mother and that she needed him was what finally brought him to. But Atanasia was never the same after losing her beloved husband.

Pricilla and Juanita visited often to spend time with their sisters and brothers, engaged in whatever games their imaginations could conjure. On those occasions the house was bustling with excitement for them. It was also a pleasant diversion for Nora from her household duties. Her creativity was constantly challenged when preparing meals for six children as they all had their favorites. The stacks of tortillas she prepared grew with each passing year and child added to the family. The house was constantly filled with aromas of cooking and baking.

Nora celebrated her twenty second birthday on May 24th. During the daily visits by Rudolf, Nora confided in him in so many ways. For her he was more than a father, he was her guardian and best friend. She trusted and adored him in every way. She drew strength from him when life seemed against her. Although she kept Ed's abuse from him, deep in his heart he knew the truth, thus his visits were frequent. In conversation he would advise her, console her and build her spirit. He instilled in her the common sense that guided her through life. He always knew ultimately she would make the right decisions however desperate the situation might be. Rudolf always left Nora feeling renewed; ready for any challenge life would bring her. In his embrace she felt safe from the harshness of life and the world. A place she wished she could stay forever.

Christine and Modesto moved near Center, about twenty five miles northeast of South Fork. On occasion Ed and Nora rented a cabin near Christine's while he worked on building cabins in the area. It was a home away from home. Sometimes they stayed there for weeks, returning to their residence in South Fork until he was needed in Center again. Throughout the spring and summer this took place. Back and forth they went, along with the children. Chores and duties awaited her wherever she went. That was a given. Hauling diapers and clothing back and forth for the children was a chore in itself. Wherever they went Ed made sure she had accommodations for those duties. And for that she was grateful. In Center the only help she had was Christine when she was able. Being close to her was enough in itself for Nora as she missed her dearly since the day she left South Fork. She not only missed her sister, but her best friend in so many ways. For hours they would visit while Christine helped her with chores and caring for the children.

On occasion, Nora and Christine ventured into Del Norte. If Hueso noticed them on the sidewalk she immediately crossed to the other side. The last thing she wanted was another physical confrontation with either of the Prien sisters. For her it was a no-win situation should that happen again. It bothered her even more when Nora and Christine merely ignored her going about their business – their laughter carrying through the summer air. It brought her to a boil to hear Nora's laughter. For her it was a mockery.

Not being pregnant was bliss for Nora. She relished it. On every occasion she was able to go to dances, she eagerly went, dancing her heart out. Knowing her children were safe with Rebecca and Rudolf gave her the freedom to have nights out with no worry. At times jealousy's ugly head would rear itself in Ed when men got a little too close to Nora for his comfort. As always, she commanded attention wherever she went. All eyes were on her the second she stepped into the room. While many wives were intimidated, husbands stole heated glances at her from across the dance floor, their desire burning in their eyes. Her legs in shimmering, silky nylon hose poised in high heels drove their fantasies to heights only they could know and secretly bask in.

The break from pregnancy was brief. In the fall she was with child again, bringing an end to her bliss. Although Nora felt something different about this pregnancy, she was nonetheless overjoyed to welcome another child into the world. Rudolf and Rebecca were not surprised; it seemed their Nora's fate was to bear a child just about every year.

Nora couldn't know it, but 1939 would be a year of deep personal loss.

CHAPTER 15

1939. GERMANY INVADES POLAND and the horrors of World War II begin. *"Gone With the Wind"* and *"The Wizard of Oz"* offer box-office escapes from the growing madness. The economy continues to sputter, bread lines persist, and unemployment goes on and on. The New York World's Fair opens. John Steinbeck publishes *"The Grapes of Wrath."*

* * * * *

FOUR MONTHS' PREGNANT IN January, Nora was as beautiful as ever to Ed. Together they danced their troubles away. For him to watch her on the dance floor made him realize how much he loved her more every day. Her free spirit, inner strength and devotion to her children captivated him. For him there would be no one other as long as he lived. Of this he had no doubt. On those rare nights of dancing and frivolity when Ed kept his drinking to a minimum, there was no arguing or fighting. It was instead a time of celebration and fun, of with music and laughter. Nora looked stunning in her high heels and silk dress, accented with the jewelry she was so very fond of. Her hair had grown down her back in a thick mass of waves glistening in the light. To Ed, her perfume was intoxicating, her moves on the dance floor sensual. She filled his senses.

Nora's heart shattered when she went into early labor. She worried for the child as she knew it was not the norm. She sensed something was terribly wrong. In labor for several days, Nora knew deep in her heart the outcome would not be good. Having the midwife at her side gave some sort of comfort, but no one could ease her maternal instincts. They were confirmed when the child was stillborn in early April. Nora was devastated. Her heart was crushed when she held the child in her arms. Its tiny, lifeless body vibrated with her trembling hands. Ed drowned his sorrow in liquor, unable to come to terms with it sober. It was the only way he knew how to cope.

For weeks upon weeks Nora mourned. There seemed to be no end to her grieving. Rudolf tried his best to console her, as did Rebecca, but nothing anyone could say would ease the pain and sorrow of losing a child. Friends and other family were there for her, but no one could soften the blow. It was her children who finally brought her out of the darkness when she gazed into their eyes and realizing she neglected them. The children needed her strong and healthy. Gradually through time she recovered and the grieving eased, but she never forgot.

* * * * *

THE NEXT MONTH NORA turned twenty three, mature far beyond her years. Her abrupt introduction into adulthood thrust her into it prepared or not. Not to mention what losing a child did. Those around her were constantly amazed. It seemed one day she was a child herself with her favorite doll in her arms, and then suddenly the doll was replaced by child after child. Still, she had a special place in her home for her favorite doll. She kept it out of sight of the children as she didn't want it to be destroyed. It was something she cherished.

Rudolf gave advice and consolation as best he could, well aware of losing a child and its aftermath. Without him it would have been far more difficult to navigate her way down the path of life she was on. His words of wisdom gave her strength, a light to find her way. He sensed the day Nora was born that she would draw upon his strength and embody it. Already, she was strong far beyond even his expectations. For that he was grateful. The need to be true to herself he had embedded in her.

On this birthday, like others in the past, he not only gave jewelry but something more precious: pearls of wisdom to fashion her life upon. Those words would always stay with her. He encouraged Nora to rise above her fears and do what was right for her and the children, even if it meant personal hardship. He resurrected the self-respect she had misplaced along the way, lost within the abuse and alcohol. He wanted to be certain those qualities were instilled in her beyond a doubt. Only then would he be certain she was safe and make the right decisions for her life. Although his precious little girl was now a woman, to him she would always be his baby Nora. Nothing would take that from him.

A worse tragedy struck in June. Rudolf was at the dentist having all his teeth removed to make way for dentures. It was a grueling experience. Within days after the procedure he developed an infection that rendered him bedridden. He lay while his grandchildren each took their turn to visit with him. Although they were far too young to understand, they sensed something was not right with this grandfather they cherished. The house felt a sense of foreboding.

In the wee hours of Saturday, June 24th a loud pounding at Nora's front door awakened her. Nora's older brothers were there to escort her to their childhood home. Half asleep and her heart on fire, Nora made her way with them to the house, leaving Ed with the children. The second she stepped inside and saw Rebecca, she feared the worst.

"It's your father," her mother said as her tears flowed.

"What's wrong with Daddy?" Nora gasped. "I want to see him."

"He's gone," Rebecca answered.

The words tore through Nora like a bullet. They seemed like echoes. Her siblings stood around her in tears. Nora couldn't believe what she heard. Her heart could not accept it. To lose him at this point in her life was overwhelming. She'd scarcely gotten over losing her child.

"I want to see him," she repeated.

"He's in our room," Rebecca said.

The longest walk Nora ever took was from the kitchen to the bedroom where Rudolf lay. She stood in the doorway looking down at him. He seemed so peaceful, as though he were sleeping. She sat at his side taking his hand in hers. He was still warm. The world took a whirl as the reality that he was indeed gone ripped through her. For once in her life she felt lost, totally alone in the world. Whatever would she do without him went through her mind. She burst into tears, resting her head on his chest. She couldn't believe he was gone. She cursed the heavens for taking her most precious of people, the source of her strength and guidance. Over his body she wept until Christine entered the room taking her by the arm leading her out into the living room where everyone else was. All were devastated.

The days following Rudolf's death Nora spent in a fog of despair. It felt like she wept a lifetime of tears, and then they would come again in spurts of uncontrollable outbursts. Although the children were a diversion, the pain in her heart surpassed anything she ever went through. It was from her children that she drew strength, for without them she didn't know what would become of her. Fortunately her friends were there for her as they always had been. They cared for the children while Nora helped Rebecca with what was needed for Rudolf's services and aftermath. Despite all their quarreling, Rebecca, too, was shattered. As self-reliant as she was, she would miss him terribly. Rudolf's words and memory would forever haunt her.

Children were kept at a distance, although from behind closed bedroom doors they heard the weeping and adult conversation. They could not comprehend the reality of what was happening; only that Grandpa Prien would no longer be around. In their own way they, too, grieved although they did not fully understand the sting of death. Rebecca's house filled with family members and friends, some of whom arrived from out of town. Cots were set up throughout the house to accommodate the overflow. Food was prepared for the dinner after Rudolf's services. For Nora it all seemed like a

During the services she sat in a daze, constantly wiping her eyes. For days afterward, the eruption of pain deep inside would not give her peace. It was there constantly, awakening her at all hours of the night, leaving her unable to get the rest she so desperately needed. She had wept a lifetime of tears. Still, they would not cease.

At the Del Norte Cemetery she stood among family and friends as the pastor paid tribute to Rudolf's life. For Nora, it felt like she was going through the motions, living someone else's life, feeling someone else's pain and sorrow. As Rudolf was lowered into the earth she exploded in torment. Reality ripped through her with no remorse. Her wails drowned out everyone else. Ed did his best to comfort her, to no avail. For Nora there was no comfort. Her life had been altered forever. The void in her heart and life would last into eternity. The person she loved most in the world was

As the crowd thinned, Nora was left at Rudolf's grave site, a lone silhouette standing in the June breeze gazing down at his grave. She pleaded to the universe to have mercy on her pain and sorrow. There she stood and cried until she could cry no more. Her eyes were swollen and red, sore from the constant wiping. Her breathing came in gasps. Walking away was the hardest thing she ever had to do. For her to walk away was to face the world on her own with only the memory of Rudolf's words to guide her.

At Rebecca's during the dinner, Nora stayed in solitude. She was numb from the pain. Her appetite was gone. She simply could not eat. When people spoke to her, all she heard were echoes. Nothing seemed to make sense to her. In her children's embrace she found solace. It was through their hugs and kisses that her heart was at peace if only temporarily. The house seemed empty without Rudolf's presence, his memory a ghost. Everything held a memory of him. She wondered what life would be without him.

In the weeks following, the void in Nora's life was evident. The constant duties of taking care of her children kept her preoccupied, but at night when she rested her head on the pillow she could hear her father's words. She missed him more than she could ever have imagined. He was on her mind constantly. The jewelry he gave her over the years took on a whole new meaning and value. Although they were special to begin with, they became precious to her beyond words. All Rudolf gave her were now invaluable. On occasion she would make trips into Del Norte to the

It was on one of these trips that she told Rudolf she was pregnant again. The joy and challenge of another baby on the way, combined with time itself, were the healers she so desperately needed. Her tears diminished, the knot in her stomach became more tolerable.

Christmas proved to be difficult for everyone. Rudolf's absence was clearly felt. Nora's grief returned, but having another life growing inside brought her joy through it all. If for nothing else she had to be strong for her children. They needed her regardless of the circumstances, pain and sorrow. The tubs filled with soiled diapers were still there to contend with, along with

CHAPTER 16

1940. HATTIE MCDANIEL BECOMES the first African-American to win an Academy Award for her role in *"Gone With the Wind."* Roosevelt wins an unprecedented third term as president. Winston Churchill is named prime minister in England. The Battle of Britain rages as Germany presses its invasion of Europe. Nazis enslave millions and sends them to concentration camps. Americans desperately hope to stay out of the war.

* * * * *

NORA WAS GRATEFUL WHEN January became February, although she was large and uncomfortable. At times she was bedridden for days upon days, unable to do what had to be done. Rebecca and friends were always there to lend a helping hand through it all. The children were well taken care of, and when needed Rebecca took them to her place to give Nora the breaks she needed for rest. Although pregnancy was routine for Nora, each one had its own challenges and joys.

On March 11th she gave birth to another son they named Delfino, after Ed's father. He would be called Dale for short. The similarities Dale had to his siblings were uncanny. They all shared characteristics passed on from both Nora and Ed. She was filled with joy to hold him in her arms, surrounded by her loved ones. The children climbed on the bed to get a glimpse of the newborn brother they now had. They were in awe of the infant.

Rebecca had her eye on a patch of land on the south end of Baxterville heading up toward the summit of Wolf Creek Pass. Nora's brothers Bill and Charlie had friends whose father owned the land. Although he resisted selling, she knew with persistence she would finally convince him. In her heart she knew the land was for her. She envisioned her home and her family there as though it were meant to be. Each and every time she saw the man, she pressured him for the piece of property. She wanted it and was not taking no for an answer. For her it was a done deal.

At times she stood near the patch of land and anticipated living there. The view was outstanding. Down the hillside ran the Rio Grande River. There would be plenty of room to plant a garden and have a chicken coop. The openness of the property gave it plenty of sunlight throughout the day. Although it was next to Highway 160, the traffic would not bother her. Plus, it was convenient for the children to catch the school bus. As with Nora, losing Rudolf awakened a reality in Rebecca that she had only herself to rely on when it came to life and its challenges.

With persistence, Rebecca finally persuaded the man to sell the property. Now that she stood at its boundaries envisioning life there, it had become a reality. She knew precisely what she wanted. The home she wanted had to be built from the ground up. That was going to take enormous energy for not only her, but for everyone involved. She made arrangements with the homeowners across the highway to use their creek to make adobe blocks for the home when the time came. First, the plans had to be drawn up, then the foundation set. There were tons of details to contend with before anything begun. She knew exactly who to call on.

It was decided that Ed along with his brother-in-law would draw up the plans and set the foundation. She knew it would be months of extremely hard work but was grateful she now had what she wanted for such a long time.

Rebecca's immediate task was raising the funds to buy the land and pay for construction of the home. Cleaning rooms in lodges, washing and ironing laundry for others, she did whatever it took to raise money. The task was difficult, but she was determined to accomplish it, Life without Rudolf at her side was challenging for her now that she was on her own with a family to raise and support.

In spring, work on the foundation began. Ed, his brother-in-law and others worked long hours on it. At times it seemed more money was going out than coming in. Rebecca did what had to be done. She kept busy not only working her jobs, but preparing for things needed for the home, everything from curtains to appliances. Locals went by the property in curiosity to check on its progression.

Nora did what she could with what little time she had to spare. With three children in diapers her household duties were never done. Constantly she was scrubbing out laundry for the next day. It was endless. With the children going through five to eight diapers per day, her hands were left raw and sore from constantly being in water. With Christine living in Center, and Rebecca consumed with obligation to the new home, she fended for herself. It was always a relief when her friends came with a helping hand. The busy schedule kept her mind off Rudolf and her stillborn child, although at night she still cried herself to sleep from time to time – Ed oblivious to her tears.

Nora turned twenty four.

On occasion Ed continued to work up at Pearl Lakes. He and Nora with the children would spend up to a week at a time there. Although life was difficult for her there, she made do with what she had. Ed made things as convenient for her as possible at those times. Once, she and the children posed for photos while sitting at the fire pit. Nora wore a cotton sundress. Behind them was the tent.

Nora with children

REBECCA'S HOME WAS TO be a two-story structure with a cellar. Porches would extend the length of the house to the north and south. Rebecca's plans were to have a garden on the northeast side where it would get full sun throughout the day. A garden was a must for her, as well as a chicken coop, rabbit hutch and pen for a pig. A well was to be dug at the front of the house. Materials were continuously gathered for the project.

Even with the work on this home and on others, Ed always found time to drink. The arguing persisted, and now that Ed knew Rudolf was not there for protection, more violence arose. It always prompted Nora to grab whatever was near, resilient in her defense. On occasion the children were exposed to it, which was totally against everything Nora believed in. She fought desperately to shield them from it, but when Ed was intoxicated there was no reasoning with him. His outbursts were uncontrollable regardless whether the children were present or not. It worsened with time, but still never was directed toward the children, always towards Nora.

The foundation to Rebecca's home was completed. She was eager for her dream to become a reality. Daily she went to the creek across the highway and made adobe blocks. The children and older grandchildren all had to help. The blocks were made with mud and straw, placed into frames, let dry enough to be removed, and then moved to the property site by the truck load. It was a daunting task. There never seemed to be enough blocks no matter how many they made. She wanted as many as possible before winter set in when more blocks would be virtually impossible to make. What time she had to herself was spent making curtains and other items needed for the home. Exhaustion drew her to bed at night.

As the blocks piled up, the shell to the house was slowly erected. By mid-summer it was nearly complete. Rebecca also was busy building the path from the house down to the river. Along the path she placed large stones and planted flowers and lilacs and other bushes. The path came to a stop at the river's edge where a swinging bench was placed with wild vines covering it. The spot she created for serenity was enchanting in many ways. River water lapping against its banks was soothing. She planted flowers surrounding the area. What she hoped to create was a place where she could sit and contemplate life in peace and solitude.

Nora visited the property site and took lunch for all. At her side were the children. She sat in wonder at the beauty of it all. Rebecca couldn't have picked a lovelier spot for the home of her dreams. It was obvious to all what had captivated her. The property gave her the beauty of the mountains surrounding it, along with easy access to everything needed. The river was near for hauling up water needed for laundry or bathing. There was plenty of room for the children to run and play safely. Locals stopped by to lend a helping hand with whatever was needed. Although daunting, it was also joyful to see Rebecca's home come to life. They all took pride in taking part of it.

The stack of adobe blocks grew. Rebecca pushed on, and pushed those who helped. At times when she felt the children had had enough, she gave them the day off to play and laugh the stress away. Pricilla, Juanita and Flora relished when those times came. Their little hands were sore from the countless blocks they had already made. Rebecca rewarded them with not only the day off, but with homemade treats and candy. She knew the way to a child's heart.

By summer's end there were finally enough blocks to make Rebecca secure that there would be plenty for the job. Nora's brothers, Charlie, William, Ernest, Henry and even a very young Ted, helped in setting the blocks into place. Ed and his brother-in-law supervised the project. With their experience the house was certain to be solid. One by one the blocks went into place using mud as mortar. Locals weren't the only ones taking notice. Curious wildlife peered through the shrubbery to the sound of pounding hammers.

Through the summer and fall the house progressed. Gradually it took shape as the adobe blocks were set into place. An early winter chill was in the air by October. Thanksgiving was a joyful event at Rebecca's in celebration of the new home taking shape. There was plenty to be grateful for in spite of the void left in so many hearts. Life just wasn't the same without Rudolf.

Christmas, although joyful for the children, once again felt empty and so very different. As usual Nora and Ed participated in the caroling events. The children were eager for Christmas to arrive to see what Santa brought them. Their laughter filled the house on Christmas morning as they unwrapped their packages. Throughout the year Nora quizzed them to learn their wishes for the holidays, then saw to it that they were met. The children's wishes were usually modest, within reach for Ed and Nora. All hoped for a better year ahead when Rebecca could finally move into her new home.

CHAPTER 17

1941. GERMANY SPREADS ITS reign of terror in Europe. The movie *"Citizen Kane"* débuts, as do *"Dumbo"* and *"The Maltese Falcon."* *"Chattanooga Choo Choo"* by Glenn Miller fills the airwaves. Bing Crosby sings *"White Christmas"* on the radio. Fast food is becoming popular. Gas is twelve cents a gallon. America stands on the verge of a war that will change everything.

* * * * *

Nora's DAYS FILLED WITH routine in the harsh winter when temperatures plunged below zero. From sunrise to sunset, and beyond, she was on the move. Dale, like all the kids, grew quickly. In that way, time moved too swiftly for her—yet, with nearly two years gone since her stillborn baby and her father's passing, time often seemed to stand still. She felt the void, and a day didn't go by that she didn't think of Rudolf. She missed him more than ever.

When weather permitted, work proceeded on the inside of Rebecca's house. Walls had to be constructed, floors installed. She hoped to move in by summer. Once the adobe blocks were set into place, the porches were constructed. The house took on the personality Rebecca had hoped for. It was everything she dreamed of. On tolerable weather days, she was there for work on the two bedrooms on the main level. The cellar was to have storage convenient for all of Rebecca's canned goods. A stairway would lead upstairs to two rooms with no doors. Cavities on the eves of the house made easy, ample storage.

By March, plants and flowers sprouted along the path leading down to the river. She was anxious to see how many came forth. The interior of the house was getting done and the well outside of moss rock and cement mortar was underway. Rebecca was there every step of the way. She knew what she wanted and how she wanted it done. There was no disputing her wishes.

The kitchen took shape. The counter was built, and linoleum in shades of green put down on the floor. The stove was set into its place, wood and coal bins near. Cupboards were installed. In the cellar Rebecca could keep vegetables buried in sand crates, with canned goods stored away on the shelving.

It was not yet Nora's twenty fifth birthday when she experienced the familiar signs of pregnancy, along with the mixed emotions. This was her ninth pregnancy. She was more than confident that this would be her eighth living child. To be surrounded by her children made all the hardship of her life worthwhile. With them at her side she could endure whatever life threw at her.

Ed could never have enough children. And Rebecca, despite knowing of the responsibilities of the growing family, knew what had to be done would get it done and be prepared to welcome another grandchild into her life and home.

Even nature seemed to celebrate the new life with all its blossoms and colors.

Christine visited from Center to celebrate Nora's birthday. She brought beautiful dresses for the birthday girl, along with clothing handmade for the children. Christine's expertise with needle and thread was unlimited.

Christine would sit and marvel at Nora's mothering skills, amazed at how she had matured through the years, had grown into the woman she now was. Having children of her own now, Christine could relate to Nora in many more ways than before. What she could not relate to was the extreme of Nora's responsibilities as a mother and wife with so many young ones. And like everyone including Nora herself, she could only wonder how many

By summer, Nora's pregnancy bloomed. Every day that went by she showed a little more and wasn't even able to wear the beautiful dresses Christine brought for her birthday. Nora began the familiar task of bringing out the maternity clothing for the impending newborn, supplemented by

For Rebecca and her family, this was also a joyous time because they were finally able to move into the house, although there was still much to be done. Pricilla's bedroom was to the right of the kitchen next to the stairwell. Rebecca and Juanita shared a bedroom at the other side of the house next to the living room. A piano was outside their room. Above the piano hung a painting of wild horses running through a thunderstorm. Lightning veined in the skies above the horses – a beautiful yet mysterious painting that caught most people's eye when they entered the room. Upstairs were two more

Out on the porches Rebecca placed chicken wire and planted morning glory vines on it. Hummingbirds hovered over the succulent blossoms throughout the morning and day. On a weather vane, Hansel and Gretel came out on nice days, but on bad ones the wicked witch ventured out to make an appearance. The children looked to it each day. The flowers and shrubs along the path to the river bloomed in an array of colors and species. Their fragrance saturated the air. Rebecca's garden sprouted with carrots, green beans, celery, bell peppers, beets, onions, cucumbers, squash,

Rebecca made frequent trips to the rivers and valley in search of wild spinach and other edible treats. As Rebecca had taught her, Nora showed her own children what to pick and how to cook it. There was no mistaking the scent of wild spinach and onions cooking in the kitchen of either Nora's or Rebecca's home. Both Rebecca and Nora were always well stocked with pinto beans and flour, both necessities for their families. They were bought in hundred pound bags and kept in cool storage. The flour bags when empty were used to make diapers. Nothing was wasted.

After two hot, dry months, August began with roaring thunder that rattled windows. Raindrops tap danced on everything in their path. The gardens rejoiced. Rebecca and her neighbors stood in doorways admiring the downpours that left puddles of liquid relief for the dry, cracked earth.

Rebecca harvested her second batch of radishes and other vegetables and planted more in their place. Fruit trucks made their rounds selling to households. Rebecca stocked up on apples, cherries, apricots, peaches, oranges and grapefruit. She baked pies with the fruit and jarred what she could for later. Children were rewarded with fruit after completing their chores for the day.

It was about this time when Nora experienced worrisome changes in her body. For days she was bedridden, unable to do anything. It horrified her, and was no surprise when she went into early labor giving birth to another stillborn baby boy. Once again her heart shattered. All who knew Nora grieved when they heard the news. The child was buried next to his stillborn

She'd scarcely gotten over losing her first stillborn son, then Rudolf, and now this one. Still, with having children in diapers and others to attend to, mourning had to take second place. Her duties waited for no one. They forced her into obligation. She had no choice.

Ed grieved in his own usual way, a broken heart and a bottle in his hand. It was the only way he knew how to cope with such tremendous loss. Rebecca tried her best to console Nora to no avail. The only person who ever could was gone forever. At moments and times like this Nora missed Rudolf more than ever. Her tears were not only for her deceased child, but for him. She doubted she would ever adjust to living without him in her life. In quiet moments, Nora visited the children's gravesites, known only to her, Ed and Rebecca. There she would weep and mourn for children she would never know or hold – voids that would forever remain in her heart.

A life had been taken, but there were two others to celebrate. In mid-August, she and the family marked Juanita's and Flora's birthdays. Despite her sorrowful state of mind, Nora would not cheat them out of acknowledgement of their entering the world and life. It wasn't in her heart to take away the joy for them on that day. For all of her girls' birthdays, she made pretty dresses and bought them dolls and toys. The boys always got shirts and toys as well. She baked cakes and cookies for these days, and

After the loss of her second child, Nora kept Ed at a distance, not wanting to ever get pregnant again for fear of losing another.

Winter approached. Flocks of geese veined the sky in their migration south. Mountain peaks tipped with snow. Elk bellowed, some locking horns in battle. Nora and Rebecca made Halloween costumes for the children and baked cookies and candy to hand out. They prepared baggies for each child who came to her door. It always brought a smile to Nora's face and joy to her heart to see the children in their costumes. To see her own was even

She would stand at the door with a happy heart and watch them go off in their quest for treats. Children's laughter was everywhere. With each knock at her door she never knew what to expect would be there but knew it would bring a smile to her face. Hoboes and witches paid their visits, as did ghosts

For days following Halloween, treats and candy had to be rationed for the children. Too much of it would send them into a sugar frenzy, keeping Nora on her toes for all the wrong reasons. Their costumes were stored away for the next year. But in knowing children, they would probably want to wear something different next time around. Hand-me-downs were a common thing in families. When one child outgrew clothing, the next child could and would use it. Every fall a new pair of winter shoes was purchased for each child.

Soon, Nora and Rebecca were busy planning their Thanksgiving dinner. It was to be held at Rebecca's new home this year. There was ample room and sitting, with plenty of food to go around. Keeping busy was key to Nora's healing. There were days she didn't feel like getting out of bed, but the children needing to be fed and readied for school pulled her from her state of mourning. As days went by she was grateful for this.

On Thanksgiving Day, Rebecca presented her best turkey dinner ever. She bought a live turkey and butchered it herself. The golden, brown bird enticed everyone's appetite. Her home smelled of mashed potatoes, gravy, cinnamon rolls and ginger bread. She had fresh garden vegetables and salad to go with the meal. Nora's brothers and Christine with her family were present. Rebecca had a house full with plenty of hungry mouths to feed. As usual she opened the dinner with prayer and scripture from the Bible. That was always a must in her home and life.

Gazing across the table at the spot at the table where Rudolf usually sat gave Nora an empty feeling inside. His absence was keenly felt. Tears filled her eyes. With one quick glance from Rebecca, her thoughts shifted. Rebecca's eyes told her it wasn't the time for sadness, but for gratitude. To convince Nora heart of this was another thing. Nothing could fill the void she felt, particularly Rebecca's admonition.

Now came Christmas. With seven children, there was much to be done. Once more Ed took to the mountains and brought home a beautiful tree. As usual he placed it in a bucket with rocks securing it in place, filling it with water to keep the tree fresh. The scent of fresh pine immediately filled the house. The children took delight in decorating it. Nora spent time with them in making the decorations, and with pride they strung them on the tree. Excitement filled them as they anticipated what Santa would bring this year. For these reasons Christmas would always be Nora's favorite holiday – the vivid colors, the joy and celebration, along with the family unity. She would always treasure these things.

The Christmas preparations were shattered on December 7th when households around the country sat gathered around radios listening to the news of Japan's attack on Pearl Harbor. Nora and Rebecca's were among them. In disbelief, they found out the grisly details of battleships damaged or sunk, many American lives lost. The shock waves were felt in South Fork, across the United States and around the world. America was at war.

All that, and what was to come over the next four years, seemed so very far away. On Christmas at Nora's house the children tore into their gifts. Ed sat next to the heater with some of the children on his lap. Their eyes lit with joy as they unwrapped presents to find what Nora had quizzed them on during the year. They never could quite figure out how Santa knew exactly what they wanted but knew their mom was a superstar.

Ed's love for Nora and his family was apparent in his eyes. There was nothing more he could ask for. His heart quivered with joy and happiness. In spite of their differences and problems, she was everything he could ever hope for. His desire for her would never die. For a moment he was lost in it all. Nora's long, black, wavy hair glistened in the morning light. Her laughter with the children's echoed in his mind, would always be in his memory.

The moment was short-lived. They argued that night about her continuing distance from him. His insecurities blinded him from the reality of a mother losing a child. As usual he resorted to the bottle, drowning his problems with alcohol, encouraging the distance between them to grow even further. In the living room he sat in the glow of the kerosene lamp until he passed out for the night. Nora left him there.

CHAPTER 18

1942. RATIONING OF FOOD and everyday supplies is a way of life in South Fork, as it is across the country. Everything across America goes into the fight against Germany, Italy and Japan. U.S. naval and air forces defeat the Japanese at the Battle of Midway. U.S. and British forces invade North Africa. The government forcibly moves 100,000 Japanese-Americans from the West Coast to detention camps. The first nuclear chain reaction is produced at the University of Chicago. Fortunately, Glenn Miller and Bob Hope offer an escape from the madness.

* * * * *

NEW YEAR'S WAS ALWAYS Nora's and Ed's night out. The children were left in Rebecca's care while they went out dancing. This year, as usual, Ed played his fiddle in the band, and Nora sat with her friends and danced at every opportunity. Periodically, Ed took breaks to dance with his wife. Nora got to wear one of the beautiful dresses Christine had either made or bought her. Her worries drifted away with the music, but from experience she knew the night wouldn't end well. She could see it in his eyes.

As expected, Ed fought with her when they got home, saying she let men get far too close for his comfort. In reality it had all been in innocent fun, but to Ed's insecurities it was something else. His voice carried from the house out into the street. Neighbors heard the arguing and Ed slamming doors and tossing things about in the house. He accused Nora of enticing men, encouraging them with her seductive behavior. Nora was grateful the children were with Rebecca. She secured a chair under the doorknob and went to bed, leaving Ed cursing until he finally passed out.

In bed she studied the ceiling, contemplating her life. How tired she'd grown of the arguing and fighting. There didn't seem to be an end to it in sight. She reflected on Rudolf's words, questioned the path life gave her to walk. Her children made her grateful for her decisions.

Through the night Nora fed the heater, making sure the fire kept going and the house stayed warm. She was careful not to awaken Ed for fear of another confrontation of who knew what magnitude. Although it was much colder in the bedroom for her, she placed more blankets on the bed instead of opening the door. She didn't want to chance Ed wandering in to continue the fighting.

Early the next morning, the door slammed as Ed went off to work, ending the latest in the long line of ugly episodes in their marriage. Like always, Nora was eager to get the children home and let her joy kick in again. Although the children were gone only one night, she missed them terribly. The silence in the house was deafening. She missed them running about playing their games, filling the house with laughter and life. She bundled up and went to a friend's house for a ride to Rebecca's. Like their mother, the children were excited at every reunion. They missed her. Rebecca fed them a good breakfast and bundled them up with clothing she made for them. She also had bags of goods for Nora to take home. More canned foods, with breads and cookies for the kids, along with more winter clothing she worked so lovingly on.

At Rebecca's, the children had rules to abide with. Running amok was not tolerated. They knew the rules the second they stepped into her home. At Nora's it was the opposite. She let them play to their hearts' content. Having them involved in games with each other meant more time for her to get her duties done. It was when they were quiet that she worried. Then she knew they were bound to be up to something. Her children were like every other child; if there was mischief to get into they found it. She kept an eye on them at all times.

On more tolerable days she would let them out to play in the mounds of snow. They loved it. Building a snowman was on every child's list of wishes during the winter season. And with newly fallen snow it meant just that. Periodically she made them come into the house for warmth, then out again to play more. With mittens and snow boots they were fully content. Nora restricted them to the front yard while she did her laundry, cooking and baking. She caught glimpses of them playing their games while hanging out the diapers and laundry on the clotheslines. Occasionally one would burst into tears, but that would last a mere thirty seconds. There was far too much fun to be had than to cry.

It seemed the minute Nora was out hanging clothes, her friends came by to help. For years it was like that. She couldn't imagine life without them. They had been true, devoted friends to her in every way. To sit and have coffee with them was always a treat for her. Many times they allowed Nora the privilege of sitting down while they did her chores. Laughter was a big part of their friendship, never a dull moment when they were together. Each had their tale to tell.

Most of them had children of their own, some the same age as Nora's. When they visited they brought their children along. The kids busied themselves in one of the bedrooms and played their games, or went outside while the women got together. Children were restricted from the adult conversations. This rule was well known to them. Occasionally heads would peer from behind doorways in curiosity, but with a simple hand gesture they retreated.

During these visits Nora and her friends discussed the pros and cons of married life and motherhood. Each had their own story to tell of what alcohol had brought into their lives. Like Nora, all of them were tired of it and fought back. They encouraged one another to do so at those times. With liquor sold in stores now, it made their struggles even greater.

Nora's attitude toward Ed softened, as it always did, and eventually she felt those familiar changes in her body. At first she hoped her instincts were incorrect but broke into tears when she realized beyond a doubt she was pregnant again, afraid of losing another child. She never wanted to go through that again. At times like this, she missed Rudolf more than ever. It was he she could turn to and consult with. It was his words of wisdom that saw her through her turbulent times as well as her times of sheer joy and happiness. Come what may, she would always welcome another child into her life. Perhaps Rebecca was right after all. She would have to keep having children until "God" decided she'd had enough. But when would enough be enough?

She was in a daze for days before breaking the news. Ed was once more overjoyed. Rebecca only echoed her suspicions of what she'd say.

Rebecca's new house brought new winter chores for Pricilla and Juanita, who had to shovel paths to the outhouse, chicken coop and rabbit hutches. They also had to clear a path down to the river for hauling up water when needed. Along with the adults, they began counting the days to spring.

The war came to Rebecca's home in that springtime of 1942. One of her sons was talking of enlisting, and there were visits from government officials asking questions related to Rudolf's German heritage. She knew they'd be back, that their questioning was ridiculous and that Rudolf would be enraged to have his loyalty questioned. Despite her strict attitude in so many ways, Rebecca had a loyal and soft heart.

Travelers going by on their way either up Wolf Creek Pass or coming down into the valley stopped for food or water. Turning her back on anyone was not in Rebecca's nature and she provided them with their needs. She always had plenty to share.

On May 24th Nora turned twenty six years old.

* * * * *

REBECCA'S WORST FEARS CAME to be when her son Bill joined the Navy. Many nights she laid in bed awake, tossing and turning contemplating his decision. On one hand she was proud of him, but on the other she was deathly afraid. Her other son, Charlie, had made reference to joining the Air Force but hadn't made up his mind. This was troublesome to her as well. She knew in her heart they would do what was needed regardless. She struggled to make peace with that. Not long after that, Charlie did sign up. Rebecca's heart sank as she bid him farewell to an unknown, unpredictable future.

The war has everyone on edge. No one knew what tomorrow would bring. Families picked up newspapers to read about it and gather spellbound around radios to listen to reports of battles in faraway places.

Having two sons in the armed services was the height of Rebecca's fears and worries. Daily she included them in the prayers at the dinner table. At night sleep eluded her. She tossed and turned, until finally drifting off. Her sense of faith carried her through. Even with her sons' service, government officials were at Rebecca's doorstep with their inquisitions every month. They confiscated guns Rebecca had in her household. Two men who had been interned in a concentration camp in the valley escaped at one point and were found sheltered in the basement of a home in Del Norte. This made things even worse for those suspected, foolishly, of being anti-American.

Rebecca kept busy with preparations for the upcoming seasons. A lot had to be done. As soon as the weather permitted the garden had to be planted. It did her heart good to finally be able to open the windows letting the cool, spring breeze sweep through the remnants of winter. Whatever the season, getting Pricilla and Juanita up and ready for school was a must. She was very strict on that. She wanted them to get a good education above all. There was no disputing this. Few dared to question her decisions. And for a child to do so was intolerable under any circumstances.

Three months into her pregnancy, Nora began to show. She tried not to overdo the work, to keep her body safe for the new little one inside her, but she still had to tend to business. She busied herself planting a garden like many in South Fork. As usual, diapers by the dozen swayed in the breeze like flags of testimony to her life and struggles. The children ran in and out of the house in celebration of the spring air. On rare occasions Nora sat on her porch watching them frolic in the sun. It did her heart good.

Nora felt good about this pregnancy. Her instincts told her this child was sure to be welcomed into the world and her life. She and the family had moved to a cluster of four homes that shared an outside water pump. It was near Chinook Cabins. The general store on Highway 160 served them well, and the house was close to Ed's job and Rebecca.

Also, the beauty of the mountains was breathtaking. Living next to Highway 160 posed no problems or issues. Nora could walk to most places she needed to go, children at her side or in her arms.

Even with the approaching birth, life at home remained unchanged, challenging for her while she guessed every day what Ed's mood would be like. That all depended on what he had to drink and how much. The second the door opened she anticipated what the evening and night would be like. Far too many were spent in turmoil. The arguing and fighting had grown too much for her. At times when she peered out the window to see him stumble toward the house, she locked the door. He resorted to spending the night at Hueso's or elsewhere. Nora's tolerance for his drinking and abuse grew thinner and thinner. The difficulties of life were enough for her to contend with without the added drama and stress.

Nora was bedridden on Halloween. She couldn't even get her children into costume, and friends came to the rescue. From her bed she watched as they walked out the door dressed as their favorite characters to merge with other children. Their laughter faded as they ventured into the night. Nora lay with her friends at her bedside. She was immobilized. For days to follow she needed help, either from Rebecca or her friends. She was unable to do for herself.

She went into labor around Thanksgiving. On November 28th she gave birth to a boy, named William. He would be known as Billy. The hue of the fine fuzz on his head foretold that he was sure to be another redhead. Ed was overjoyed to have another son. He fully accepted his red hair and would not tolerate outside influence from anyone. He loved his children more than life itself, regardless of what anyone said. In his mind, he was not about to make that mistake again. He damned himself for allowing Hueso to poison his mind from what common sense could only explain.

Nora now had eight children and wouldn't trade them for anything. To have the children surround her, pulling at her apron was the highlight of her life. They scampered about the house filling it with laughter and joy. It was they who made their house a home.

Nora was dancing again, in her heart and on the dance floor. On New Year's, she sang along with the band, threw her head back and laughed a hearty laugh.

* * * * *

MORE MODEST PROGRESS IN the war comes in 1943. U.S. and British forces invade Sicily. U.S. Marines advance in the Pacific. Race riots erupt in Detroit and New York. Dozens die. Paycheck withholding taxes take effect. *"Oklahoma"* opens on Broadway.

* * * * *

REBECCA WAS BUSIER THAN ever putting in her garden that spring. It grew to impressive proportions to feed everyone she loved, and working in the dirt helped calm Rebecca's fears for her sons.

Both Bill and Charlie sent her money every month, but instead of spending it she opened savings accounts for them when they returned. Rebecca toiled long and hard hour to make ends meet. Work began at sunrise, lasting many times into the wee hours of the mornings. She had a set clientèle for whom she did laundry and ironing. Washing laundry was done on days off from her regular job, and ironing during evenings when there was solitude in the house. At those moments was when she also reflected on life.

When she could, Nora sat on the front porch with Billy in her lap as the other children played, sometimes dashed in and out of rain. Their laughter filled both the air and her heart. Billy's hair turned to a brilliant, copper red mass of curls. The dancing raindrops took her thoughts to Rudolf and the children she lost. She reminisced fondly about him. She had come to peace with his passing but would never get used to being without him. She would miss him forever. Nature seemed to sigh when the storm settled into a soaking rain.

Ed seldom had a day off. The needs of his growing family kept him constantly on the go, What free time he did have was spent tending to Nora's needs at home, finally capturing what little sleep and rest he could.

On weekends he still tried to take Nora dancing as he'd promised when he married her. Although his insecurities and jealousies overwhelmed him at times, he managed to find it in his heart to fulfill his promise and her desire. He knew dancing was Nora's only escape from the trials and tribulations of life. At the dance hall Nora met up with her friends for a night filled with laughter and escape. For him to put his jealousy and insecurity aside just to give her that was worth the effort. Those times were rare, but they meant everything to Nora.

Nora turned twenty seven on May 24th.

* * * * *

IN AUGUST, NORA KNEW she was pregnant again, her dancing days on hold once more. At age twenty seven, she had had ten children, with eight surviving, and an eleventh on the way. That was astonishing to anyone who met her for the first time, and even those who knew her. To many, she was extraordinary. To Nora, this was simply walking the path of life she was meant to walk.

What totally surprised Nora and everyone else was when she thought she felt two babies stirring within in her. Nora's mid-wife confirmed her suspicions. The mere thought of having twins was mind boggling to her. There was much to celebrate and be grateful for this holiday season. Both Rebecca and Ed were ecstatic with the news. Although this was to put even more pressure on Ed, Nora and Rebecca, it was still a very joyous occasion. Nora smiled when she felt the babies stir, and tenderly stroke her stomach to comfort them.

Strangely, with this pregnancy Nora's voice faded to a whisper for no apparent reason, was thought to have been laryngitis, but no trace of it was to be found. It made for difficulty in calling for the children to come in after sunset and getting her point across when needed, but she made do with what voice she did have. Many were there to offer their home remedies for the cure, but to no avail. She was this way for days and weeks.

For Christmas, although large with child, Nora participated in the caroling even though she could not sing. Each house she came upon offered her tea with honey to sooth her throat, which was not sore in the least. Some suggested a shot of whiskey in the tea, but Nora was dead set against it. Being pregnant merely gave her more a reason to refuse. She was not about to participate in what was destroying her home and family. Still, many made claim to its medicinal purposes when used in moderation. She would not budge in her decision.

She also took the children to the local fire station, where they awaited Santa's arrival in a sleigh drawn by two horses. The horses had bells around their necks the size of baseballs. They looked enormous to the children. Santa handed out mesh bags containing apples, oranges, a popcorn ball and various candies. From infants to toddlers to grown children, all were taken there for the festivities. Christmas carols filled the background.

Without delay after Christmas, Nora was busy sewing. She wanted to be well prepared for the twins. The thought of having ten children in her life was still hard to grasp, but it was her reality. Nora often felt their movements inside her. She was eager to meet them and prayed they would be healthy. With this pregnancy she counted the days, weeks and months as they went by.

CHAPTER 19

1944. THE WAR REACHES a turning point. The Allies land in Normandy, preparing to free Europe and defeat Hitler. The Soviet army smashes the German forces on the east. In the winter is the Battle of the Bulge, a last-ditch offensive that costs 80,000 Americans killed, wounded or missing but that proves to be Hitler's last gasp. In the Pacific, U.S. forces move closer to the Japanese mainland. Roosevelt is elected to a fourth term. Meat rationing ends. Bing Crosby's *"Swinging on a Star"* entertains.

* * * * *

NORA WENT INTO LABOR in late April. For hours upon hours she struggled through the pain, giving birth to two-dark haired daughters on April 30th. They were named Charlotte and Rebecca. Charlotte was born first, Rebecca, to be known as Becky, minutes after. Charlotte had straight hair, Becky curly. Nora held the tiny infants in her arms with pride before dozing off to a much-needed deep and restful sleep. Out in the front yard Juanita held Billy in her arms. The other children played around her. Felipé, one of Nora's friends, walked out of the house grinning.

"Now, you have two more to play with," he told Juanita and walked away.

She didn't quite realize what he meant until later when she discovered she had two more sisters. The children gathered around the infants in curiosity and awe. They had never seen twins before.

During this time Rebecca took Billy to live with her along with Pricilla and Juanita. Rebecca did all she could to help Nora with the struggles and burden of a growing family. Rebecca knew with so many young ones in diapers and others to care for, Nora needed all the help she could get. If this meant raising some of her grandchildren to help, so be it. She would love them and care for them as if they were her own. Pricilla, Juanita and Billy were free to go to Nora's whenever they needed or wanted, or if Nora wanted them to be near her. None were deprived of each other. Flora, Rudy, Lawrence, Lucy and Dale kept each other entertained with games and things children notoriously do.

Children ran in and out of the spring rain showers and puddles. Nora had her hands full with the twins and their constant needs. The joy they brought into her life and home was far worth the sacrifices. In her spare time, she handmade their clothing, usually in matching sets. Rebecca and others contributed with clothing and diapers as well. Many were involved with the twins' introduction into the world.

Nora turned twenty eight on May 24th.

Rebecca kept busy constantly with not only her daily job and odd jobs, but also helping Nora with her needs. Pricilla and Juanita came with her to Nora's to help with the sewing; washing and doing what all had to get done. It was a constant task keeping up with garments for the growing children. It seemed from month to month they required new clothing as they outgrew what they had. Nora's daily meal planning grew along with them.

Drifters continued to stop at Rebecca's house for food and water. As usual, Rebecca would allow them to sit at her porch while she prepared, sending them on their way with full bellies and a bag of other supplies for their journey. She kept the children at a distance from them.

Disheartening to Nora was that Ed's drinking didn't slow. The arguing and fighting persisted. Sometimes he hit her in front of the children, which broke Nora's heart. As usual she lifted whatever was available to her for defense. While other wives kept their abuse a secret, thinking it might be a cultural happening best kept a secret, Nora was open with hers. Common sense told her she'd look foolish trying to hide it with bruises. It was what it was. For her there was no denying this. It was something she incorporated into her life whether she liked it or not. So many times she thought of walking out, but where would she go, especially with so many children to feed? Still, she knew in her heart the day would come when she'd have her fill. It seemed many wives in South Fork shared the same dilemma. Ed's gentle, loving nature when he wasn't intoxicated was what kept Nora at his side. It was her diminishing hope.

* * * * *

TIME FLEW BY AS Nora kept busy with the twins and other children. Before long summer came to an end and fall's red, oranges and yellows speckled the mountains and valley. The crickets' concerto that started at sunset into the wee hours of the night served as nature's lullaby for many who slept with their windows and doors open. Already Nora was planning ahead for winter and the Christmas holiday. It seemed like only yesterday that it had ended. Now within a few months it would be there. She pulled out boxes of warm clothing, patching and preparing them for the coming season. The children who could use the hand-me-downs were set, but for those who couldn't it meant a lot of sewing and handmade work.

Luckily, Ed's saw mill boss would bring down a large box filled with new shoes of various sizes for the children. They detested and refused to wear shoes during the warm seasons. For them running barefoot through the wild grasses and mud puddles was bliss. They were not about to let that go. If Nora and Ed put them on, they were off within minutes. Once Ed's boss brought the box they instinctively knew their days of running barefoot were ending.

Thanksgiving was a particularly joyous occasion as they had much to be thankful for with the twins now in their lives. Nora also enjoyed not being pregnant. Her time on the dance floor was enjoyed to its fullest when she was able to go. Ed made sure she had that time taking her out every chance he got. Although the times were far and few, they were enjoyed to the max.

After all this time, Ed still peered at Nora on the dance floor with admiration – plus the usual insecurities and jealousies.

At Christmas, the children were mesmerized by the horses drawing Santa's sleigh to the fire station. Gladly they accepted their gift packages of candy and other surprises, eager to tear into them. Families gathered at the fire station by the dozen for the annual event. It was a social event that brought families together if only for an afternoon. There Nora would see many of her friends with their children.

Rebecca arrived with Pricilla, Juanita and Bill. It was cold out, but the festivities made it all worthwhile. Nora made sure the children were bundled up warmly before venturing out into the elements. She didn't need colds or flu to contend with, and neither did the children. When one child got sick, the others were surely to be infected. Many times Nora and Ed themselves were too.

As a young girl, Flora had taken an instant enjoyment to decorating the house and tree. For her there were never enough trimmings or decorations. She worked endlessly on decorating the house and tree, taking pleasure with those who enjoyed it. That was her reward. Although a child herself at age thirteen, she had creativity about her – a talent she was learning to utilize.

Flora's favorite game with the other children was playing priest. She wrapped curtains or drapes around her shoulders and pretended to be the priest while the other children confessed to her. It was her way of learning their deepest secrets. This game among many occupied their time closed indoors during harsh weather. Otherwise they were out making snowmen, snow angels or whatever else they could find to occupy their time and imaginations. Some learned ice skating from Rebecca. Often she joined them. She skated well, and safety was a must for her. She taught the children where to go, and where not to take their chances.

Christmas morning all the children were up at the crack of dawn eager to open their gifts. Although they tried to remain quiet and not awaken Ed and Nora, the giggling finally brought them to. All sat nervously awaiting the permission to open the packages. Once the word was given, there was no stopping them. The twins got matching outfits Nora had made for them. In a second package were more outfits from Rebecca.

Christmas dinner was filled with laughter and excitement from the children. It was a moment Nora wished would never end. To have her entire family surrounding her was joy beyond compare. She couldn't ask for anything more. With the economy getting better, so was life for the residents of South Fork. All had much to be grateful for. Many were back to work. Nora always contended that the Depression never had an effect on the poor because they had little to begin with. It was the wealthy who were hit the hardest. For her life was a struggle no matter what state the nation was in. Her top priority was putting food on the table for her children and making sure they were healthy and kept warm and safe. Very little else mattered above that.

Nora danced the night away to end the year.

* * * * *

April 1945 BRINGS THE tragic news of President Roosevelt's death, the nation's savior not living to see the end of the war he so courageously managed. Harry S. Truman takes over. Germany surrenders in May, the horrors of the concentration camps made known to the world. Japan surrenders in August after Hiroshima and Nagasaki are devastated by atomic bombs, thus ending World War II. Gas is fifteen cents per gallon.

"*Spellbound*" and "*Anchors Away*" hit the silver screen. Television, the latest fad, is in 5,000 American homes.

* * * * *

THANKFULLY FOR REBECCA AND the family, Bill and Charlie survived the war and returned home to South Fork.

April brought peals of laughter from Nora's children playing the familiar game "Red Rover-Red Rover". The month also brought another pregnancy for her. She grew exhausted just thinking about it.

Ed showered Nora with hugs and kisses upon the news, the gentle, loving man behind the drinking. Attention from him was something Nora never had to do without. In spite of their differences he loved her and made sure everyone around them was aware.

Nora turned twenty nine on May 24th.

This year Pricilla would be fifteen, Flora fourteen, Juanita twelve, Rudy ten, Lawrence nine, Lucy seven, Dale five, Billy three and the twins one. The familiar preparations by friends and family commenced. And Nora had no other choice but to put her favorite dancing dresses back in the closet and pull out her maternity frocks. At times she resorted to using some of Ed's shirts, which fit her comfortably.

Christine and Modesto made frequent trips into South Fork to visit and brought their own children along to see *Tia* Nora and *Abuela* Rebecca. Christine was amused and amazed to see Nora with the twins in her arms and a swelling belly of another child on its way. She marveled at her sister in so many ways.

These visits were short but sweet. Nora cherished them. On occasion she and Ed took drives to Center to visit, but with Ed's very busy work schedule the trips and visits were rare. As usual, Christine showered Nora with gifts of garments she either made or found in a catalog. Either way, Nora was constantly on her mind and in her heart.

Having the children out of school for the summer kept Nora on the go constantly. Most of the time they were outdoors playing, unless severe thunder or hailstorms hit, forcing them to retreat inside. Otherwise they were out from dawn to sunset. The older children were there to watch over the younger ones.

Meantime, Nora was either leaning over the stove cooking or with her hands in a tub using a scrub board washing out diapers and laundry. The second the smell of fried potatoes, tortillas, meat and chilies swept through the air, the children were there with appetites to match their enthusiasm. For them there was nothing like their mother's cooking. The aromas coming from the kitchen lured them like nectar to bees.

With summer ending, the children were ready to go back to school. This would give Nora more time and space to get things done. This also meant more clothing was needed for them. She spent hours upon hours mending dresses, shirts and pants before sending them off in the school bus. With the twins in her arms she walked them down to the bus stop on Highway 160, and then watched as the bus drove out of sight taking them into Del Norte for schooling.

The twins had begun walking and at this point were into everything their inquisitive minds and eyes could come upon. They kept Nora going from one end of the house to the other. She relished nap time when solitude was her only friend. In that space she could get done what she needed. But like clockwork, when one twin awakened the other soon followed. People adored them wherever they were. Nora's friends fully embraced them; bringing gifts and things they needed whenever they visited. The twins were alike in so many ways, yet with differences as plain as night and day. Nora found humor in their personalities as did everyone else.

$$* \quad * \quad * \quad * \quad *$$

THANKSGIVING AND CHRISTMAS WERE the best for Nora in years. She and Ed were getting along better; the children were in good health. What more could she ask for? Flora once again decorated the house beautifully, an artistic flair in whatever she did.

Other than Nora losing her voice once again with this pregnancy, all else went fine. As before, she simply woke up one day and her voice was reduced to a whisper. Nora was very large and uncomfortable, yet eager for the arrival of her next child. In bed she wondered who was to enter her life and what would they name him or her. Like Rebecca's, Nora's nights were short and the days long. Lately her time was consumed with making the newborn clothing along with patching and making more clothing for the rest of the children. It seemed from one week to the next they were outgrowing theirs. She had become an artist with the needle and thread, making the twins and her other daughters clothing with vibrant, floral fabric. She used mostly cotton for the boys' shirts. Other clothing she usually found in the thrift stores on her trips into Del Norte. She formed friendships with many of the merchants there.

CHAPTER 20

1946. HUNDREDS OF THOUSANDS of workers, led by the mine workers, go on strike. The U.S. grants independence to the Philippines.

"It's a Wonderful Life" hits the silver screen. Frank Sinatra, Perry Como and Nat "King" Cole entertain music lovers.

* * * * *

IN MID-JANUARY, NORA SHE was bedridden for several days before going into labor. On January 22nd Caroline was born. Carole, as she would be known, was another redhead and an instant sensation for her brothers and sisters. They gathered around to see their new little sister, running their fingers over the soft, silky fuzz on her head. The following days Rebecca took care of Carole while Nora recuperated. She bonded quickly with the infant. Although Rebecca loved all her grandchildren, there were some that the bond was stronger. Once Nora was back on her feet she brought Carole back home to the familiar duties that awaited her.

It was a long, grueling process doing the laundry with so many diapers. The two tubs she had for them usually had to have the water changed at least twice before she was done. Indoors a fire blazed constantly to heat the water. The scrub board was always there calling her name. It gave her no peace.

One of the streams of friends who stopped by to help, chat and hash out their troubles was Nikki, an artist with needle and thread who taught Nora plenty. She had a heart of gold, with generosity almost to a fault. She radiated compassion wherever she went. Nikki loved Nora like a sister, would go to the ends of the earth for her. After Rudolf passed away, Nikki and these other friends became a lifeline for Nora.

Nora was worry free living close to Highway 160. She let the children out to play knowing they wouldn't wander too far from home or get too close to the road. From the kitchen window she kept an eye on them while doing her daily duties. She relied on Flora and Rudy to look after the younger ones. They were protective of their younger siblings. Regardless of the outdoor elements, for them it was always about fun and games whether in the snowfalls of winter or the mud puddles of spring and summer.

Lawrence was a funny one. He could lock his knees into place standing against the wall, and then fall asleep next to the warm heater. He loved wearing bib overalls and had a knack for acquiring nickels. He asked for them wherever he went – usually ending up with a pocketful. In early spring, he, Lucy and Dale posed for a photo sitting on a large rock at the base of the mountain. This photo Nora kept close to her heart.

Nora turned thirty with nine children at home to care for. She was grateful that the older ones helped with the household chores. They were put to scrub out diapers when they were old enough. Each had their daily chores to do when they got home from school. She also taught them how to cook and bake. The skills that were passed onto her she was now passing onto them. She knew they would be needed in their journey through life. She taught them all the same things. Pricilla, Juanita and Billy were also taught the abilities needed for their journeys. Pricilla, Juanita and Flora blossomed into beautiful, young girls taking notice of the boys. Each girl had a unique personality. To Nora, they grew up far too quickly.

Although having some of the children in school gave Nora more time, it also put pressure on her for more and better clothing on a daily basis. There was no rest from this. First thing every morning Nora prepared the tubs for laundry, having the clothes hung on the lines before noon. With the twins getting into everything and Carole an infant, it was difficult to find time and space in to get things done. But through experience Nora had it down to a science. She learned multitasking through trial and tribulation.

In the late afternoons, Nora stood on her front porch waiting for the school bus to arrive and unload her children. Chores were first, then fun and games. Clothing had to be brought in from the lines before dark, folded and stored away until needed. Each also had to get their clothes ready for the following school day. Wood had to be brought in for the stove. Even on hot days the stove had to be fired up for cooking. School lunches were prepared the night before.

On Halloween, Nora broke out her own costume – maternity clothes. Yes, she was pregnant again. The words the priest told Nora when she consulted him about having so many children echoed in her mind. For Nora and Ed it didn't matter as they would welcome and love every child brought into their lives. For them each child born was a blessing.

At least this baby was due before the intense heat of summer, something she was grateful for. "Child number fourteen," she told herself. "I will love you as I love my other eleven on earth and my two in heaven."

Christmas was a major production as the family grew. The joy Flora got from decorating was worth its weight in gold for Nora. To see the joy and happiness her daughter got out of it was immeasurable. The stack of packages under the tree grew steadily through the years, as did the laughter and excitement from the children.

At fifteen, Flora was old enough to be left in charge of her siblings while Ed took Nora out dancing for New Year's. Flora had proven her sense of responsibility to them. They trusted her in the care of her younger siblings.

As Ed watched Nora on the dance floor that night, he was never more in love with her, his world, the love of his life. For her, he always wanted to be an honorable man, hardworking and devoted to his children, never raising his voice to them regardless of what they did. The taskmaster's job was left to his beloved Nora.

CHAPTER 21

1947. Elizabeth Short, known as *"The Black Dalia,"* is found murdered in Leimert Park in Los Angeles. Al Capone dies of syphilis at age 48. Arthur Miller's *"All My Sons"* premiers in New York City. Gas prices are still fifteen cents a gallon. The war gone and the Depression over, Americans are full of hope.

Bing Crosby and the Andrew Sisters are popular. Americans are on their feet dancing the jitterbug and swing, troubles hopefully behind them. Fashion, particularly for women in silk and nylon, starts to blossom. Shoes sport a bold new look.

* * * * *

NORA LOVED THE DANCING craze sweeping the country and joined in the fun. She wasn't pregnant enough to stop her from putting on her favorite dresses and high heels. She would never lose her thirst for beautiful clothing and jewelry. Those were embedded in her. Her collection of jewelry grew through the years, and she ran out of space to keep it. The jewelry boxes were filled. Necklaces hung from her dresser mirror, earrings on stands she found in thrift stores. Her favorites, the pair Rudolf gave on her wedding day, she kept safely stored, bringing them out only on special occasions. Her closets were stuffed with beautiful dresses she either bought or were given to her by Christine or others. Although she could only wear them when she wasn't pregnant she took full advantage of them when she could. She wore them with grace.

A fresh snowfall was always a treat for the children in more ways than one. If they weren't outside playing in the mounds of snow, Nora made them ice cream, mixing canned milk and vanilla with the snow creating a smooth, delicious, frozen dessert. It was a delight for the children, who ate to their hearts' content.

Snowmen decorated nearly every household in the neighborhood. Children pulled out their sleds and ice skates. Down the mountainside they slid on their sleds, and over the frozen lake, ponds and rivers they skated. Their laughter rang throughout the neighborhood. Other than an occasional minor injury, all went well.

Indoors, Nora's older children put the twins on swings in the bedroom, swinging them as high as they could, nearly touching the ceiling with one swoop to the other. The twins' laughter carried throughout the house. For them it was bliss. Although mere toddlers, they knew what fun was, and swings were their favorite.

As Nora swelled, she was left to wonder if she'd lose her voice again. It had her and those around her baffled as well as the mid-wife. Actually, it was something Nora had come to expect and would surprise her more not to lose her voice.

With the older children able to care for the younger ones and trusted to be on their own, Nora took more trips into Del Norte on weekends as the weather got nicer. She bought sacks of flour, potatoes and sugar, heading to her favorite thrift stores for summer clothing for the children as well as for herself. She visited with friends who sometimes went with her for lunch or coffee on their shopping sprees. Nora always looked forward to these visits into Del Norte. She often thought of living there but could not imagine leaving the beauty and serenity of South Fork. She wasn't ready for that yet.

Rebecca took Carole for the day when Nora was gone and sometimes made a surprise visit to the rest of kids at home, just to be sure everything was in order. No one ever knew when or where she would show up; only that she could at any given moment. This kept them on their toes.

Ed, too, was known to take breaks from work and show up unexpectedly when he knew Nora was out of town. Between him and Rebecca a very close eye was kept on the children and household. The consequences were much too dire for the children to chance with. They all had their chores and knew they had to be done first. Before they took to playing their games and having fun, the wood was chopped and stacked near the house, water was brought in. Diapers and laundry were washed and hung out to dry, and the house cleaned from one end to the other. This was what Nora expected when she came home, and what Ed and Rebecca demanded to find when they came to the house on their surprise visits. It was a given.

When Nora turned thirty one on May 24th her voice was back to the familiar whisper, as expected. This time it lasted for weeks upon weeks. Although she could only "yell" at a whisper, she got her point across to the children when needed.

By late June, she was bedridden with the mid-wife and Rebecca at her side. On July 8th Cordelia was born, Cordie for short. She had Nora and Ed's dark, curly hair and eyes and Nora's olive complexion.

Shortly after Cordie's birth, Ed, Nora and Rebecca decided Carole would join Pricilla, Juanita and Billy in staying with their grandmother. This would leave Nora with eight to care for at home. All were at peace with the decision.

Two weeks later, on July 22nd headlines of a UFO crashing near Roswell, New Mexico, shocked South Fork, the nation, the world. The debate over whether this was an alien spacecraft or just a weather balloon would never be settled completely and conversation about the infamous Area 51 where the alien bodies were supposedly transported never really ended.

Nora suffered a severe toothache, resulting in having all her teeth pulled to make way for dentures. Although she was uncomfortable with the situation, there was no other choice. She resigned herself to the fact that she'd have to be without teeth until they were able to afford dentures. She sighed with this realization.

Household duties resumed when she was strong enough. Plenty of diapers in the tubs were always there. Flora turned sixteen in August and was always a great help. To Nora, it seemed like only yesterday when she was sixteen, although at that age she already had children. To have children that age and older was incredible to her. Pricilla was now seventeen and working in the sawmill office part-time during school and full-time when school was out. These children were Nora's pride and glory – her world.

Pumpkins for the coming Halloween were always a great joy in the fall. Children anticipated picking the largest to carve and set on their porches. They nursed them with love, measuring them daily. Finally in mid-October they were ready for picking and carving. Oddly carved pumpkins decorated households in South Fork and throughout the valley. Candles were placed in them to light once the sun set, bringing to life the creations of their carvings and art.

As Nora stood at the porch watching as her older children took the younger ones trick-or-treating on this night in 1947, she smiled radiantly. She was to stay home and greet her own witches and goblins who came calling. She had made candy, popcorn balls and fudge, and had apples and oranges for them as they arrived. She scarcely recognized who was behind the ghost sheets and masks of those who came to her door. For her it was a pleasure and joy greeting the children and seeing the creativity in the costumes she greeted. At times, Nora reflected on her own abbreviated childhood and vowed she would never cheat her children out of the joys of holidays like this.

For Thanksgiving, Nora cooked and baked a feast of feasts. Rebecca brought Pricilla, Juanita, Billy and Carole to join them, along with goodies she prepared. The table was no longer large enough for everyone, so the smaller fry were at their own table. It did Nora's heart good to have all her children occupying the same space. Many times she missed the four staying with Rebecca, but she knew it wouldn't be fair to uproot them from a home and love they were accustomed to. Rebecca was very good to Pricilla, Juanita, Billy and Carole. There was never a doubt of this. She loved them as though they were her own. Although there was a void in Nora's heart having them gone, she knew they were well cared for and loved as she loved them. This brought peace to her heart. In many ways Rebecca was able to give them what she couldn't with so many to care for.

Ed, Nora and the children celebrated a joyous Christmas. Mom and Dad stayed up into the wee hours preparing for Christmas morning. Those hours when Ed and Nora were together and making sure their children were happy were more precious than any gift. This night was a time of peace, love and fulfillment. To have Nora and his children to himself was all Ed could ever have wished for. He was truly content. Nothing else mattered.

CHAPTER 22

1948. Harry Truman ("the buck stops here") defeats Thomas Dewey for president despite the famous headline declaring Dewey the winner. Alger Hiss is indicted for perjury resulting from investigation of a Communist spy ring. The Kinsey Report on sexuality is published. The Soviet Union blockades West Berlin.

* * * * *

NEWS OF YET ANOTHER pregnancy caused Rebecca to question for the first time her decision on marrying Nora off at such a young age. But what was done was done, and Nora was destined to walk whatever path fate had for her. Nora and Ed fully accepted that, and whatever challenges they knew would lie ahead, nothing stopped them from being happy with another child in the household.

Pricilla turned eighteen in May and proudly graduated from high school shortly after. She took a job full-time at the sawmill office. Juanita graduated from eighth grade and received a Bulova watch as a present from Nora's brother Ted, who was in the Navy stationed in the Aleutian Islands. For Nora's thirty second birthday, she received something more practical from Ted: money to pay for the dentures she needed. She didn't like being without teeth. Her beautiful smile was restored.

Nora took time out from her birthday festivities on May 24th to reflect on all that happened in the world and to her in just a couple of decades. It seemed like only yesterday that she was thirteen and taking her marriage vows. So much had happened in her still young life. The twists and turns taught her an abundance of the rules on life. The common sense Rudolf implanted in her served its purpose. She was a strong, independent woman – a person of strong conviction and devotion to her children. Nothing would change that. The passing years only ripened those qualities Rudolf had embedded in her. She was ever so thankful for this. He gave her the right tools needed for her journey. She used those qualities time and time again, knew she would for the rest of her life.

At age seventeen, Flora was a beautiful, young woman favoring Nora in many ways. Her long, black hair was reminiscent her mother. She discovered the art of make-up, bringing her natural beauty to life. Like any teenager, Flora did whatever she could get away with. Still, she was very helpful to Nora and her younger siblings.

Despite bouts of arguing, life was many times at its best. Ed knew now what Nora would and would not tolerate, and Nora had come to terms with Ed's ways that she knew would never change. No matter what, the children were always there, filling Nora and Ed with unbridled joy.

After consulting with Rebecca and her friends, Nora and Ed decided this would be their first child to be born in the Del Norte Hospital. Giving birth was getting more difficult for Nora, and her mid-wife was in agreement. This would be a total change for Nora as she was accustomed to home births.

She didn't know quite what to expect. She'd already seen a doctor there a couple of times during her visits into the town. The doctor and hospital staff was intrigued with Nora, a mother about to give birth to her fifteenth child.

It was on one of these trips that she met a man named Joe. Married with a family, Joe took an instant liking to Nora. And she sensed something different about him, as though their paths would cross again. On what grounds and to what degree were yet to be seen and known. Joe noticed Nora at dances, but before their chance encounter on Main Street he never approached her for fear of angering his wife. So, he admired her from afar.

Some of Nora's friends moved from South Fork into Del Norte and told her life was much easier there for them. There were grocery stores, the hospital and the thrift stores. Nora kind of liked the idea of moving but was concerned that Hueso lived there as well. Would the town be big enough for the both of them? Still, she wasn't about to let Hueso dictate her future.

Spending so many days there gave a glimpse of what life might be like. Of course she would miss the serenity and beauty of mountain living. And what friends she had left living in South Fork she would miss tremendously. A move like this she wasn't quite ready for. Still, it was at the back of her mind, and her friends discussed it whenever she visited. Nora sensed that in due time life was going to shift for her in many ways. This both excited and concerned her. She spent more time in Del Norte.

As Nora grew larger, she felt this would be a big child and difficult birth. She was already larger than usual with her other children. The child was active, sending bursts of happiness through Nora each time it stirred. It was though the child was eager and impatient to enter the world. A smile glowed on Nora's face with each movement.

In late November she went to the Hospital and on December 3rd had another daughter after a very difficult labor. They were unsure as to what to name the child until someone suggested naming her after Nora's brother Charlie. Thus it was. As Nora suspected, Charlene weighed in at over nine pounds. She was also another redhead. Charlene was an early, joyful Christmas gift for Nora, Ed and the growing family.

* * * * *

POSTWAR POSTERITY BOOMS IN 1949. Cars pour off Detroit assembly lines. RCA introduces 45 rpm records. Millions of television sets in black and white are in American living rooms, and color TV is around the corner. The Volkswagen Beetle is imported to America. *"Mule Train"* by Frankie Laine fills the airwaves. Los Angeles has snow. Gas costs seventeen cents a gallon. The minimum wage is seventy cents an hour. The soap opera *"These Are My Children"* debuts.

* * * * *

Nora's FAMILY WAS NOT among the millions to have television. She relied on friends, newspapers and radio for headlines and entertainment. She marveled at the latest technologies, wondering when she would be able to enjoy them. Recuperated after having Charlene, Nora was able to slip into her favorite dresses and high heels and escape, however briefly, the endless chores to go dancing with Ed while Rebecca took care of the new baby.

Nora turned thirty three in May. One day not long after Nora's birthday, Becky was caught in the crossfire of play when one child threw a book at another, hitting her in the eye. It caused severe damage and resulted in her having to wear glasses. Her siblings were intrigued by them, taking turns trying them on.

Mid-August brought Flora's eighteenth birthday, Juanita's sixteenth and shocking news. Flora announced she was three months' pregnant. Although Nora noticed signs of it, she hoped they weren't what she suspected. Rebecca was infuriated, while Ed simply took it in stride like he took most things his children did. Rebecca felt it brought shame to a family having a child born under the circumstances and voiced her opinion loud and clear to Nora, Ed and Flora. She was as non-negotiable in her decision as she was with all she decided. There was no swaying her.

Nora did what any mother in this situation would do. She educated Flora with what she learned through her own experience. Flora quit school even though she was close to graduating. Small communities could be very harsh on her. Nora knew she would love this grandchild as if it was her own and wished Rudolf was alive to experience it with her.

When Nora announced her own pregnancy in September, it was anti-climactic.

CHAPTER 23

1950. ANOTHER DECADE, ANOTHER war. American troops are embroiled in Korea as part of the United Nations forces. Kids watch *"Howdy Doody"* on TV and spend Saturday afternoons at the movies for a nickel. Gas is eighteen cents a gallon. *"Sunset Boulevard"* graces the silver screen. Times are still simple, automobiles big and luxurious.

* * * * *

REBECCA WAS DETERMINED THAT Flora would marry shortly after the child was born. She was dead set on this, would accept nothing else. For Nora it was a reflection of what Rebecca had done to her. In many ways she resented it, but she was also fully aware of the challenges that would face Flora if she stayed on her own. Thus, reluctantly she consented.

In February, Flora gave birth to a son named Richard at Del Norte Hospital. She was surrounded by family. Even with her own experience, this was somewhat daunting to Nora to be a grandmother at thirty three. Tomorrow had never ceased to amaze her time and time again. After several days in the hospital, Flora returned home with the baby. Flora's fiancé visited on a regular basis. Flora continued to stay with Ed and Nora for a while after Richard was born, then she and her fiancé married and moved into their own home not far from Nora's. Lucy turned twelve at the end of February.

March brought Dale's tenth birthday along with spring, when Nora could visit Del Norte more. Her friends, having planted the seed of it being a better place to live, tried to make the idea blossom and urged Nora more and more to take the big step.

April brought Rudy's fifteenth birthday and the twins' sixth. Nora's family, always growing, now was growing up as well. Nora wouldn't trade it for anything in the world.

Pricilla turned twenty on May 8th. Two days later Nora gave birth to a son, named Dwayne, and then two weeks after that turned thirty four. In the months before Dwayne was born, Nora crossed paths with Joe on more than one occasion. Despite them both being married, his attraction to her was obvious, his persistence difficult for Nora to ignore. With feelings long past just a physical attraction, he admired her in many ways. A bond had been created.

Meanwhile, Nora's marriage to Ed hung by a thread. Her resentment toward his drinking was to the point where she felt better when they were apart. When they went dancing, she simply ignored his insecurities. Their moments of bliss became fewer and fewer, and she longed for the gentle, compassionate man she married. At least his hostility was never directed toward the children, for whom he always showed love and compassion.

At home, with Flora gone, the older children had more chores placed on them. Rebecca made her trips to help out in any way she could, and she brought Pricilla, Juanita, Billy and Carole to help when they weren't working or in school. Raising Nora's family was a joint venture.

Over the years, July Fourth was always a festive occasion. The family gathered to watch fireworks shot up into the night sky where explosions of color would entertain all. Ed always made it a point to bring fireworks to light up at home. But this year was different. Following the fireworks display he erupted into one of his jealous episodes. While the kids were outside playing, he struck Nora severely and often and left the front room in shambles. Nora bled from gashes on her face and mouth. When he'd followed her inside she knew something was up, but the ferocity of the attack shocked her. She resented him more than ever and wanted nothing more than to get as far away from him as possible.

The next day she went to Del Norte, only to have another encounter with Joe. This time she was more receptive toward him. When Joe saw the cuts on her face, he knew what happened and was enraged. His compassion toward Nora was the key to unlock her heart. Her perspective of him changed on that day. He lay heavily on her thoughts for days to follow. Cordie's third birthday was celebrated on July 8th.

It took Nora over a week to heal from her wounds. Although the older children suspected what happened, the younger ones were oblivious. Sharing the same bed with Ed had become a challenge for her, she resented him so badly. Alcohol had destroyed the kind, compassionate nature in him she once loved. Nora was losing all hope for the survival of her marriage.

On August 17th Juanita turned seventeen, and on the 18th Flora turned nineteen. The days were long, with plenty for all to do. Nora had completely healed, although the inner scars were there for good. More of Nora's friends left South Fork, moving into Del Norte. She missed them immensely. Those who remained were still there for Nora come rain or shine. Through the years they taught Nora the art of being a mother and wife and principles of life she lived by. Many of those principles echoed what Rudolf embedded in her. She missed him more as the years passed.

On her trips into Del Norte she visited his grave, sat in solitude and quiet conversation with him. To leave his grave site was just as difficult for her as the day they laid him to rest. She always left with a lump in her throat, tears in her eyes, heaviness in her heart.

September brought summer to an end and fall to a beginning. Ed worked around the clock at times. Nora's job in raising a family was also 24/7 at times. But the illusion of this being a family was just that.

In November, Nora ran into Joe in Del Norte. This time it was different. Her loneliness had gotten the best of her. Joe said the right things, did the right things to gain her trust, and Nora was intimate with him. When it was over she wept, not only for Ed and the trust that had been shattered, but for herself and the self-betrayal of what she believed in. This was a sure indication that their marriage was near its end, if not there.

Although there was much to be grateful and happy for at Thanksgiving, things just weren't the same for her after the intimacy with Joe. How could they ever be, she wondered. She blamed herself, blamed Hueso and Ed. She also welcomed a part of her that Joe had revived, the yearning for the life she had when she first married. He revived the zest she so longed for.

December had Nora busy with the holidays. Flora came by with her husband and child and decorated, as always. December also brought those familiar changes in Nora's body, but with a big difference. She knew this time it was not Ed's child. It was Joe's. Alone in her bedroom once the children had been put to bed, she sat at her dresser in front of the mirror. How was she to break the news to Ed? To Rebecca? It seemed every emotion she had came to the surface. She wept. Happy to have another child, this one came at great cost, the loss of trust and love for Ed and their marriage.

CHAPTER 24

1951. MORE ROADS ARE needed to handle all the cars. Unemployment drops to 3.3 percent. Children get Encyclopedias, bought by parents from door-to-door salesmen. The average family income is $3,700. Cars are more luxurious and powerful and have options like two-tone paints and mechanical turn signals.

"I Love Lucy" airs. Tests for color TV are broadcast from the Empire State Building. Direct dial coast to coast telephone service is introduced. *"The African Queen"* and *"A Street Car Named Desire"* premiere. *"The Day the Earth Stood Still"* piques sci-fi fans' curiosity. *"Life After Tomorrow"* is the first movie to be X-rated. The term rock 'n' roll is coined by Cleveland disc jockey Alan Freed.

* * * * *

LIKE MOST WINTERS IN South Fork, January was arctic. The cold was unbearable at times. Both Nora and Ed struggled to keep fires going in the heater 24/7. By day it warmed a little, but at nighttime temperatures plummeted. The children had to be bundled especially warm when sent out to the school bus. Yard dogs were brought inside for warmth. On the 22nd Carole turned six.

In Nora's home things were not at their best. Word had spread of her involvement with Joe, putting more pressure on her marriage and home. Ed struggled with the rumors, which were blown out of proportion at times. They hoped, as with most gossip, the rumors would eventually wear themselves out. Hueso had her say and contribution to the rumors. Did not let them rest. She added fuel to the burning fires whenever she was able.

Rebecca got wind of the situation and confronted her daughter.

"Are they true?" she questioned.

"We all make mistakes," Nora replied.

"Not like this," Rebecca said. "This is not right. It's immoral. It's against God and everything he stands for. You are a married woman. Married women aren't supposed to do this."

"Only married men?" Nora answered back. "Why is it okay for them?"

"That's the way of life," Rebecca said. "A woman's duty is to be a devoted wife regardless of what the husband does."

"Not with me. Not anymore. I've had enough. He will never change. He can't put that damn bottle down long enough to change."

"Your duties are to be a wife and mother. Never mind what he does. It's God's way. It's in the Bible."

"Well, it isn't mine. I have to be happy too. And if he can't make me happy I'll find someone who does. It's a simple as that. Is that in the Bible?"

"You're not making sense. Just do your wifely duties. That's your obligation. Have you told him?"

"He knows. He knows without me having to say a word."

"The whole town knows."

"I don't care what this town knows. I'm not here to please anyone but my kids and myself. This town gossiped about me long before this happened. And they'll continue long after this passes. No matter what I do there will be gossip. I'm used to that."

"It's wrong. Against God. That's all I'm going to say."

"Well, let's just let this 'God' deal with it then. There are enough judges in the world. It'll be okay. You'll just have to believe like I do."

Rebecca was not pleased with Nora's response to her confrontation. She hoped she had taught her daughter better than this. She also knew Nora was strong and determined, and regardless of what anyone said would do what she wanted and needed. She was grateful in many ways for this strength in her daughter. After all, she had inherited it from her mother.

* * * * *

THE FIRST SIGN OF spring came with robins making their appearances. All were relieved to be leaving behind another brutal winter. Nora confided in Ed about the baby, reminding him of his own past behaviors. In those days, men were patted on the back for extramarital affairs, while a woman was chastised. Nora found that out the hard way.

Shockingly, Ed came to terms with the pregnancy as the year went on. His love for Nora and his family brought him the realization that he had been wrong in how he abused her. He continued to drink, even more, but struggled to keep away from Nora at those times so he wouldn't go into a rage against her. He wanted to keep his family together.

Many of those in South Fork weren't so accepting. Hueso had a field day with it. Since that day spent with Nora, Joe developed an attachment to her. He drove through the neighborhood trying to get a glimpse of her. Nora pleaded with him to keep his distance as it would only reflect on her. Joe's wife eventually found out and gave him an ultimatum that he leave town with her or she would leave him. In summer, Joe and his family moved near the New Mexico border. That in itself gave Nora peace, and a small measure of it to Ed, who wouldn't be quite as haunted by a man he knew little of.

Strong winds blew through in March. At times it was difficult for Nora to hang out diapers and laundry with the wind carrying them away or ripping the clothing from her hands. Standing at the bus stop in the mornings, the children had to hang on to each other.

The wind howled mysteriously through the night, bending tree branches, scraping them against the house and making peculiar sounds that awakened and frightened the younger children. Both Nora and Ed tried to calm them, but the ghostly shadows cast against walls from the branches only made it worse. Were the winds portending something evil or sweeping away all the bad that had happened in the Marquez household? Only time would tell.

The children grew. Rudy turned sixteen and talked of going into the service even though he was too young to do so. The twins were seven and growing like weeds.

In May Pricilla turned twenty one, a full-time secretary at the sawmill and a beautiful, responsible adult. Dwayne, at one, was walking and into everything, Nora turned thirty five on May 24th.

Progress came to Highway 160. It was paved with a composite of gravel and tar, a relief to drivers. The potholes and bumps would be a thing of the past. As they paved next to Rebecca's, eleven year old Billy befriended the workers and made lemonade for them.

One day in late June, Nora had water heating in a tub on the stove. Rebecca was patching the children's jeans, Flora, pregnant with her second child, was ironing, and Juanita was mending clothes on the sewing machine.

"Watch the baby now that he's walking," Rebecca cautioned as Dwayne bounced around.

No sooner had she said that than the boy fell head first into the tub of scalding water. Nora screamed at the sight. Dwayne cried uncontrollably as Juanita pulled him out, badly burned and blistered. Nora wanted to rush him to the hospital, but Rebecca said no and flew into action. She ordered Flora to seek out white feathers in the yard and chicken coop and Juanita to the general store for ointment of her specification. Meanwhile, she sterilized the crib with bleach and ironed the sheets to destroy bacteria. When Flora returned with the feathers, Rebecca sterilized them as well. She heated the ointment to a liquid and with the feathers spread it lightly over Dwayne's blistered body.

Once all that was done, she laid Dwayne in his crib, covering him with a sheer curtain to prevent flies from getting to him. The child cried non-stop from the pain. Nora's heart was broken as she felt defenseless at a time when her child needed her most. Rebecca tried to comfort her as she wept. She reasoned with her, finally convincing her that the ointment would eliminate much of the pain and the baby would be much better in a few days.

For the following days and nights, Dwayne continued crying. Nora sat on the front porch rocking him, hoping to bring comfort. All he wore was a diaper, along with the ointment that was applied to his wounds throughout the day and night. Finally, on the fourth day he was better. The blisters scabbed over and were healing well. Rebecca's advice was to allow them to heal naturally to avoid scarring, which was exactly what Nora did.

Cordie turned four on July 8. She loved riding a horse and delighted whenever she knew it was time. The horse knew it, too, and seemed to almost smile as it walked around slowly, letting the little girl have her fun. Through this pregnancy there was distance between she and Ed. Rebecca forbade Nora's relationship with Joe from continuing. Nora assured her that it had ended as Joe had left the valley.

The change in Ed was obvious to those who knew. He drank more heavily than usual, spending more time away from home with his friends. His heart was broken, but his love for Nora and his family surpassed anything he felt. He restrained from fighting with Nora under the circumstances.

That didn't last.

One weekend, he arrived with whiskey and wine strong on his breath. Nora tried avoiding him to no avail. He was determined to confront her. He couldn't hold it back any longer. Alcohol gave him the courage needed for the confrontation. He followed her into the kitchen.

"How could you?" he asked. "How could you do such a thing?"

"This is not the time or place for this," Nora said, making her way toward the living room.

He grabbed her by the arm. "Was it worth it? Look what you've done!"

"And what is it that I've done that you haven't already done?" Nora said in her defense. "How easily you forget all the hell you've put us through, and all the women you've gone through."

"At least I didn't do this," Ed said. "At least I didn't bring it into our home."

"And how do I know this?" Nora said. "How do I know you don't have children of your own out there?"

"That's it! Put the blame on me! It's you with another man's child!"

"Don't you think I know that?"

"Do you love him?"

"Please, not now. You'll wake the entire household."

"I need to know. Damn it! I need to know!"

"Yes. Yes, I do. Now, are you satisfied?"

"Damn you! Damn the hell out of you!" Ed shouted, sweeping his hands and arms across the dinner table.

Dishes shattered when they hit the floor, making enough noise to wake the dead. Nora stepped into the living room making sure the children weren't awakened and startled.

"Please leave," she told Ed. "Leave before you do something we will both regret."

"I won't until I get everything out of my system. I don't want you seeing that man again. Is that clear?"

"Or what? What makes you think you have the right to tell me what I can and cannot do after what you've done? I've had to forgive all you've done. Maybe now it's your turn. Forgiveness is a two way street," Nora shot back. She was furious.

"I don't give a damn! This is about you, not me! And I don't want you seeing that man again."

"I'll do as I please. You lost the right to tell me what I can and cannot do. Now get out! Go to Hueso's. I'm sure she'll have what you need as usual."

"Leave her out of this. She's got nothing to do with this. This is about what you have done."

"She is to blame for more than what you think, more than what you will admit to," Nora said. "But I know you won't face that fact. To you, that woman can never do wrong. Now, get out of here!"

Ed shoved more dishes onto the floor. His face was red, the veins on his temples throbbed with fury. He grabbed Nora by the shoulders, ready to strike her.

"Go ahead! Hit me like you know how! But don't think for one second that I'm going to take it!" She screamed, daring him.

Ed struck her once, then lowered his fist, shoving her aside and storming out the house. He couldn't strike her more while she was in her condition although he came close. Despite the alcohol, he had the awareness that leaving would be the best thing for him to do. His heart was heavy. His heart beat hard against his chest as though it were on fire. He hurt unlike he ever hurt. The sound of his spinning tires faded as he drove away.

Nora cleaned up the mess. Tears filled her eyes at her mistake made. She'd realized it long ago. But for her, the child she carried would never be a mistake. Nor would she allow anyone, including Ed, to treat this child as though it was.

In his heart of hearts, Ed knew this was his own fault. He stayed away drinking to deal with his depression and to avoid abusing his wife again. Both of them hoped desperately that those days were over.

On August 22nd Nora gave birth to Theodore at the Del Norte Hospital. He was named after Rebecca's brother and Nora's younger brother. They called him Teddy for short. He had light skin and very light hair – almost the color of butter.

In the hospital room next to Nora was Rose, who had given birth to a daughter the day before. Rose was a beautiful woman, with a sense of humor to match. She lived in Alamosa and was a cousin to Nora through marriage. Nora and Ed had known Rose for years. Ed's Uncle Antonio was Rose's father.

When Nora returned home with the baby, Ed left to spend his days drinking, drowning his sorrow. But he also took time reflect, think and conclude. When he returned, he knew what had to be done and embraced Teddy as his own. He gave the child his last name and helped raise him along with the rest of his children. He knew it would be wrong to begrudge this innocent child. To him, the boy would be a reminder of what of what he drove his beloved wife to do. This was the heaviness in his heart. He felt responsible in so many ways. He made promises to Nora he hoped he'd be able to keep.

* * * * *

IN SEPTEMBER, NORA AND Ed finally made the transition into Del Norte. They moved into a home in a section known as Sleepy Town. Dwayne healed from his burn wounds and was back to himself. Flora gave birth to a daughter she named Peggy. Flora and her husband, Ben, lived with Ed and Nora in a room set up in the back of the house. In this room they also kept Peggy in her crib. Both Ed and Ben worked for the sawmill in South Fork and rode to work together.

Nora quickly felt the benefits and convenience of living in Del Norte. She felt closer to Rudolf because Sleepy Town wasn't far from the graveyard. At Rudolf's grave she could sit and ponder her life. She had much to think about. How she wished her children could have known their grandfather. She knew they would have loved him as she did.

Sleepy Town got its name because folks there retired for the night earlier than most others. The people there were hard workers and lived by the mantra "early to bed, early to rise." It wasn't ritzy there nor poverty-stricken like the west side of town. The Westé lacked street lights, making for dark and scary walks for youngsters at night. Tales of the child-seeking La Llorona thrived and often drove the young ones into their homes after sunset.

On weekends, people could see a movie at the Princess Theater on Main Street for a dime. Ushers led them to their seats, then walked the house with flashlights keeping tabs on everything. Dances were held at the Parish Hall on Friday and Saturday nights. The thrift store next to the theater was one of Nora's favorites. She befriended the owner, Sofia, who treated Nora with the utmost respect. Nora thoroughly enjoyed walking down Main Street window shopping with friends or some of her children. The difference between living in Del Norte and South Fork was like night and day. She was happy they made the decision to move. Life was so much easier for her.

Halloween in Del Norte also was very different. There were many more children. Soaping windows and toilet papering homes that didn't give out candy was a nasty tradition. Nora's children were eager to go out on the town in their trick-or-treat hunt. Neighborhoods were abuzz with groups of children moving from house to house, neighborhood to neighborhood. Streets were filled with children's laughter and various costumes. It was fun for all involved.

Thanksgiving was enjoyable for Nora because she could see more of her friends in Del Norte. They paid visits the day before with a dish of sorts in hand, adding to Nora's family dinner. Lawrence turned fifteen on November 27th and Billy turned nine on the 28th.

Since it was nestled in the mountains, winter in Del Norte wasn't nearly as rough as it was in South Fork. The fire station featured Santa, who rode in on a sleigh and gave out bags of candy and goodies to the children. The town's Main Street was lit with Christmas decorations. A large star hung strung across Main Street near the library. Although there was snow on the ground, Main Street was abuzz with shoppers. Merchants were overjoyed. The lighted star on the D Mountain, which Del Norte set at the base of, made its statement, as it did every year for the holidays. Charlene turned three on December 3rd.

As in South Fork, people living in Del Norte ventured from home to home singing Christmas carols in English and Spanish on Christmas Eve. Some took guitars. Adults usually ended up at someone's home to finish off the celebration with drink and dance. Del Norte burst with energy during Christmas season, and Nora and all in her family loved it. Flora decorated their new home both inside and out, bringing the spirit to life.

On Christmas morning, children poured outside with their new sleds and ice skates. They took to the D Mountain with inner tubes and sleds forming lines to slide down the hillside. The morning air was crisp, full of children's laughter and sometimes tears from those who had taken falls. From sunrise to sunset the children played on the mountain, until finally it was time to go home.

CHAPTER 25

1952. THE UNEMPLOYMENT RATE is all the way down to 2.9 percent. Consumer goodies pour into American homes. Dwight Eisenhower, military hero of World War II, is elected president. The Korean War drags on. The first hydrogen bomb is tested by the United States. Nat "King" Cole has a hit with *"Unforgettable."*

* * * * *

A RAGING BLIZZARD HIT Del Norte one day in January. Those fortunate to have televisions and telephones kept tuned in with the forecasts. Nora's family was not among them, so the radio was going continuously. People shoveled through snow drifts to make paths to wood sheds and outhouses. Most walked to their destinations as the roads were far too bad for driving.

Nora prepared well for the blizzard. She baked enough bread for the week and had plenty of canned goods to see them through. The pressure cooker was going for beans on the menu. The house smelled of chili, tortillas, beans and frying potatoes.

She rose at dawn to begin her day and bundled up the children, who were insistent on going out to play in the freshly fallen snow. For her the blizzard made no difference. She had duties to tend to regardless of the weather. As usual she had water heating on the stove for washing diapers, to be hung throughout the house for drying as the snow was much too deep to get to the clotheslines.

Ed dug paths to the outhouse and coal and wood shed, as well as to the clotheslines. Luckily, children were still out of school for Christmas vacation, so this storm was just fun and games. They made snowmen and snow angels, had snowball fights and came inside to enjoy the ice cream Nora made from snow. Carole turned six on January 22nd.

Early one cold morning, Flora's screams awakened Nora. Her little daughter Peggy had died overnight, a sad victim of crib death. The news sent shock waves through the entire family. Comprehension was beyond reach for all, particularly Flora, who fell into a deep, disheartening depression, as any mother would. Nora herself had felt such sorrow on two occasions. Peggy was buried in the Del Norte Cemetery just south of town.

Nora hurt deeply in watching her child suffer and felt helpless to her. What could anyone say to a mother who lost a child? Words eluded Nora, as they had around her when she lost her own children. She knew from experience that time would be the healer of sorts, but never would Flora forget. The memory of her lost child would haunt her forever, as Nora's memories haunted her. How could they not? She also knew that patience was a virtue.

In mid-February, Nora became pregnant with her eighteenth child. People around town were getting more curious about this woman not yet forty years old who had all these children. They had all heard stories of her when she lived in South Fork, but now with her living in their own community they wanted to actually see her. Heads turned on Main Street at the sight of the town novelty. But for Nora it was merely a way of life.

Flora and Ben wanted to move back to South Fork in due time. Nora and Ed decided to move within Del Norte once winter was over. They not only needed more space, but they also had the need of change after losing Peggy in the house. The memory was too much for all of them

When Dale turned twelve on March 11th Nora packed in the event. They found a home with immediate occupancy. She wanted to be ready. The blooming flowers and lilac bushes of spring brought a sense of newness to the town and the two households trying to put their grief behind them.

Nora's friends Julia and Roberto told her of a home next door to them that would be available soon. Upon visiting Nora had a chance to glance at the home getting an idea of what it looked like. Julia told her she'd let her know the second it became vacant and available. It was at the opposite side of Del Norte near the hospital. Since the streets were unpaved it was somewhat of a dusty walk for Nora into town, but that didn't faze her as she enjoyed walking. It was also convenient to shopping with Skaff's Grocery nearby. Julia and Roberto had moved there from South Fork and had children of their own, the same age as some of Nora's kids. She hoped it would be available to her in due time.

On April 16th Rudy turned seventeen and informed Nora and Ed he wanted to join the Marines. He was unyielding on his decision. Ed and Nora were not pleased but knew he wouldn't have it any other way so they consented. On April 30th Charlotte and Becky turned eighteen. It seemed every time Nora turned around there was another birthday.

In May, Flora and Ben found a place on Church Lane in South Fork and the house next to Julia and Roberto became available. Nora and Ed took it immediately with plans to move in as soon as possible. The two-story house had two rooms on the main level and two on the upper. There was no running water, but a well was in the front yard. A water bucket hung and glistened in the sunlight. A chicken coop and rabbit hutch were in back of the house and a swamp to the east. Pussy willows swayed in the breeze. The children loved the baby chicks and baby rabbits Lawrence had and played with them for hours. Nora turned thirty six on the 24th.

Once occupied by Nora's family

NORA LOVED THE EVENINGS at her new home. The song of crickets and frogs filled the air. The full moon rising over the marsh was mystical and mysterious for her and the children. When mating cats howled and cried into the night, Nora cautioned the children it was La Llorona – to beware if they were not good. The children took heed to the warning, snuggled next to each other in the upstairs room Lawrence had sectioned off with sheets so he could have his own space. Now sixteen, privacy was a major issue for him. Over the years he grew his hair down to the middle of his back. It was his crown of glory. He took great pride in it.

On the main level were the living room in which sat a pot- belly heater for those cold winter nights, and the kitchen with a coal and wood stove along with a long, wooden table with benches made of timber on each side. Ed built the table himself for the family. The luscious smell of tortillas filled the house and yard during the day when Nora had them baking on the cast iron stove. The valve on the pressure cooker danced as she cooked beans or other items on her menu.

On summer evenings when the mosquitoes were too intense, Nora burned cow manure as a repellent. It worked like a charm, an old fashioned remedy passed from one generation to the next simply because it worked. Nora and her family were content in their new environment. She was pleased to be next door to these good friends.

One summer afternoon, Lawrence was viciously attacked in the front yard. Bigotry and prejudice fueled the assault. Lawrence was tossed to the ground and held down while his head was shaved. A cloud of dust covered his futile struggle.

At the front door, Nora stood with Teddy at her side in his diaper. She positioned him to the back of her so he wouldn't witness what was happening, all the while screaming at Lawrence's attackers to stop and go away. The other children watched in horror as well, unable to understand the dramatic scene unfolding in their front yard. Torn between going to Lawrence's aid, or leaving her young ones unattended, all Nora could do was shout and hope to bring the assault to a stop. It didn't work.

When it was over, Lawrence stood, grabbed his head in horror and retreated into the house, his coal black locks scattered about in the yard. Up in his space the terrorized, traumatized boy could only weep as he looked at himself into the mirror. His attackers walked away bloated with arrogance and hateful pride in what they did, their venom temporarily satisfied.

Only late at night when everyone else was in bed would Lawrence venture down from his hiding space to eat. He wore a scarf around his head all the time. The space he took so much pride in had become a prison. Not even his friends could convince him to come out.

Weeks later, Rudy enlisted in the Marines. He left for boot camp leaving Nora with a lump in her throat. All the kids missed him as well. Her family was close knit, took care of each other for the most part consoled each other. Nora hoped the closeness would last a life time.

His hair turned butter blond, Teddy turned one in August. To some he was spoiled, very attached to Nora. His cries echoed through the house whenever she left on a night out of dancing, or merely to go shopping. His tantrums were common whenever she left without him or he didn't get what he wanted. When he started walking, he followed his mom everywhere.

Julia and Roberto's children bonded with Nora's. Some were in the same classes at school. The friendship Nora had established with Julia and Roberto grew stronger through the years. They were always there to lend a helping hand to Nora, and she to them. They were merely two of a very strong friendship base Nora had built. Most of those friends now lived in Del Norte within easy access for her.

In fall, Nora was large into her pregnancy with weeks still to go. She was a sight to behold down Main Street going in and out of stores, swollen with child, a pile of other kids at her home. Even strangers wondered when her childbearing would end.

Ed rented a space in South Fork for his convenience because of his heavy workload there, Often he put in eight hours working on homes, then went to the sawmill for the graveyard shift. His growing family had demands and needs, and he worked with no complaint. His children and Nora were foremost of importance to him.

He usually came home on weekends. This gave Nora further breaks from the drama that many times unfolded but placed a greater burden on her as she had to tend to the children on her own. Fortunately she had older children to help. A great deal of the burden was on their shoulders – the cooking and cleaning as well as the washing out and hanging of diapers and laundry. She taught them cooking skills, so each had their duties when it came to mealtime. With nine children in the household it had to be this way.

The chickens and rabbits were well-fed and fattened, the supply of fresh eggs steady. On occasion Nora would have lamb, elk or deer to add to the menu. Driving along Highway 160 into South Fork were crews of potato and pea pickers. As soon as someone came of age they were put out into the fields. It was a way of life.

On November 13th Nora had son number seven. Named Andrew, he favored Ed in many ways. Teddy was delighted to have his mother home at last after what seemed like an eternity.

Andrew cried for hours upon hours and like clockwork started every night about eight. Why, no one ever knew. Nora tried her best to comfort him, but his tears simply would not cease. Bouts of peace between these episodes were enjoyed and appreciated by all. His crying soon became part of the household.

For his second Christmas, Teddy got an electric train from Rebecca. She sat on the floor showing him how to use it once she set it up. He was in a diaper and marveled as he watched the train move on the tracks in circles.

For him it was bliss. Santa was good to him this year. The other young boys received clothing, toys, wind-up cars and trucks; the young girls got clothing and dolls. Nora and Ed never had a lot of money, but they saved as they could during the year to make the day special in every way for the children. The wreath on the front door was homemade, the tree cut down by Ed.

CHAPTER 26

1953. AMERICA IS BREAKING out. Sex symbol Marilyn Monroe stars in *"How to Marry a Millionaire"* and *"Gentlemen Prefer Blondes."* For the kids (and some adults too) *"Peter Pan"* is popular. Gas is twenty cents a gallon. The armistice suspending the Korean War is signed.

$$* \quad * \quad * \quad * \quad *$$

NOT YET THIRTY SEVEN years old, Nora had sixteen surviving children.

When she walked down Main Street with most or all of them at her side, there was always a stir. Some people pointed, others whispered, still others gossiped. She didn't care. Holding her head held high, she walked in stride doing her business. And she and Ed went to the local dances. To slip into one of her favorite dresses and high heels, and fix up her long, coal black hair was pure bliss. There at the dance she congregated with her friends for a night filled with dance and laughter, celebrating a joyous life of diapers and high heels. She could ask for nothing more.

In spring, the dirt roads beside Nora's new home turned into mud puddles the children loved to play in. They found pleasure in the simplest things in life, found fun in whatever situation they were. Doing without the trappings of money did not strip them of the joys of childhood. The quality of childhood was found in each other, in the closeness they shared. Many times Nora sat back and observed the closeness of her children, hoping it would last a lifetime.

Nora turned thirty seven on May 24th and became pregnant again less than two months later.

In June, Ed's mother became very ill. She was bedridden at the home of his sister Cresalia. Nora's children went to Cresalia's, seated and instructed not to move until given permission to visit Atanasia at her bedside.

Cresalia was immaculate and her home spotless. She was a large woman, wore glasses and had a light complexion and sharp features that gave her an unmistakable appearance. She looked very little like her siblings. She was stern, and what she said was the word. Children knew instinctively she meant what she said. So when instructed not to move from where she seated them, they obliged with no complaint. She cared for Atanasia with loving care, as any child would a mother.

Atanasia grew sicker by the day, lying in bed and observing as the daytime shadows were consumed by nightfall. Adults knew her time was limited, but the children just saw their grandmother as being ill, totally oblivious to the severity of her condition. As time went on, she grew weaker and lost a lot of weight. Her skin discolored, and at times she barely had the strength to lift her head. Through it all, she smiled at the sight of the grandchildren around her bed.

August brought Flora's twenty second birthday and Juanita's nineteenth – and Nora still had three children at home in diapers.

Lawrence began to come out of hiding. His hair grew again to the middle of his back, thicker and more luxurious. His self-esteem was something else. The damage inside had been done, perhaps forever.

At age twenty, Juanita married her fiancé, Albert, at the Justice of the Peace in Del Norte on December 4th. Ten days later, Atanasia slipped away and died peacefully in Creselia's home. Ed's heart was shattered, but watching her those months in bed suffering had been even more difficult. With both of his parents now gone, Ed knew more than ever what Nora meant to him, how she was the center of his life and universe. Atanasia was laid to rest in the Del Norte Cemetery on a cold and cloudy winter day, as though nature herself seemed to mourn with them.

Christmas time was dismal for the adults, particularly Ed. Nora prepared her usual feast, but Ed sat in silence most of the day, just taking part in the children's exuberance from time to time. His heart just wasn't in it this year.

* * * * *

"**F**ATHER KNOWS BEST" makes its television debut in 1954. Marlon Brando stars in "On the Waterfront." Elvis Presley comes out with "That's All Right," his first single. The music craze rock 'n' roll is taking off, inspiring teen dance moves that make adults around them blush and wonder what the country is coming to. The austerity of the 1940s is a thing of the past. Gas is a staggering twenty two cents a gallon.

* * * * *

ON APRIL 8th NORA gave birth to her fourth son in a row. He was named James, Jimmy for short. He favored Ed, and his dark hair and bronze skin were a reflection of his dad's heritage. Jimmy looked a lot like Nora's brother Ernest.

As usual, Teddy clung to Nora's side everywhere she went once she returned home. He'd missed his mother terribly. His crying frustrated everyone, and some of the kids taunted him about it. All were relieved to have Nora back home to finally put the episodes to an end.

When Ed came home on weekends he usually was so worn out that all he could do was fall asleep in front of the pot belly heater. But he always found the strength to show affection to his wife. Constantly he attempted to hug and kiss her even after all the years. To him she was more beautiful than the day he married her. Although his jealousies and insecurities drove him to distraction when she got dressed up, and he loathed other men admiring her, he admired her himself at those times. He loved to see her dressed up in her best. It made him proud to have her as his wife.

One day, out of the blue, there was Joe. He stopped Nora while she was downtown shopping, taking her by total surprise. Joe still lived near the New Mexico border, but it was not a chance meeting for him. He made the trip into Del Norte to see her. When he knew Ed was at work, he drove by her home to make sure she took notice, then met her downtown where she would always wear her trademark high heels. Their feelings for each other had matured past the affair stage to the point of being intimate friends without sexual intimacy, two people who had much in common, particularly a son named Teddy.

Amazingly, Nora got pregnant again in August, just four months after Jimmy was born. This would be her twentieth child, and she wore the news with pride. The smile on her face was usually the dead giveaway. It was such a norm for her that she couldn't imagine life without her pregnancies. The priest was right after all.

With Joe back in town, the rumors flew. It didn't take long for them to reach Ed. He was not pleased, and the drama came back and escalated on the weekends when he was home. During the week while he was gone, she often wished he would not come back. Things were so bad that it didn't matter to him if the children were present or not. He said what he had to say, sometimes did what he wanted to do. Even the children expected trouble when he came home. For Nora this was inexcusable.

Juanita gave birth to her first child, a son she named Jerry, on September 30th. On Halloween, Nora went out dancing with her friends at the local Parish Hall. Although pregnant, she was able to get into some of her favorite clothes and high heels. People gawked, whispered and gossiped, talking about her pregnancy and Joe being back. But Nora didn't need their approval, or anyone else's. She was out to have a good time with her friends. That ate at the naysayers even more.

By Thanksgiving, Nora knew her marriage was dissolving. She felt in her heart that the end was near. The distance between she and Ed had become far too great to reconcile. They could barely be in the presence of each other without quarrelling. It was an aggravation and stress she no longer wanted or needed. They ignored each other on Christmas.

CHAPTER 27

1955. IT'S A TIME OF McDonald's, TV dinners and Coca-Cola in cans. Cars are everywhere, now with seat belts. People dance to Fats Domino, Bill Haley and the Comets, Chuck Berry and the Platters. Little Richard and his unique style and sound are on the scene. Young men's fashion matches the times with shades of pink shirts and charcoal grey suits.

"Rebel Without a Cause" and *"The Seven Year Itch"* hit the silver screen in Hollywood. Pocket transistor radios become popular with the youth. An African-American seamstress named Rosa Parks refuses to give her seat to a white man on a bus in Montgomery, Alabama.

* * * * *

ONE WEEKEND IN MARCH when Ed was home, Nora chose to go out with her friends dancing. She simply wanted to get away and be around laughter and anything else but arguing and fighting.

When she arrived home that night, Ed was waiting for her. He'd been drinking, fuming as the hours went by. When she went inside, Teddy was there to greet her. Cordie was sleeping on the sofa. This didn't stop Ed from pouncing on Nora. Three-year-old Teddy screamed, cried and tried to shield her, but it was no use.

The other children heard the commotion, ran in and started to cry and scream. Lawrence ran downstairs in questionable attire, where he found Ed standing over his mother in a fetal position holding her stomach to protect her unborn child. Lawrence struggled with Ed.

He shouted, "Get this screaming brat out of here!" to keep Teddy away as he battled with his father.

Finally, Lawrence pulled Ed away. Ed flopped down on a chair in front of the pot belly heater, both fuming and disappointed with himself that he'd gone to this extreme.

With Lawrence's help, Nora lifted herself and went into the kitchen to wipe away the blood from her mouth and nose. She was furious that he had struck her in her condition, and in front of the children, no less. His apologies fell on deaf ears.

"I just want you out of my house and life!" she yelled. "Now! I don't want to ever see you again."

This time she meant it. It didn't matter anymore what she had to go through in being a single parent with this many children to care for. She'd do what she had to do to get away from all the hell and chaos.

Finally she was able to calm the children and put them to bed. It was difficult. They did not want to leave her side for fear of him hitting her again. Most of them cried themselves to sleep that night. Her heart ached as she saw the effect on them. The one thing she wanted so badly to shield them from had come to pass.

"Stay out of our bed!" she screamed at Ed as he tried to talk to her. He fell asleep on a chair in front of the heater, where he passed out.

After that night, things were never the same between Nora and Ed. She hated the sight of him, shivered at the thought of his presence. He tried desperately to mend the damage, but knew instinctively that it was too late. He'd come to know Nora well enough to realize when she'd made up her mind there was no convincing her otherwise. His promises fell on deaf ears, for her a mockery and patronization. Ed went back to South Fork, where he knew the cabin he rented would be his permanent residence from then on.

On weekends he drove down and picked up some of the children, taking them back up to South Fork to spend time with him. The children knew each had their turn when it came to staying with him on his days off. Most of the children were oblivious to what was happening. To them he was simply working at the sawmill as usual. They could not comprehend what separation meant. After awhile, their laughter returned. Whether in South Fork with Ed or in Del Norte with Nora, they stayed outdoors playing games until sunset, sometimes beyond. Many times both Nora and Ed had to force them in. For the children there were never enough hours in the day.

Jimmy celebrated his first birthday on April 8th Rudy turned sixteen on the 16th Charlotte and Becky eleven on the 30th. The constant birthdays were reminders of how not only Nora was getting older, but also how her children were growing up. She was so proud of them.

Shortly after her thirty ninth birthday, Nora had a baby daughter on May 29th. Nora named her Bernadette, after a nun she befriended at the hospital. She would be called Benny for short. Benny was a beautiful baby with a very light complexion, virtually no hair, but with fuzz the color of butter.

Nora was in the hospital for nearly a week. The children gathered around her the minute she stepped back into the house with the baby in her arms, all eager to see their new sibling. There also to greet her were tubs and mounds of soiled diapers. The older children did their best in keeping up with the demand, but without her supervision they fell behind. No sooner did the baby fall asleep for her afternoon nap, Nora's work began. There was plenty to catch up on.

Nora hadn't been home but for hours when friends showed up to congratulate the family, bring what was needed and pitch in to help. One by one they entered the house with baked goods, stacks of tortillas and pots of beans and other goodies. With four now in diapers, some brought fresh ones to add to Nora's growing collection. Within hours the mounds were washed and hung out to dry, along with other clothing the children needed for school. Nora felt good being home in her own element, although the one advantage to being in the hospital was getting the rest she needed.

Lawrence was a fixture at the chicken coop and rabbit hutch, where he lovingly took care of his animals. His rabbits were special to him, especially while they were just bunnies. Daily he stocked up their food supply of lettuce, carrots and other vegetation. His love and compassion for his brood was obvious to all. He was also very protective of them. He could be found there tending to them come morning, afternoon and evenings. The rabbits knew him well, knew they were safe with him. The smaller children watched in awe as he took care of the furry creatures. He let them hold bunnies now and then, as he would the chicks when they were little.

As weeks went by taking Nora well into June, her workload kept her on the go constantly. Neighbors were accustomed to seeing her at the clotheslines hanging out diapers and laundry to dry. They could almost time their clocks by Nora's visits to the lines.

Ed stayed up in South Fork much of the time, other than coming down on weekends to pick up whose turn it was to go back up with him. He hadn't stayed at the home in Del Norte since the incident with Nora and Lawrence. For Nora the separation was permanent, but for him there was still hope. He wasn't about to give up on her and his family that easily. His love for them wouldn't allow for it. Although he gave Nora money for the family, she had to go on government assistance to make ends meet.

On July 4th Ed came down to pick up as many children as he could for the annual fireworks display at Beaver Dam. He knew the children looked forward to that every year since they'd started the tradition. He would also pick up fireworks for their own use once the sun set. It was an exciting time for the children. They had plenty to tell Nora when they got home.

Cordie turned eight on July 8th. She spent a lot of time with Rebecca up at the homestead, sometimes for weeks. As the other children, Cordie grew accustomed to Rebecca's stern, sometimes harsh ways. None dared question Rebecca's rules and requests. It was a given that things were just done the way she wanted in her household. Each had their daily chores to be done, prayer at each meal and before bed, with Bible readings whenever Rebecca chose. Those requirements were non-negotiable.

On weekends, Nora slipped into one of her favorite dresses and high heels and went dancing with friends around the valley. Sometimes it was in Del Norte, in others Seven Mile Plaza, Center, La Garita, Alamosa or Fort Garland. They had plenty of places to choose from. A night out with her friends was exactly what she needed after a long week of hard working at home. Without Ed's jealousies and insecurities to contend with, it was always a night of frivolity. She had friends all over the valley and reunited with relatives she'd lost contact with through the years. She was content with her life once again, and slept peacefully without having to worry what mood Ed would be in when he stepped through the door. Anyone who approached and smelled of liquor was quickly sent on his way.

More birthdays in August – Flora was now twenty four, Juanita twenty two and Teddy four. Nora had her hands full trying to wean Teddy off diapers. When he wasn't in them, she had to contend with bedwetting, something neither she nor the older children could understand. Whether it was his fear of rising in the dark and using the portable commode set in the room or something else they were oblivious to, they could never tell.

Teddy often spoke of witches and ghosts up in their room but could only elaborate on it as much as any four year old could. Words eluded him although the horror of what he experienced stayed. He was awakened one night to a large hand creeping under the covers feeling their way to him. He pinched at the hand trying to keep it from him. When that didn't work he scratched at it with his tiny fingers.

Finally out of desperation, he pinched at his brothers who were sleeping with him. When that didn't awaken them, he resorted to digging his tiny nails into the hand, scratching it until it retracted. His next move would be biting the hand. He lifted the covers to watch the hand sink below the bed before he had to resort to that. For the rest of the night he stayed under the covers, huddled next to his brothers for fear the hand would return. The next morning all he could was tell Nora and whoever would listen what had happened. For him they were real.

Days later when Teddy had done something wrong and was being disciplined, for punishment Rebecca put him upstairs in the room alone. He cried at the open window telling Rebecca and Nora, who were outside, that there were witches and ghosts in there with him. For them it was a child's imagination, but for Teddy it was very much a reality – one that brought constant terror into his young life. At the window he sobbed and pleaded with them to bring him down – his words falling on deaf ears. Eventually, he cried himself to sleep.

Trouble of another sort came in the fall when a local female gang known as the Spiders was involved in a fight. Three of the girls were sent up to Morrison to a girl's facility, and authorities made sure the gang was dismantled. Much to Nora's disappointment, one of her daughters was among the three girls sent up. The legalities were frustrating for Nora, a source of constant worry and sadness. All she could do was accept the facts for what they were and hope her daughter turned out right.

Andrew turned three on November 13th, and Lawrence nineteen on the 27th and Billy thirteen on the 28th. Ed joined the family for Thanksgiving dinner, then returned to South Fork when it was over. As angry and frustrated as Nora was with him, she would never deny him or her children of each other. Ed was on his best behavior. The separation had done both of them good. For Ed, it had sunk in that Nora was dead serious, and there was no turning back for her. For Nora, she finally had had enough and was sticking to her guns. His empty promises only nauseated her and irked her that she fallen for them all those years. She'd heard them all a million times, a patronization more than anything else.

On December 3rd Charlene turned seven. Winter covered the valley with several inches of freshly fallen snow. A white Christmas was predicted. Lawrence and Dale cut a tree for decorating. With Flora living with her own family, the decorating was up to the older children still at home. In no time they had the tree up and dressed for the season. The bubbling candlestick lights amused the younger children, along with those who sat observing the multi-colored lights glowing through the web of angel hair and silver icicles.

Other decorations were lovingly made at school. The popcorn garland and craft paper garland they displayed with pride. They took turns filling the bucket in which the tree sat, keeping it fresh. The scent of evergreen filled the house.

Nora and Ed collaborated on the Christmas gifts. For the boys there were toys and various games, for the girls, dolls and tea sets. All got jeans and other clothing. Board games like Monopoly were shared. Puzzles kept them entertained for hours upon hours. In no time the children were involved in their own little worlds with their gifts, wrapping paper spread across the front room. No matter what they got, the children all loved everything and every minute, as did Nora, who would let them have their day however exhausting it might be for her.

Christmas night she lay in bed pondering her day and life. So much had changed for her. She could hear giggling but that soon ceased as the children dozed off. She was only thirty nine years old and had eighteen children living with her or nearby. The love she had for them all brought a lump to her throat. Her children meant the world to her.

CHAPTER 28

1956. ELVIS PRESLEY IS all the rage. *"Don't be Cruel"* and *"Hound Dog"* top the music charts. The heartthrob's first movie *"Love Me Tender"* opens in New York. He makes his first appearance on the *"Ed Sullivan Show"* but is forbidden from being filmed below the waist because his gyrating pelvis is too much for the prudish.

A flamboyant Little Richard releases his high-energy *"Tutti Frutti,"* getting people off their seats and onto the dance floor. And then there's Bill Haley and The Comets, Chuck Berry, Jerry Lee Lewis, Johnny Cash and Ella Fitzgerald.

The soap opera *"As The World Turns"* debuts on CBS. *"The King and I," "The Ten Commandments"* and *"Around the World in Eighty Days"* hit the silver screen. Portable black and white TV sets are sold.

Eisenhower is re-elected president. Martin Luther King gains national prominence as the civil rights movement gains momentum. In Alabama, bus segregation laws are declared illegal by the U.S. Supreme Court.

* * * * *

To NORA'S DISMAY, HER children began moving as time went on. Juanita and Albert packed up and moved to San Francisco in 1956. Later, Lucy went there to stay with them, and Dale went to stay with Lucy when she got her own place.

On occasion, Ed came into Del Norte to bring her money, wood and coal for the month, as well as the new rage – disposable diapers. Nora was accustomed to cloth and didn't take well to the disposables. Rebecca was totally against them. For her it was a mother and wife's duties to scrub out diapers for her children.

In late January, despite all the troubles and distance from Ed, she experienced the familiar symptoms again. She hoped it wasn't true, but the Del Norte Hospital confirmed her suspicions. He, as well as his staff who knew Nora, were amazed. Many people couldn't understand how one woman could have so many children. While large families were common at this time, they didn't come close to the size of Nora's.

This winter was exceptionally cold. In nearby Alamosa, temperatures sometimes plunged to forty degrees below zero. Still, on those very cold days Nora made her weekly trips into town to stock up. If she needed help, the older children went along. She wouldn't expose the young ones to the bitter elements. When one child got sick, the others usually followed. During winter she was well-stocked with Vicks Vaporub and other remedies she came to know and rely on. She considered herself lucky if she made it through a winter without some sort of illness hitting the children.

In early April, Nora had a miscarriage. She went into a mourning depression, but obligation and duty forced her to her feet. In the quiet of the nights to follow, she could only wonder who this child might have grown up to be, like the two others before. She wept herself to sleep thinking of what might have been. Having now lost three children, Nora doubted that she could withstand another. It was just too much for her to take. All her children were of value to her whether they were alive and well or never had the joy of birth. To Nora, she had twenty one children now.

At the end of April, Charlotte and Becky celebrated their twelfth birthday. At this point, there were only three months in which she didn't celebrate a birthday, a thought that always brought a smile to her face.

Nora's separation from Ed was becoming difficult on the children. Having some of them in South Fork during the weekends helped, but the younger children couldn't grasp why he wasn't home. Ed lived in a two-room cabin at the end of Church Lane at the base of the Beaver Mountain near the small chapel. Behind the cabin were the dump and an abundance of chokeberry bushes with other edible vegetation. The children spent hours upon hours in the dump, playing in and on the abandoned cars piled on each other.

When the weather permitted, Ed took the children on fishing trips along the South Fork River. Usually after such a trip the smell of frying trout filled the cabin. Having no electricity, they dined by kerosene lanterns.

The family living next to the chapel also had a bunch of kids. The mother gathered her children and Ed's around her chair and told tales of La Llorona, sending Ed's kids' home screaming through the darkness, only to return for more fables the next night. The woman was a master at her tales, setting the mood with her kerosene lanterns, manipulating shadows around the house creating the atmosphere for her stories. She was beloved by all.

In May, Nora turned the big four o and little Benny one. Pricilla turned twenty six and married a man named Bud.

The kids always found creative ways to entertain themselves during the summer months out of school. They made horses out of twigs and stilts out of branches. One June day, the children played out back jumping off the chicken coop. Only four feet high, it looked like a mountain to them. When Teddy took his turn, he landed on a broken bottle, slicing through the arch and out the top of his foot. His screams brought Nora outside to find him covered in blood. Helped by the other children, she carried him inside, wrapping his wound and heading for the hospital.

Teddy's screams carried through the halls as the doctors did their best to treat him. He was terrified. The pain was unbearable. He kicked at the doctor who tried to give him shots in the foot to numb for treatment. The staff had to hold him down while the doctor did what needed to be done. Pieces of glass were taken from his foot along with pieces of flesh that needed to be removed. After a few days' stay, he was sent home for recovery and was immobilized for weeks as the wound healed, a real task for Nora as Teddy was so hyper. Creativity by her kept him off his feet.

In mid-July the stitches were removed. Once again his screams carried down the hallways of the hospital. Although the pain was minimal, the doctors and nurses terrified him. The staff seemed almost relieved to have Nora leave with him at her side. They would not soon forget his visits.

Teddy resumed life as though he'd never been injured. He ran around, jumping and playing as before. Freedom from bandages was overwhelming after being off his feet for weeks. He was eager to join his siblings in games they had enjoyed while he had to sit back and watch. He was also eager to show off his scar to anyone who would agree to see it. Like any little boy, he was proud of it, totally forgetting the pain involved. He was certain the scar would last as a lifetime reminder of that day. He turned five on August 22nd.

Nora became pregnant in September with child number twenty two on the way. Although joyful, she couldn't help but think of the challenges yet another child would add to her life along with the fear that something could go wrong. Plus, she was now forty years old.

CHAPTER 29

1957. UNEMPLOYMENT IS 3.3 PERCENT, and gas costs twenty four cents a gallon. Slinky and Hula Hoops are popular toys. Little Richard and Elvis continue to dominate the music charts with hit after hit. Elvis' movie *"Jailhouse Rock"* is released. Elvis and his family move into Graceland mansion in Memphis, Tennessee.

"American Bandstand" is all the rage as teenagers across the nation tune in to their favorite artists and songs. Hollywood releases *"Three Faces of Eve."* People by and large are content with their lives and situations, although poverty remains for millions. The civil rights movement continues.

* * * * *

AT FOUR MONTHS PREGNANT, Nora was doing okay, though she had stopped dancing out of concern for her baby. The winter was cold and difficult for all in Del Norte. Feet of accumulated snow covered the ground, temperatures often below zero. Nora's pot belly heater and stove were constantly going. Still, the children made their way to school every day through the elements, even playing outside afterward despite the arctic elements. Rock 'n' roll music blared from Lawrence's space upstairs. A day would not be complete without the beats blasting in his room, along with his joyful laughter, awakening the children for school.

When weather permitted, Nora made her usual trips into town. One of her favorite places was still the second-hand store next to the theater owned by her friend Sofia. Nora spent hours rummaging there, often going home with several bagsful.

From the thrift store Nora met friends for coffee or lunch in the Model Café or the We Ask You Inn, both on Main Street. Teenagers were usually there having sodas, sundaes or hamburgers and listening to their favorite tunes on the juke boxes. Nora and her friends spent hours upon hours reminiscing on the joys and sorrows of their lives. Lucy turned nineteen on February 28th.

Nora's concerns about the pregnancy turned out to be true in the second week of March when she went into labor at six months. She feared for the worst and was immediately admitted into the hospital. On March 11th was Dale's seventeenth birthday. The day after, Nora gave birth to a girl weighing twenty four ounces and not even twelve inches long, her arms like pencils. The baby was unlike anyone the hospital staff had ever seen.

Ed and Nora named the little one Frances. She came to be known as Pee Wee. She was placed into an incubator and covered with cotton because her skin was so delicate not even fabric could touch her. Nora's heart was gripped by fear all the while. The chances for the infant's survival were dim. Nora's heart broke each and every time she gazed into the incubator seeing the fragility of her child. She so wanted to lift and hold her, but that, too, was forbidden. Nora was released and reluctantly went home, to return day after day to check her baby.

When Nora turned forty one on May 24th the baby was still in the hospital. She had gained weight and size, but Nora was told it would still be awhile before the child would be big or strong enough to go home.

Luckily, winter was behind them and the weather was good. It allowed for Nora's walks to the hospital at any given moment when things came up. Her family did not have the luxury of a telephone, so she relied on word of mouth for news at the hospital. She spent countless hours at the incubator yearning for the day she could hold the child in her arms, love her like she wanted. It seemed she'd lived with a broken heart forever. There was a lump in her throat and a never-ending feeling of impending doom. The hell was the waiting, not knowing what tomorrow held. Every ounce her child gained was a milestone toward her recovery, closer to the day Nora would finally be able to take her home where she belonged. She lost count of the times weeping on her way home and was ever so grateful to have the older children watch over the young while she was gone. She had taught them well.

Finally in mid-June, the baby emerged from the incubator. Although still tiny and fragile, she was stronger and nursing on her own. Nora was exhausted, physically and emotionally. It had been months since she had a solid night's sleep. Now she could resume life.

Nora brought the baby home several days later. She put the little one in a shoe box, near the stove for warmth. The other children peered in at her, afraid as they'd never seen such a tiny person before. The infant had a head full of curly, black hair and a dark complexion. Wherever Nora was in the house, she made sure the shoe box was within sight. At night she placed the shoe box next to her bed, awakening on and off checking on her. It was round the clock care for the wee one.

By Cordie's tenth birthday on July 8th the baby grew more and put on weight. Nora took great precaution in caring for her. The shoe box went out into the yard while Nora and the older children did daily chores. Wherever Nora went the shoe box went too. Thunderstorms knocked out the power for hours, so Nora would light up the kerosene lanterns.

Word spread about the newborn, and everyone in town wanted to see her. But Nora wouldn't take the risk of bringing her along downtown. Most of the time, she sent the children to run her errands while she cared for the baby. On the odd occasion that Nora had to go herself, the older children kept a constant watch on their little sister. She was getting stronger by the day.

She also learned the art of getting her way by going into crying episodes that literally robbed her of her breath. Nora, or whoever the infant was in care of, had to sprinkle cold water or snow in her face to bring her out of it. This was a constant thing with her. She frightened everyone involved, especially the children who cared for her on those occasions when Nora was gone. The older children went into a panic each time it happened but also knew the procedure in getting the infant out of it.

The August days were long and hot. In that day and age, people could still leave doors and windows open with no concern. On the second floor, the children's space was sometimes intolerable because of the daytime heat, and leaving things open left nighttime breezes cool everything off. Teddy was six, his fondness of Nora growing with each passing day. He was constantly at her side, holding on to her dress. The other kids called him spoiled.

Nora wanted another house, one with more room and more conveniences for her large family. Before summer was out she found one to rent on along Highway 112 northbound toward Center, next door to her best friend Julia's son and daughter-in-law.

Within a week she was finally moved and settled into her new place. Living nearby was a family known to the residents of Del Norte as the Répos. Why they were called that was never known. They had the reputation of being a rowdy group. One of the older daughters was in a gang rival to the onetime Spiders.

Nora's wishes for more modern conveniences were satisfied in this home. It had indoor running water and a gas cooking stove, things Nora had done without all her life.

Nora also was grateful for a furnace, something else she never had before. The harsh winters of the valley were already looking less burdensome. She no longer would have to go outside for water, only to find a frozen well, or send the children out for wood and coal in the harsh elements. School was a straight shot down the road, a fifteen minute walk. Main Street was a mere block and a half. The children seemed eager and happy to be in their new environment. As usual, they were outdoors most of the time playing games the minute they got home from school. The highway was of some concern to Nora, as it would be to any parent, but she felt secure in their safety as she knew the children cared for one another.

On weekends when they weren't in South Fork with Ed, they went to the movies for a matinee at the Princess Theater for a dime. In South Fork, Billy had a job changing the coming theater attractions at the post office in exchange for passes, popcorn and a pop. Nora often sent a group of her children to the movies escorted by their older siblings. The theater done in red velvet was always a treat for the children, as it was for adults. The aroma of freshly popped popcorn swept into their faces the second they stepped through the doors. Cartoons before the main feature were something the children all looked forward to.

Ed

THE HOLIDAYS WERE EVEN more festive in the new home. The conveniences were a godsend in preparing the Thanksgiving feast, and everyone could more easily share in the town's Christmas celebrations. The downtown decorations were a short walk away, lights adorned homes everywhere. Snowmen were in many yards. In stores Christmas music filled the air. Teenagers cruised up and down Main Street in heated automobiles passing time away, rock 'n' roll music vibrating from inside. Many of them sang along with the songs, moving to the beat. The liveliness of the music was a mantra for the times, days of optimism and hope for the future. Nora couldn't help but tap her feet in happiness when the teens drove by.

Christmas was especially joyful. Life had turned a page for Nora in many ways. The hardships of the past were gone, the children warm and cozy in their nice, toasty house. As usual they were up before dawn ready to tear into their packages the second Nora gave them the word. Rebecca came down bringing with her Carole and Billy. Ed came with bags and bags of gifts for the children.

A white Christmas settled over Del Norte that wonderful year of 1957. Streams of smoke rose from chimneys throughout town. Adults sang Christmas carols around town. Men played along on their guitars. It was the time and season to be grateful, to reach out to others. Finally, silence swept over the town leaving memories of another year gone by.

CHAPTER 30

1958. THE GOOD TIMES don't last. A recession hits. Unemployment shoots back above 7 percent, and hard times return for millions for the first time since the Great Depression. Gas is twenty five cents a gallon. But it is also a time to rock. Jerry Lee Lewis' *"Great Balls of Fire"* is a smash. Joining him in popularity are the Everly Brothers, Ricky Nelson and Billie Holiday. Rock 'n' roll sweeps across America becoming a national phenomenon. In cafés, juke boxes are constantly going with high-energy tunes. Teens don't just sit and listen; they get up and dance in the eateries. The Edsel goes into production. Hula Hoop sales top a hundred million.

* * * * *

NORA'S LIFE WAS A roller coaster ride living on Highway 112 in early 1958. The children were content even in the freezing winter. The baby got sick with pneumonia and spent nearly a week back in the hospital. Nora never knew from one day to the other what to expect. She could only hope for the best. After her bout with pneumonia, the baby grew and put on weight. Her fragility diminished as time went by.

Nora lived in a different house, but winter was its usual miserable self. Many automobiles were left stuck and stranded on the side streets when snow fell by the foot, which was a common occurrence in the valley. While the children took it all in stride and played games in the mounds of snow, it was difficult for the working adults and those trying to raise families.

On rare occasion Ed was in town and able to give the children a ride to school. He drove a greenish 1951 Chevy, which many times overheated, thus he had to pull over allowing it to cool. For the children it was all fun and games each time it happened. They would simply entertain each other in the back or front seat. For Ed it was a frustration. The twenty minute drive from South Fork usually ended up being forty-five

Ed and children

CAROLE WAS TWELVE NOW and worked as a crossing guard directing school kids and traffic before getting on the bus bound for South Fork herself. On occasion Rebecca brought her down to Nora's to spend time with her siblings, but most of the time they only saw her in school. Cordie was back and forth from Rebecca's to Nora's during this time. On weekends the children still took turns spending time with Ed in South Fork. Up there they had the chores of hauling in firewood and coal for the day and night, also bringing in drinking water as Ed did not have the conveniences Nora did.

Being over forty and having been pregnant twenty two times didn't stop Nora from her favorite activity. Everyone was amazed at how great she looked after all those children and still taking care of so many at home. She wore her long, black, wavy hair with great pride. Sometimes it was piled on top of her head, but mostly it hung down her back. She loved having long hair. Simmering, silk stockings completed her look when she stepped out of the house in heels.

On March 5th Flora had twin boys – Jerry and Larry. Seven days later, Nora's youngest and littlest celebrated her first birthday. Living in Del Norte, Nora often found time to steal away to Rudolf's grave and wonder while kneeling there what he'd say of her life now. She'd given him a multitude of grandchildren. Great-grandchildren would soon come, too, with certainly many more. She couldn't help but ponder the legacy she'd leave. It all seemed so surreal.

Nora loved the lilac bush next to her new home. With spring, the scent swept through the house as soon as she opened the window. Lilacs and roses were her favorite flowers. On the 8th Jimmy turned four. Rudy turned twenty three on April 16th. He visited from San Francisco but not very often, and certainly not as much as Nora would have liked.

Time moved swiftly that year. It seemed the days, weeks and months flew by. In May, Pricilla was twenty eight, Dwayne eight. Outside of having rowdy neighbors Nora was content with her life. She and Ed worked out a schedule for the children as they loved spending time with him in South Fork. This also gave Nora a break herself; though on sunny days she never tired of taking some of the children on expeditions in search of wild vegetation for meals along the river and in meadows. Wild spinach, for one, was always welcome on the dinner table. She turned forty two on May 24th. She had six children twenty years or older, yet still had two others in diapers.

To say the least, Nora was surprised when she got pregnant again. Ed was rather taken aback as well. Rebecca found it difficult to believe. Rudolf's words haunted her.

As usual Ed gathered the children on July 4th, taking them up to Beaver Dam for fireworks, hot dogs and hamburgers. Eagerly they piled into the car squeezing into the front and back seat, finding space wherever they could. Ed's car overheated regularly, so as usual, he pulled over to let the engine cool down. The children found it amusing, making a game out of it. The drive was an adventure for them.

Finally they arrived at Beaver Dam and set up for the day and evening. Through the day the children spent their time wandering the mountainside, fishing or swimming when they found a calm spot in the river feeding the dam. After the long day of excitement, they piled back into the car and headed home.

July was hot, August hotter. Harvest season neared, giving work in the potato and pea fields. It was hard, grueling work from sunrise to sunset. Much of the produce picked was sold to locals, who stored it in the cellar for use in the winter months. Hundred-pound bags of potatoes also were loaded onto trucks and 18-wheelers and transported across the nation. Potatoes from the San Luis Valley were known throughout the country.

Crews piled in back of large trucks and were hauled to the fields. The pea pickers carried baskets and earned a penny a pound. Teenagers worked hard to get money for movies and partying or clothing for the incoming school year. Nora's children did it for both reasons.

Older residents worked the fields to make ends meet or to buy things for Christmas. The money they earned was often spent at Sofia's, so she, like everyone who worked the fields, looked forward to the harvest.

At times some of Nora's children went to the Western Slope near Grand Junctions to pick peaches. They stayed there for the season, returning home worn out, but with full pockets. Christine and Modesto also brought their family to the region for harvest season and rented cabins at Jessup's. This was nice because it gave Nora time to spend with Christine.

Tragedy struck in August. One day, Rebecca went to the chicken coop to gather eggs and check on the hens. She left Billy and her son Ted inside the house. They grew concerned when she had didn't return. Billy found her sitting on the ground near the chicken coop; her face drooped on one side.

Billy tried to lift her, to no avail. In a panic he ran inside to get Ted, who was able to get Rebecca to the house, then ran across the highway to use the neighbor's telephone calling for help. Within minutes two family friends of Rebecca's arrived. They helped get her in the car and drove to the Del Norte Hospital.

Doctors confirmed that Rebecca had had a stroke. The left side of her body was weak and immobile. When Nora went to the hospital, she found her mother in grave condition, slurring when she tried to speak. Nora's heart sank. She sat with Rebecca before returning home to her children. She wept along the way. She'd never seen her mother like this, a shadow of who she used to be.

Juanita, in San Francisco, turned twenty five on August 17th. Nora heard from her pretty regularly via mail. Nora still did not have the luxury of a telephone, nor did any of her friends. It was on her wish list, especially with Rebecca in the hospital. Thankfully, Rebecca began to recover somewhat, gained strength on the paralyzed portion of her body and spoke without slurring her words. But she was never the same and swore she couldn't go back to the homestead after this incident, too attached to her independence to return like this. She walked with a crutch and missed the wonderful life she'd had. She missed being who she was.

At seven, Teddy was still very much the mama's boy. He threw tantrums whenever she left without him, falling to the floor kicking and screaming a common sight. Some of the children even got a kick at goading him into going ballistic.

When harvest got underway in early September, Nora's older children were up at the crack of dawn waiting for their ride to the fields. Those who gave the workers a ride often gouged them, charging as much as possible. It wasn't fair, but it was common. The older children gone, Nora was back in the diaper business full-time. It was daunting doing all that and keeping a keen eye on the little ones. But, like always, she did what had to be done. It would be that way for weeks.

Rebecca was released from the hospital in September and moved into Del Norte, to a spacious home at the base of D Mountain. Ted, Billy and Carole joined her there. She later moved to a log cabin in the area. Nora visited frequently, helping take care of her needs.

Also in September, one of Flora's twin boys, Larry, got sick and passed away. He was only six months old. To lose a first child was devastating enough for her, but now two by the age of twenty seven was beyond comprehension. Little Larry was buried in the Del Norte Cemetery. It was a mournful day. The sky was overcast and gray, as though nature herself seemed to mourn the loss of another angel.

Through September and into October, harvest season was in full swing. Anyone driving Highway 160 into South Fork could see crews of potato pickers, harvesters and bail buckers in the surrounding fields. It was a common sight every year. Crews of Native Americans were always noticed in their velvet garments, adorned with turquoise jewelry.

Going on sixteen, Billy hitch-hiked from South Fork into Del Norte to spend time with his siblings and friends during the weekends when they were free to go out and do things. They piled into one car and went to drive-ins, the theater or cruise around town. If he didn't find a ride back to South Fork, he just hung out at the Model Café or the We Ask You Inn and hitched a ride with a truck driver. Either way he made it back home.

Lucy and Dale left San Francisco by bus and arrived back in Del Norte that fall. Nora was pleased to have her son and daughter back home. Dale was equally shocked to find the tiny infant lying on the bed next to the heater vent. At first he thought Nora had gotten a cat. He quickly was introduced to his little sister's knack of getting attention.

In mid-October, Nora miscarried again. Doctors told her she was going through the change of life, something Nora was not familiar with. Rebecca never discussed it with her, considering it just part of being a woman. Nora hadn't gotten over her last miscarriage thirty months ago and concluded this was nature's way of saying that her child-bearing years were over.

CHAPTER 31

1959. THE ECONOMY TAKES a turn for the better with unemployment falling to 5.5 percent. Gas is twenty six cents. It's a year to remember in the entertainment world. *"Rawhide," "Bonanza"* and *"The Twilight Zone"* are popular television shows. *"Some Like it Hot"* hits the silver screen bringing laughter to millions as Tony Curtis and Jack Lemmon play cross dressing band members fleeing gangsters. *"Ben Hur"* starring Charlton Heston and Alfred Hitchcock's *"North by Northwest"* are also popular. The Grammy Awards debut.

A lot more happens. Alaska and Hawaii are admitted as the 49th and 50th states. The Boeing 707 enters service. Girls love their Barbie Dolls. Fidel Castro takes power in Cuba. February 2nd is the day the music dies when Buddy Holly, Ritchie Valens, "The Big Bopper" JP Richardson and the pilot are killed in a plane crash near Clear Lake, Iowa.

* * * * *

DOWNTOWN WAS STILL DRAPED in holiday decorations as the year began. The big star on D Mountain lit up the night sky. Teenagers cruised Main Street during the evenings listening to K-O-M-A out of Oklahoma, the only rock 'n' roll radio station available in the valley. It faded in and out regularly. Cars rumbled from the bass as they eased down the icy road. We Ask You Inn and Model Café kept busy with teenagers going in for sodas, hamburgers and floats.

The life cycle began anew in Nora's household. Often in those winter months the diapers and clothes froze when hung outside and Nora had to bring them in to thaw.

The March winds blew in cold air, but the kids in town, including Nora's, loved them because it meant they could fly kites, colorful creations of all sizes and colors that filled the sky like sails. Nora was taken by surprise when she discovered she was pregnant again. Her doctor at the Del Norte Hospital confirmed it.

Dale turned nineteen on March 11th. The youngest celebrated her second birthday on the 12th. She was gaining in weight and strength. Nora wasn't as much on edge with her anymore. With the exception of her crying episodes and losing her breath, her health was on the rise. Nora was content knowing she was a healthy child, but still kept a close eye on her, as did everyone else in the household. She took her to the doctor on a regular basis for check-ups, growing more secure with the reports each time she left.

Apple trees blossomed and tulips bloomed in yards, even in the poor areas. Beauty had no prejudice, nature's canvas there was for everyone. The lilac bush next to Nora's home bloomed, sending its fragrance throughout the house. She loved the scent, had perfumes with lilac fragrance, and looked forward to spring and summer once again. Despite its hardships, winter was always Nora's favorite season because it meant the festivities of

Thanksgiving and Christmas. And now with these modern conveniences, the winters were easier to deal with, making them all the better.

One sunny day in April, Teddy was on his way home from school when he saw a small crowd near the house on Highway 112 watching two entangled bodies in a fight. One was the Répo girl from next door and the other a friend of Nora's older children. The neighbor being somewhat older and larger had the advantage. Helping the friend up, one of Nora's older daughters quarreled with the neighbor, warning her to stay away. It was only a matter of time before they, too, locked horns. Nora went out and took a very curious Teddy inside.

This incident and others involving the neighbors gave Nora second thoughts on where she was living. She hoped for a place near the school and downtown. Charlotte and Becky turned fifteen on the 30th.

On May 3rd Lucy gave birth to her first child. Nora turned forty three that month. It seemed like only yesterday that she had Pricilla, who turned twenty nine two weeks before. Now she had been pregnant twenty two times, had nineteen living children and more and more and grandchildren, yet was still young, strong and healthy. But that was challenged when she went into early labor, having her third miscarriage in mid-May. Once more her heart broke. Once more she was left to ponder on who this child may have grown to be. This time she knew beyond a shadow of a doubt that there were to be no more pregnancies for her. She had fulfilled her destiny, and then some.

* * * * *

SUMMER SET IN, AND Nora stepped up her search for a new home, wanting to be settled before another winter arrived. The children were outside most of the time playing games or wandering around town. Downtown always buzzed with activity involving the teens, who were lucky if they found a parking space. If not, they cruised up and down Main Street, going from one side of town to the other, rock 'n' roll music and laughter blaring. Carloads of boys chased after carloads of girls, the cat and mouse routine that has been and always will be played in towns across America. The library, not far from where Nora lived, was also a popular hangout. Girls sat on the steps or at the pillars out front having a bird's-eye view of the boys that went by in cars or on bikes.

Pricilla gave birth to her first child June 6th a daughter she named Karen.

Charlotte fought with one of the neighbor girls in the bathroom of the We Ask You Inn Café on Main Street. The manager disrupted the squabble and kicked out both of them. Charlotte was tired of the girl's bullying, putting a stop to it once and for all. Both Ed and Nora had taught their children not to instigate trouble, but not to run from it either. Bullies were a common thing in town those days for both girls and boys.

One day, Charlotte, Becky and Carole took the liberty of driving Ed's car while he was at work. He had exchanged the Chevy for a gray 1938 Pontiac. They drove it up and down Church Lane with the rest of the children standing on the running boards or chasing after. Since all three girls were still in their early teens and none had experience driving, they burned out the clutch and demolished the gears.

Later, when an unsuspecting Ed tried to drive it, he couldn't imagine what had happened when the thing wouldn't move. The children feared telling him but eventually broke down and told him the truth. To their delight (and surprise), he showed no anger or hostility, although his frustration was obvious as he worked on the car trying to get it back into running condition.

More frivolity, if you want to look at it that way, came in August, a month of mosquitoes and bats that the children got fun out of dodging. One day, the residents of South Fork were puzzled as the chapel bell rang out from the hillside. It usually only rang on Sunday's during services. Curiosity drew the attention of the priest and officials.

When they entered the chapel, standing at the altar were Teddy along with Flora's daughter Tonnie clothed in the priest's robes. They broke a window, put on the priest's garments, played the organ and rang the bell. Flora, who with her family was living in South Fork next to Ed on Church Lane, was notified immediately. Ed had moved out of the cabin into a house next door to Flora. He came with her, and they arrived to find the two children draped in the priest's finery. Although finding humor in the situation, the parents still meted out consequences. Likewise, the priest laughed but also lectured the children before sending them home.

Nora's time living on Highway 112 didn't last much longer. Under the extreme circumstances and stress the family was under, she chose to rent a home temporarily closer into town, about a block off Main Street due north. The home situated across the street from the Moore's, a local family. Some of Nora's kids were classmates with the Moore children. Nora lived there for a brief period before searching for another home more suitable for her family.

Between helping care for Rebecca and house hunting, Nora was busier than ever but that didn't stop her from joining the annual Halloween festivities. Nora, as always in a favorite dress and high heels, and her friends attended the dance at the Parish Hall, where they met up with other friends and relatives from towns around the valley. A local band called the Challengers, popular with young and old alike in the valley, played Spanish and English music, and a lot of rock 'n' roll.

In November, Rudy and his family returned to California. Nora, seeing the yearning in Billy's eyes, consented to his request to go along. Snow fell as she looked out the window watching him leave.

Teddy, now eight, was in the Christmas school play as an elf dressed in green tights and hat with brown shoes curled up at the toe. He was shy and terrified of crowds, so when the teacher pushed him out onto the stage he was in tears and froze. Clumsily and reluctantly, he did what he was taught to do, but from that point on he became even more shy and insecure around people. Social anxiety, not the career of an actor, debuted that day.

Christmas morning the children were up early, pumped with anticipation. They were eager for Ed to arrive so they could open their gifts. He arrived later than expected due to the icy roads. Rebecca, Carole and Billy were with him.

Rebecca sat in a chair taking it all in. Although still struggling to get around, she wanted to be near life and activity and couldn't think of a better place than here with her children and grandchildren.

CHAPTER 32

1960. GAS COSTS TWENTY SEVEN cents a gallon, and people are upset about it. Unemployment is 5.5 percent; a first-class stamp costs four cents. Martin Luther King follows other great leaders throughout history using non-violent means to bring change. He is loved by many, detested by many. John F. Kennedy defeats Richard M. Nixon for the presidency, changing the face of American politics.

Skateboards, mini-skirts and go-go boots are popular. The Beatles and other British pop groups catch on. Chubby Checker's song *"The Twist"* sets off a dance craze. Neil Sedaka, Jerry Lee Lewis, Paul Anka, Del Shannon and Frankie Avalon top the music charts. Motown is on the scene with Gladys Knight and the Pips, Martha and the Vandellas, the Supremes, Aretha Franklin, Smokey Robinson, James Brown, Jimi Hendrix and the Temptations. Bob Dylan, Joan Baez and Peter, Paul and Mary popularize folk music. And then there are the Beach Boys and the Righteous Brothers.

Alfred Hitchcock's *"Psycho"* scares everyone in the movie theater. Ninety percent of U.S. homes have televisions. Poverty and discrimination remain widespread. The poor live off the land or at numbing menial jobs, working grueling hours to make ends meet.

* * * * *

NORA'S HUNT FOR ANOTHER home came to an end when she found one in the middle of town near Main Street at the west end of town on Highway 160. The Sandoval's owned the L-shaped, adobe dwelling. Nora and her family moved in as soon as the home was available. Unfortunately the move was in the dead of winter, but it had to be done. She was more than anxious to get out of the place they were in.

Once again hardships set in. The new home wasn't as nice as the one she'd left, nor was it insulated. Still, she was relieved to have gotten out of the previous place. She piled blankets over the children at night, and sometimes the little ones crawled in with her and snuggled for warmth. But there also were advantages. Nora could walk downtown in ten minutes. Walker's, a grocery, was on the corner at the end of the block. Ed had credit there. Nora would make purchases which he paid for monthly. He had good standing with the Walkers. They knew he was a man of his word.

Rebecca moved into a vacant apartment next to Nora not much later. She, Ted, Billy and Carole were to stay there. She struggled with the damage left behind from her stroke, still resorting to a crutch and cane for mobility. On January 22nd Carole had her fourteenth birthday. She spent it in Oakland, California, where Pricilla lived.

In February, Teddy got a scolding from his mom for painting a storage trunk Rebecca gave her. This trunk was in the family for many years. With wounded feelings, Teddy climbed into the trunk when no one was looking and closed the lid so he could pout in peace. He fell asleep chomping on a candy necklace.

Hours later after frantically looking everywhere, his mom found him there burning up with fever. She could not get the fever down, took him to the hospital and was told he had double pneumonia.

Nora went to his side over and over at the hospital in the following days. He told her of a nun who periodically stopped by to visit him. Her name was Sister Bernadette. At one point a priest was present at the foot of Teddy's bed praying. Nuns and priests always frightened Teddy anyway, and this made it worse. Teddy's illness made Nora realize they would not spend another winter in the home they were living in. After a two-week hospital stay Teddy went home. Once more he was his energetic self, clinging to Nora wherever she went.

Rebecca helped as she could. Her slurred voice carried through the air as she stood at her doorstep scolding the children for misbehaving. As usual, she rewarded them with baked treats when they listened and obeyed.

Many times when he worked the graveyard shift, Ed took Dwayne, Teddy and Flora's son Richard to the boiler rooms, which had sawdust mounds twenty feet high used as fuel. The boys took turns helping Ed feed the boiler fires, shoveling sawdust into the furnaces. The warmth of the boiler room was welcoming when the elements outdoors were freezing. On those mounds the boys played for hours, finally falling asleep wherever they found it comfortable enough. At times it was in the sawdust itself. Sometimes Richard's sister Tonnie went along on these overnight excursions, something all the kids greatly looked forward to.

In spring, Juanita, with a growing family of her own, asked Nora's permission for Charlotte, soon to turn sixteen, to go out to San Francisco to finish school and help her with babysitting. After careful thought, Nora put Charlotte on a bus bound for California for the two-day trip, hoping that all worked out and that she, indeed, would finish her schooling out there. For both she and Carole in Oakland, California would be a totally new experience, a drastic change from Del Norte and South Fork. Carole was scheduled to come home soon.

Whatever the hardships of the new house the family was content. School kids walking by the house on their way home every day, filling the air with laughter. Many stopped at the Phillip's 66 gas station across the street for sodas or just to hangout before going home. The bus, whenever a family member took it, would drop them back off in front of the house. On occasion a squabble between teen girls could be witnessed while going by.

Nora, for the first time in thirty years, had time on her hands. Her latest born was the only one in diapers, so Nora gladly packed up most of her collection in bags and passed them on to her children for their own kids or others in need. Either way she was delighted to almost rid herself of this decades-long chore.

Nowadays it was her high-heels and dancing whenever she was able, and she took full advantage. She and friends traveled from one community to the next on their dancing excursions, never a dull moment when they were around.

Spring was in full bloom when Pricilla's thirtieth birthday came on May 8th. Children took to the outdoors the second the sun rose. While in South Fork, they loved to climb Beaver Mountain at the end of Church Lane.

Once, Cordie stayed frozen in fear near the summit at an eagle's nest. It took hours for the rest of the children to coax and lead her down safely. The children also spent time at the local dump near Church Lane where abandoned vehicles were in abundance in which to play. Some days the children weren't seen until the sun set. Ed, Nora and Flora seldom ever worried as they knew the where the children were. They trusted they were safe as they watched over one another. The children marveled at the sight of a passing deer, raccoon or other wildlife. Truly they were at peace with nature.

At times, Richard and Teddy liked to ride hogs for entertainment. Through the fields they tore through bushes and shrubs, oblivious to the danger. For them it was merely fun. They rode until either they got tired or the hogs did. If there was mischief to be found, Richard and Teddy found it.

Once they were severely disciplined after breaking into a neighbor's boarded-up house. Through the house they roamed getting into whatever they came across, including a collection of coins. When they were noticed spending the money, the adults around them become suspicious. When the neighbor came by to report the vandalism, Ed and Richard's dad Ben put two-and-two together. Ed rarely used the strap when he disciplined his children, but this was one of those times. The same went for Ben. Richard and Teddy had sore bottoms for days, not to mention bruised egos.

$$* \quad * \quad * \quad * \quad *$$

THAT SUMMER, PRICILLA AND her family returned to the valley in late July and moved into Rebecca's homestead. Pricilla was pregnant. Nora heard regularly from Juanita, whom she missed terribly, as she did all of her children who moved away. A week didn't go by without a letter or call on a neighbor's phone. Nora was happy to hear that Charlotte and Carole both were doing well in California and that they loved the beauty of the state. But they missed their mom, dad, grandma, brothers and sisters. The valley called to them. It was long before Carole was on the bus headed for home.

In the fields that year, Teddy was at work, too, handing out the string to those who sewed the potato sacks as they were filled. Flora was among the sewers at one point. Lawrence, Dale, their brothers and sisters and friends also worked the fields. Teddy was intrigued by the Native Americans who worked in the potato fields, wearing velvet gear and magnificent turquoise jewelry. Another of his favorites was a horse named Matilda, who pulled the plow to dig up the potatoes. She stopped and proceeded upon command and was a gentle soul, reliable and strong. There was laughter coming from the fields throughout the day.

All were eager when quitting time came as they wanted and needed to wash away the dust and dirt. Nora usually had a hot meal waiting for those who stayed with her when they got home. The others went to South Fork, where they stayed with Ed.

In South Fork, Teddy eagerly went to De Bois market at Chinook to proudly cash his first check of $1.60. For him it was monumental as it was the first time he'd ever earned wages. He paced the aisles of the store in debate of what to spend his earnings on.

After these hard days, and any time for that matter, music was a joy, and always was present in Nora's home. Her favorite radio program, *"Mananitas Alegres,"* aired on the radio on Sunday mornings. She listened to it for years and knew most of the songs by heart. The radio seemed to be on constantly, Nora singing along as she prepared meals for her family. In the mornings, the children were awakened by the music and her singing favorite Spanish songs. This music always brought a smile to their faces, joy and warmth to their hearts.

In October, Rebecca moved to the base of D Mountain to a log home owned by the Fuchs. It was larger than the one she moved out of and accommodated her, son Ted and Billy.

Nora was pleased to find a home for rent on the northwest side near Ed's niece and next door to Christine, a family friend. Unfortunately, on the other side of her lived another rowdy family she knew her children would have issues with. One of the daughters was another bully of the town, a large person who used her size to back her attitude, especially against the vulnerable.

Behind Ed's niece lived one of Nora's best friends, Angelica, who had moved from South Fork years before. Across the street at the corner lived another of her friends. She was grateful to find the house before the cold set in. She didn't want to go through moving in the dead of winter again.

At Halloween, Nora had company from her family when she went out dancing. Lawrence and Dale also dressed to the hilt, with hair to perfection, and stepped out, as did the older daughters.

Nora was grateful to have indoor heating again in her new home. She'd long since had her fill hauling in coal and wood. The hardships of the past were too difficult for her today. She wanted a more comfortable, convenient life and had grown accustomed to the modern conveniences.

For Ed in South Fork, life went on as usual. While Nora wanted conveniences, he was comfortable with life as it always had been for him. He knew no other way, was a hard worker, had been and would all his life.

CHAPTER 33

1961. KENNEDY IS INAUGURATED as the 35th president. He challenges Americans to step up for themselves and the world. The Cold War is in full force, the Vietnam War not far away. Gas maintains at twenty seven cents a gallon. Freedom Riders get aboard interstate buses to challenge segregationist laws in the South. Some are attacked and beaten by white supremacists. The civil rights movement forges ahead.

Disney's *"101 Dalmatians"* hits the silver screen. Westerns like *"Wagon Train"*, *"Bonanza"* and *"Gunsmoke"* along with *"The Andy Griffith Show"* and *"Alfred Hitchcock Presents"* remain fixtures on television.

Teens listen to the Shirelles' *"Will You Love Me Tomorrow."* Chubby Checker's *"Pony Time"* feeds a new dance frenzy. *"Surrender"* by Elvis Presley, *"Running Scared"* by Roy Orbison and *"I Fall to Pieces"* by Patsy Cline also top the charts. Mini-skirts and Go Go boots continue to test the patience of the straight-laced.

* * * * *

WINTER WAS NOT NEARLY as difficult for Nora and her family. It was so refreshing to be near people she cared for and who cared for her. Angelica, a kind and generous person with a heart of gold, visited Nora or Nora paid a visit to her. There was nothing Angelica wouldn't do for Nora. Her kindness went beyond, her generosity had no limits. Although neither family had much, there was little each wouldn't do for the other. Angelica's younger son was good friends with some of Nora's boys.

Nora's family ultimately adjusted living next door to the bully by simply avoiding any kind of contact with her if at all possible, although at times it was unavoidable. Her younger brother was just as bad, pushing those around him in the neighborhood or in school. The sister didn't care if you were small or young. Once you were on her hit list, it was only a matter of time before she'd get you. Many hoped for the day someone would put her in her place. Nearly everyone in town disliked her.

Nora's kids liked the shorter walk to school, but it was still a drag in the winter. Snow-covered ice patches made for slips, slides and bruises. Girls were prohibited from wearing pants or slacks, even in the cold, so they put them on under their dresses or skirts, then rolled them up or took them off when they arrived at school. It was a smart, common sense approach to an unreasonable, unrealistic regulation.

For the boys, the codes were strict in another way. With the Beatles more and more popular, longish hair was a common desire, but school restrictions forbade boys' hair to be over the collar. Some boys were sent home until they had their hair cut. There were occasions when boys were taken by school authorities to the local barber and had their hair cut to specification. It only made them rebel even more.

Those who disobeyed rules were bent over to touch their ankles and then paddled in front of the class. Many were reduced to humiliation and tears. The paddles were long, inch-thick boards with a handle and had holes for better air flow. They hurt like hell. Many parents were outraged, but helpless. The targets often were children of color as bigotry, prejudice and discrimination were common everywhere.

Nora had changed her last diaper, a newfound freedom that took some getting used to. With the children now old enough to care for each other, she had time for herself. She and Ed would discuss the children, keeping their personal issues out of the conversation. If she smelled liquor, she told him to leave.

April Fool's Day came with the children playing pranks on one another throughout the day. Pricilla gave birth to a baby girl she named, fittingly, on April 8th. Rudy turned twenty six on the 16th. Although Nora seldom saw him, he was always on her mind. He and his wife had given Nora several grandchildren, some around the same age as Nora's youngest.

Nora couldn't help but marvel at how her family had grown. It seemed every time she turned around another grandchild was there from Pricilla, Flora, Rudy, Juanita or Lucy. She loved and treasured them all, and it did her heart good to see the red hair on some of them. Rudolf would have been proud in so many ways, she thought time and time again.

Nora held a special bond with her children, each in its unique way, and was grateful that her children were happy kids. Although they'd done without much, it didn't rob them of their joy of life, of happiness they found in each other. They were not only brother and sister, but friends as well. As most children do, they'd quarrel but quickly forget and return to playing games and laughter. Some of the older children even carried scars from their past confrontations, but no matter.

Flora and Ed talked of moving into Del Norte, to share in some of the conveniences and perks that Nora enjoyed. Although Ed continued working the saw mill, life in general would hopefully be easier since he was now fifty four years old.

On May 24th Nora turned forty five and felt very much at the peak of her life. She was pretty much free to dance to her heart's content and dated whom she wanted, when she wanted, as did Ed. Though still legally married, she dated openly, needing no validation from anyone. Although it drove Ed to distraction, he knew in his heart there was nothing he could do about it. He'd had his chance with her. There was no turning back the hands of time.

One day in early May, the kids walked home to Ed's in South Fork when they suddenly heard the screeching of tires. An 18-wheeler slammed on its brakes, smoke bellowing from below. Rose, one of the kids' friends, had been struck and killed on site. She was just eleven years old. Nora and Ed's kids went into shock as they had shared the bus ride with Rose home only minutes before the accident. She was a good friend to the kids. Some shared classes in school with her. Children wept when they heard the news. South Fork residents were equally shocked that something so tragic could happen.

It was in June that Flora moved into Del Norte when she found a vacancy on the edge of the west side. The home was owned by the Atencios. The moment she finished unpacking, the conveniences of living in town were appreciated. She was much closer to shopping and only about a hundred yards from Nora, just down an alley. From the front door Nora could see Ben's green panel truck parked in front of the house. Nora was pleased that Flora now lived so near.

In South Fork, Ed immediately felt the void. He missed her and her family. Things just weren't the same without her. He realized how much he relied on her. Nora's children also missed Flora's kids when they went up to stay with Ed. Things weren't the same for them either. The familiar calls of "Red Rover, Red Rover" from the kids playing out in the yard seemed to echo into eternity. It brought sadness to Ed's heart.

Rebecca's life was challenging recovering from her stroke, but an additional stress came into her life from her son Ted, who had continued drinking. His belligerence was intolerable at times, and with Billy no longer around to control and intervene, he could be out of control – disrespectful and obnoxious. Many family members would not tolerate him when he was on his drinking binges. His dark side was just too much to take. Nora had no tolerance for Ted whatsoever. She didn't want him near her home when he was drinking, much less around her children.

Nora's children, like many others, spent the hot summer days playing in water a mile or so north of Del Norte near the city dump. The Cement Bridge served as a built-in diving board. Broken bottles were a constant hazard. Many children were taught the art of swimming there at the Cement Bridge. Mud paddling was another favorite. Some smoked driftwood out of curiosity. Many took inner tubes and floated for hours, diving in and out of the tube.

Before long the day ended. Regretfully they headed home, eager to return the following day. They were usually exhausted and ready for a hot meal. But the games didn't end there. Once they got home and filled their bellies, there were more games to be played. There was never enough laughter in their lives and days. Sleepovers were very common within the children. If Nora's children weren't sleeping over with Flora's, they were sleeping over with cousins or other friends.

Ed finally made the move into Del Norte, renting the home next to Flora. In no time he had a house and yard full of children. Once more, laughter and childhood games filled the space around him. It was a place of joy on July 4th, kids playing with sparklers and watching fireworks light up the night sky.

Juanita, twenty eight, and Flora thirty, soon welcomed new additions to their families as more children were born. Juanita's absence was felt by Nora each month that went by. She missed having her near. California seemed like such a very long distance between them, and she still had no telephone or TV for that matter.

By August 22nd Teddy's tenth birthday, summer was in its glory. Days were long, sometimes hot, but to be enjoyed to the fullest. Life was good for Nora, Ed and Flora. Time had healed the tragedies of the two mothers' lost children, but the void would never be filled. Nora and Flora shared this common tragedy. Each knew the pain and loss, and though it was seldom spoken of, both inevitably knew.

Nora's concerns living next door to the town bully were confirmed when Cordie was walking home one day and was assaulted. Word spread fast. Teddy and Richard ran to the We Ask You Inn Restaurant to tell Nora's older daughter, who was a waitress there.

Shortly after, Nora and the bully's mom got into a shouting match in the back yard. They spoke in Spanish, so the children around didn't understand. But it was obvious that Nora was fuming. She pointed her finger in warning. The police were called and a complaint filed. Cordie was a mere fourteen and the bully in her twenties. The bully was notorious for assaulting kids far younger and smaller than she.

Days later, Teddy stood at the window peering between the drapes as the bully along with her sister were in verbal conflict with a few local girls who were friends to some of Nora's daughters. One of these friends had a vivid reputation for even taking down men in confrontation. It was rumored she'd taken down as many as three men at the same time. And it was she who beckoned the bully out onto the street. Wearing a white shirt with the sleeves rolled up, her hair styled in a popular duck tail and penny loafers and jeans with white socks. She was an intimidating sight even for the bully.

Nora quickly pulled Teddy from the window and closed the drapes. But to everyone's surprise, the bully never did come out onto the street. She just stood there shouting out obscenities and idle threats. She turned out to be the typical bully who could dish it out but was afraid to take it.

Nora didn't want to take any chances and vowed, yet again, that she would have to move to avoid further conflict. After searching for days in September but finding nothing, she was resigned to the fact that she'd probably have to spend the winter there. She cautioned her children to stay clear of the bully and her family. She was grateful harvest season was here. It would keep the children busy and out of harm's way.

Every passing day made Ed pleased with his decision to move closer to his family. In fact, so many people moved from South Fork that it just wasn't the same. Church Lane was almost deserted, only ghosts of the past left behind. The small chapel stood alone at the base of the mountain, seeming to whisper out its loneliness. What few families remained also explored the possibility of moving in due time.

If he wasn't with his kids, Ed had the pool hall in Del Norte to sit and play cards with other locals, engaging in idle conversation. Two of his sisters lived in Del Norte. With his kids' and Nora's houses so close, the children ventured from one household to the other throughout the day and night.

Ed might be in sight now, but he was out of mind for Nora. She was accustomed to being on her own and no longer entertained even the slightest possibility of being with him again. Even when he was sober she barely tolerated him. If Ed was drinking, he knew not to go anywhere near Nora.

The first snowfall arrived in October, but Halloween night was warm enough that the children didn't need coats to cover their costumes. The streets were abuzz with children going from home to home in their quest. Nora's children were among them. In certain parts of town, outhouses were overturned in tradition for the occasion; the owners frustrated come morning to find they'd been targeted for tricks for not handing out treats. Windows also were soaped and yards toilet papered for those who refused to participate. It was a yearly thing. Still, there were those who resisted regardless of the consequences.

Dances and costume parties went on throughout the valley. Nora and her friends attended those of their choosing, dancing the night away dressed in their best. Nora was grateful to wear her favorite high heels without the restriction of pregnancy. She was free in so many ways now. Her laughter on the dance floor came from the heart and soul.

Nora was amazed of the time and obligation the daily diaper routine had consumed as she looked back. She enjoyed this freedom, using it for more pleasurable things that she had sacrificed. She was free to visit friends and family more, free to spend more time on her shopping sprees in town visiting with local merchants she befriended. Her friends could be found visiting up to three times a week, always with a helping hand, or with something in hand when they came to her door. It was the way of the land. She always returned the favors.

In school, Slam Books, spiral notebooks with a student's name on each page, were all the rage. They were prohibited but could not be stopped. A Slam Book was passed from one student to another and words written of praise or ridicule, usually circulating the entire student body by the time it came back to the original owner.

Those ridiculed retaliated, resulting in fights on school grounds or on the streets and alleys off grounds. Girls were constantly in physical battle over what was written about them in the Slam Books by another.

Rebecca attended the Christmas dinner, along with many of Nora's children and family who lived nearby. Nora's brother Ernest and his wife Vera were among them. Ernest was a quiet, soft-spoken man. His relationship with Nora was very close. Nora was especially protective of him due to his sensitivity. In spite of his drinking problem, Ernest was gentle and compassionate. On the other hand, Vera was a character on her own. Both knew when they came to Nora's home drinking was strictly prohibited. They also knew not to arrive with alcohol on their breaths. Ernest had a severe stuttering problem. It frustrated him.

Simply Nora

On the west side of town where Nora lived, as did Flora, Ben and Ed, they and friends ventured from home to home for the traditional playing guitars and violins singing carols in Spanish. After caroling, Nora gathered with her friends to celebrate the holiday. Others ended up at Flora's, which Nora avoided because there had been times these celebrations ended up in conflict with alcohol involved, fiascoes only to be forgotten the following day. Nora wanted no part of these. She wanted to celebrate in peace. Freedoms she now could enjoy.

CHAPTER 34

1962. KENNEDY IS BELOVED by millions as he promises them the moon and stands up to the Russians in the Cuban missile crisis. But unemployment is back up to 6.7 percent, and gas is twenty eight cents. On August 5th Marilyn Monroe dies. Hollywood loses a legend, one of its greatest sex symbols of all time, and her passing is mourned by millions.

Chubby Checker's *"The Twist"* is banned in some religious arenas as the famous dance is deemed immoral. Not so with the nation's youth, who also flock to Little Eva's *"The Loco-Motion."* Gene Chandler, Bob Dylan, Roy Orbison, Neil Sedaka, Brenda Lee and the Beach Boys make hit after hit. From across the ocean comes the Beatles' first American hit *"Love Me Do,"* climbing the charts quickly. Music is an escape for youth; dance a release for their frustrations. People's hopes have been renewed with this youthful, vigorous president in the White House. It is a time of music and dance, laughter and joy for most.

"To Kill a Mockingbird" draws droves into theaters. The civil rights movement is in full force as people demand equality, tired of being treated as second class citizens. The music of the day also reflects the restlessness. Still, there are many millions with frozen hearts who cling to their sense of superiority.

$$* \quad * \quad * \quad * \quad *$$

As THE NEW YEAR dawned, the new, popular tunes constantly blared from the record player in Lawrence's space. Children awoke every morning to the lyrics of some of their favorite songs. Although it was winter outside, cold and harsh, inside it was warm and cozy both in body and spirit. And every Sunday morning, there was Nora listening to her favorite Spanish music program. She listened to all her favorite hits like *"Sentimento," "Tres Balas," "Frijolitos Pintos"* and *"Un Ratito."* Her singing along while preparing breakfast was sheer bliss for the children, who often lay in bed listening. They felt the love and compassion Nora had for her family in the notes she sang or hummed. The children wrestled and giggled in bed awhile before rising to meet the day. The smell of fresh tortillas and frying potatoes along with other familiar aromas ultimately pulled them to the kitchen. Luckily they were still on Christmas break from school.

The pressure of living next door to the bullies took its toll on Nora. She wanted to move. Her friends helped in the search. Still, there were no prospects. The one positive was that Nora did not feel much like moving in the dead of winter. She hoped for a change in spring or summer if she could hold out that long without drama or consequence erupting. With the tension between the families, anything was possible at any given moment.

Nora cautioned her children to stay clear of the bullies, avoiding them at all cost. But one of Nora's daughters was not about to be bullied about. For her to do battle would be icing on the cake, although she would not be the one to provoke it. She'd stand her ground at all costs, regardless of the outcome.

In February, Nora heard of a place to rent. On the north end of town across the tracks near the river, a good friend of hers owned several one-room dwellings. Her friend *Doña* Juana told her one would be available soon. Although it wasn't what Nora wanted by a long shot, it was something that would do temporarily.

Nora made arrangements with Ed that should she move there, most of the children would stay with him until she found permanent housing. Nora knew the families that lived in the region where *Doña* Juana's dwellings were and was friends with most of them. It was a ways from downtown but under the circumstances might have to do. It was food for thought.

Meantime, Nora began the grueling task of sorting and packing in preparation of moving. What she didn't need she was to be donated to her friend's thrift shop. If she lived in one of *Doña* Juana's places, nearly all her belongings would have to go into storage until she found a more suitable home. The space, a one-room dwelling with a small kitchenette, was just enough for one or two adults, and maybe three children. It would be a very tight squeeze. Nora yearned for the day she could live at peace. Although she had what she considered a lifetime enemy, her philosophy was kindness and compassion. This philosophy had been tested time and time again. Still, she chose to live by the standards Rudolf embedded into her. She had a joyful heart, and no one was to take that from her. That was her gift and hers alone. She cherished that above all. If there was anything she could pass on to her children this would be it. She knew the power behind it – the strength.

Through February, Nora sorted and packed for the inevitable. Having only one child at home now to care for during the day, she had plenty of time to do what had to be done. It wouldn't be long before the youngest of her children would also be in school. That would free her up for even more. It was surreal to her to gaze out her kitchen window to the clotheslines and not see row upon row of diapers waving in the breeze. Instead she saw pants, blouses, socks, underwear and dresses. Where had all the years and decades had gone? It seemed like only yesterday she exchanged vows with Ed. So much had happened to bring her to where she was today. Many times she reflected like this on her life, the path she walked.

In March, the remarkable youngest daughter turned five and was ready for kindergarten the following fall. *Doña* Juana informed Nora that one of her dwellings would be available in early May. That would give Nora plenty of time to prepare for moving into there or into something else if she found it. Either way it was time to go. Nora knew if she didn't do something quickly the battle with the bully would happen. She wasn't about to take that chance. If it meant inconvenience for her temporarily, then so be it. It was better than having one of her children possibly hurt in conflict. Flora's husband and the bully's oldest son had already done battle, a brawl that resulted in blood and black eyes.

Moving would also mean another change for the children. Because Ed and Flora lived a mere hundred yards from Nora, the children spent a lot of time there. Once school was out their yards were always filled with children playing games. They also liked playing baseball in an open field behind Nora's home next door to her dear friend Angelica. Moving away from Angelica would be yet another sadness.

In May, relatives came to Nora's doorstep with the tragic news that her brother Ernest had passed away. Nora lost her breath. Instantly she broke into uncontrollable tears, escorting her children out of the room so the adults could have privacy. The hearts of the children who witnessed Nora in tears were broken. Some went into tears themselves. To see their mother hurt was a very difficult experience for them. They had never seen Nora in tears before. To the children Nora was a pillar of strength and endurance. From the other room, all the children could do was listen as the other adults wept along with their mom.

Services were held, and Ernest was buried in Del Norte Cemetery. Nora could not adjust to his being gone. She would miss him forever. Having to move was what kept her mind occupied, packing and sorting always a daunting task. *Doña* Juana's dwelling would be her home for now, along with her two youngest daughters. The rest were to stay with Ed until she found suitable housing for all. *Doña* Juana had a liquor problem Nora was not comfortable with, but she respected the kind soul and heart she had.

Nora celebrated her forty sixth birthday on May 24th before making the move, and right about this time Benny turned seven. Her new home was one of five one-room spaces backed against the river on the north side of town across the tracks. On one side of the dwellings lived two Martinez families, and on the other side lived the Sanchez and Romero families. Nora was well-acquainted with them all. She had befriended them long before the move. One of the Martinez boys was a close friend of Lawrence's and Dale's. The Romero girls were close friends with some of Nora's daughters. Although the dwelling was room enough for just Nora and her two youngest girls, many of Nora's children visited, sometimes spending the night. Nora always managed to find space for those who wanted to sleep over. For the children it was all fun and games. Never would she turn them away. If she could, she would have had them all there.

At one point, a drunken neighbor threw rocks at the children as they played in the front yard. After going inside and telling their mom, Nora grabbed a stick, closed the door behind her and went outside. What she did was never known, but the fury in her eyes told the tale. She would never tolerate anyone abusing any of her children, much less a drunk. The gravest boundary she had was her children. She would go to any extreme for them if need be.

Nights were challenging for Nora living there. *Doña* Juana had her daily and nightly guests over for drinks. They could be heard into the wee hours of the mornings. Sometimes uncontrollable outbursts broke out when too much booze circulated. Nora kept her door locked with a baseball bat next to her bed. She would never leave her children alone. Where she went, they went. If she went to visit neighbors, the children were with her. When alcohol was concerned, Nora had very little trust. She'd learned well through the years.

Charlotte was surprised when she returned from California in summer to find Nora at *Doña* Juana's and Ed in Del Norte. So much had happened since she left. Her siblings were growing up. Those who were babies were out of diapers, walking and running about. In so many ways she was happy to be home. She missed her dad and mom and twin sister immensely.

Everyone in the family was relieved to hear that Nora was looking for a permanent home. Constantly she was on the hunt. She for sure didn't want to spend a winter where she was. She'd never survive, not to mention the two young children, certain it would be like an icebox. Although a challenge, Nora made do with the living conditions she had and knew in her heart something would come along soon. With each visit into town she scanned the area for a vacancy. Her friends were on the lookout as well. Nights were warm for them where she lived, but she would not leave her door open for fear of who might lurk in the darkness. The nightly noise coming from *Doña* Juana's dwelling made her worry.

With luck on her side, Nora found a home to rent near *Doña* Juana's on the opposite side of the tracks. It was in front of Pete Whittaker's junkyard and owned by him. The home was rose colored with a crabapple tree in the front yard. In the back yard next to a six-foot wooden fence separating the homes was a row of lilac bushes, perfect for Nora.

Mr. Whittaker was a kind man known to the local children as the "Candy Man" as he would toss candy out of his car window to groups of them as he passed in his vintage 1951 green Chevrolet. All the children were familiar with his generosity and congregated at the sight of his car coming down the street. Nora had a good feeling about this home, sensing she'd be there awhile. It had plenty of room with the large front and back yard for the children. Across the street lived a good friend of hers, whose daughter was good friends with Nora's girls. Nora's heart was content.

Within a week she and her family settled in. The long dusty road into town meant a good twenty minute walk, going to school a half hour. Still, the children made the trip frequently to play with Flora's kids. They were inseparable and on the go constantly, spending hours upon hours swimming at the Cement Bridge. Thus far, the move proved to be a very good decision. There were no problems with neighbors. In fact, the children made friends with the children nearby. The two bedrooms were put to full use. One was for Nora and the youngest ones along with some of the girls, and the second for the boys. Lawrence got the back porch. A one-room cabin in the back yard was used primarily for storage.

A convenience store was near. Jessup's had been in business for decades, had served the neighborhood well. What wasn't there she found at Skaff's across the street from the hospital on Main Street. She went to them weekly. Generally she would take some of the children with her to help with packages.

In August, Juanita turned twenty nine in California, Flora thirty one and Teddy eleven.

Fall brought out a favorite pastime for the kids with cars. After dinner, they drag raced on the road going by the Del Norte Cemetery. It was perfect for racing. Local police made frequent trips up there, but that that didn't discourage the teens. Indeed, it was all the more challenging and exciting. The thrill of it was not getting caught. Blueberry Hill, another teen hangout mid-way up D Mountain, was very popular at night for young lovers who parked for the privacy of their romance. Amid the music, steamy windows told the tale of what was happening.

Nora had indoor heating in her new home so no more lugging in coal and wood. Enough was enough. She'd long since grown tired of cold indoor nights. The difficult times she'd endured all her life she now wanted to leave behind her. She couldn't imagine struggling with the issues she dealt with in her younger years at her age today. Although many folks, including her friends, still did, she was grateful not to have to. Life was a struggle as it was without adding other burdens to it.

Weeks away from his twentieth birthday, Billy returned from California in a beautiful 1958 Ford Fairlane convertible. It was blue and white with a red and white interior and a white top. The second he drove into Ed's yard, the children surrounded the car in excitement. Never had they seen such a magnificent machine. It was in showroom condition. Billy was very proud of it. They all wanted a ride before he even had time to be welcomed.

After visiting a short while he took the girls out for a ride about town with the top down, laughter spilling out as they drove away. Disappointed, the younger children were left behind awaiting their turn for the ride he promised.

Within a couple of hours Billy piled up the small fry. For them it was the ultimate. They waved at friends along the way as they drove down Main Street. As the sun set, their ride came to an end as Billy pulled up to Ed's home dropping off those who were staying with him, then off to Nora's to drop off the rest – their adrenaline still at a high. Rock 'n' roll music pounded from the car radio as Billy drove away.

During the year, Rebecca suffered a series of minor strokes adding to her disabilities. It was getting more and more difficult to maneuver and do for herself although she did what she could. Carole, Billy and Ted did what had to be done. With Ted's severe alcohol problem she could never anticipate his actions or his dependability.

Despite her mom's diminishing condition, there was much to be grateful for during the Christmas season. Nora didn't lose sight of this. In her heart she gave thanks to the universe for her children, her life and all she'd been given. The difficult times she'd been through had become distant memories. Most of her days were filled with such joy from her children and ever-increasing grandchildren base that it brought tears to her eyes.

Simply Nora

On Christmas night, Nora's two youngest girls lay beside her in deep sleep. She stroked their hair as she thought, finally drifting off to sleep herself. There was peace and calm in Nora's home. Throughout town, Christmas lights twinkled through the darkness—a reminder of gratitude and happiness.

CHAPTER 35

1963. A FIRST-CLASS STAMP goes to a whole nickel, and gasoline is still a relative bargain at twenty nine cents a gallon. The sensual Elizabeth Taylor in *"Cleopatra"* is on the silver screen.

The Beatles release *"Please Please Me"* and *"Ask Me Why."* *"Louie Louie"* by the Kingsmen, *"Up On the Roof"* by the Drifters, *"It's My Party"* by Leslie Gore, *"The End Of The World"* by Skeeter Davis and *"Walk Like A Man"* by the Four Seasons all grace the Top Ten List. The Ronettes, Crystals, Chiffons, Angels and Martha Reeves and the Vandellas have teens on their feet everywhere. When Sonny and Cher make the scene, girls imitate by growing their hair as long as they could get it.

But events unfold in 1963 that make anything else that year pale in comparison. On August 28th Martin Luther King makes his "I Have a Dream" speech attended by hundreds of thousands and watched on TV by millions. King and the civil rights movement make their mark on history.

* * * * *

THE NEW YEAR BROUGHT excitement of another marriage – and with it the prospect of more grandchildren. Carole, newly turned seventeen, was engaged to be married June 1st. Plans were already in motion, and both families were very happy. Del Norte was abuzz. News traveled fast, even when one didn't want it to. But there were hardships. It was difficult for the kids to make the longer walk to and from school in the harsh winter. Occasionally, Billy gave them rides.

Nora had to make frequent visits to help her mom. The once independent, domineering, stern and strict woman was resentful for having to rely on others as her condition worsened. Although helping was done out of love, for her it was a humiliation. Her heart broke. She resented using a cane and crutch to maneuver around. Her independence was slowly being ripped from her. Nora treated her with patience and compassion. Both sensed the inevitable.

Ernest's death also took a toll. Nora missed him dearly, longed for his regular visits. She had a soft spot in her heart for him, always had. His trials and tribulations seemed monumental to her at times. She often wondered how he could endure them. Through the years she learned that abuse of any sort was not limited to women and knew several abused husbands in her time. Abuse as she came to know it had many faces. Each had a fury of its own.

Every time she left Rebecca's home she could only wonder what tomorrow would bring. She saw the sadness in Rebecca's eyes, felt the sorrow flowing in her heart. She was no longer the strong mother she once was. It saddened her to witness it. Mentally and emotionally she began to prepare herself. Fate was in motion.

Nora thought of bringing Rebecca to live with her, but others felt her living conditions weren't suitable, plus there were far too many children for Rebecca to contend with. For Nora, she would do whatever had to be done for her mother. She would care for her no matter what. She made that clear.

There was talk among some of Nora's siblings of placing Rebecca in a nursing home should her condition decline further. This brought Nora's blood to a boil. She was dead set against it and made her opinion known loud and clear. It appalled her that any of her siblings even suggested it. She couldn't understand it. For her that wasn't an option, not when there were far better alternatives. She stood her ground.

Nora continued visiting Rebecca's home tending to her needs three or four times a week, much like Rebecca had tended to hers in her early years as a mother. She would not forget that. The reality of Rebecca's condition brought back familiar pain of when she lost Rudolf.

In early February, Rebecca had another major stroke that left her paralyzed. Later in the month, her son Charlie decided to take her back to Denver to live with him. Although it was not what Rebecca wanted, she had no say in the matter. It broke the hearts of those who knew her wishes.

Nora not only missed Rebecca in the following weeks, but also worried for her. From what she heard, Rebecca was not happy with her living situation. She spent much of her time alone in her wheelchair. Although Charlie had a beautiful home and provided well for her, the loneliness was unbearable. Rebecca yearned for life around her. She also felt isolated from many of those whom she loved. She missed Del Norte and the rest of her family. She missed the joyful sounds of running children.

Charlie found it difficult to handle Rebecca with her feeling like this. Constantly she nagged him to bring her back. She became furious when they cut off her long hair, and this proved to be the straw that broke the camel's back. He relented and brought Rebecca back to live with Pricilla at the homestead in South Fork. There, too, Rebecca didn't want to be. Her heart was set on being with Nora and her family in Del Norte. She would settle for nothing else and complained constantly.

Nora's brother Ted was seldom around, and when he was it was only to cause havoc. His drinking was totally out of control. Along with the drinking came disrespect. Pricilla tolerated it until she could take no more. She put her foot down and ordered him to stay away. It wasn't long before Rebecca's unhappiness and demands to be in Del Norte with Nora got the best of Pricilla as well. She had no other choice but to take her where she wanted to go.

Thus, Nora had no other choice but to be there. Rebecca moved in with her and the family. It did her heart good to care for her mother, repay all of what Rebecca had done for her throughout her life. The indifference between them would not keep Nora from helping her. In those quiet moments with Rudolf she'd promised him she'd care for Rebecca should it ever come to that.

By mid-March it was obvious to all that Rebecca's condition was very much on the decline and she required more and more attention. Although Nora did what she could, even she seemed to have come to the realization of the reality she faced. She cooked, baked and cleaned for Rebecca and her own family. The more talk she heard of nursing homes among her siblings, the more frustrated she became. She couldn't imagine a woman like Rebecca being in a nursing home. Should that ever happen Nora knew it would destroy Rebecca and all hope that she had for even the slightest quality of life. Nora sensed the sadness in her mother in those quiet moments they shared together, reassured her that she'd be taken care of should the worst happen. Words of hope were what Rebecca needed, not pity or isolation from those she loved. Fortunately, Rebecca's friends never forgot her. They stopped by to visit and to bring her things.

The twins turned eighteen on April 30th.

This year there would be no garden for Nora, who didn't have the time or energy. She did housework in exchange for garden vegetables. She also continued to do laundry for certain folks as she'd done for years. The odd jobs came in handy, putting extra funds into her purse. At times she even worked in the kitchen of one of the town's restaurants helping out a good friend of hers when needed. Through years of experience Nora learned the art of stretching a dollar to its max. She always had a nest egg. Dwayne entered his teen years on May 8th. Sixteen days later, Nora turned forty seven.

Nora kept busy as Carole's wedding day neared. Getting the children new clothes for the day was one thing at the top of her list. Between doing odd jobs, tending to Rebecca's needs and preparing for Carole's special day, when she finally laid her head to rest at night it was from exhaustion. Her heart was content in spite of Rebecca's decline.

Toward the end of May, Rebecca declined even more. She required constant help from those around her. Nora feared for the worst, hoped she was prepared for whatever the universe had in store. Despite Rebecca's decline she insisted on trying to do what she could for herself. She was not ready to let that go yet. She doubted she ever would or could. At times she sat in the wheelchair and gazed out of the window in heavy thought. It broke her heart to see the reflection in the window of a woman she hardly recognized. Bible in hand, she spent hours in prayer.

The lilac bushes bloomed in Nora's new back yard. She set out arrangements, their fragrance filling the home. On the back porch, Lawrence's geraniums bloomed in different shades. Plants were his passion. This reflected in his care for them. He nurtured them with gentle care. He grew sweet potato vines in a jar, where he placed the seeds secured with toothpicks. The vines climbed walls and onto the ceiling. Because the porch was enclosed and insulated, the space was usable year round.

June 1st was a day of celebration for all. Charlotte and Becky were bridesmaids and Billy a groomsman. He escorted Carole's fiancé's sister. The bridesmaids wore pink. The Catholic Church was packed, as was the

Parish Hall cafeteria when the ceremony was done. Rows of tables and chairs were set up across the room, each table decorated accordingly. People went far and beyond to make Carole's day special for her and husband Tony.

Billy's car was decorated for the event, along with several others. In his car were Charlotte and Becky along with Tony's sister. Billy had the top down. In Rudy's car, a turquoise and white 1955 Ford Crown Victoria, were he and Lena in the front and Tony and Carole in the back. Following tradition, they drove about town blowing car horns. It'd been that way for decades. The row of cars cloaked in various flowers and ribbons got the attention of everyone on the street as they drove by.

Rebecca was unable to attend, another major stroke having left her near helpless. She was confined to her wheelchair permanently. She was left in Lawrence's care. Billy's first stop after the wedding was to see her, then it was off to continue their rounds about town, then to Monte Vista and Alamosa, finally back to the Parish Hall to resume the celebration.

Before dinner, Nora and Ed, as tradition was, gave away the bride. Folks wept as the Challengers played the traditional wedding march. It was a beautiful sight for all. The dinner hall was packed with hungry folks to feed. Plenty were on hand to hand out the food and see to everyone's needs. Children, dressed in their finest, ran up and down hallways and aisles before settling down to eat.

Following the dinner, people went home to change and prepare for the wedding dance in the evening. Nora dressed in her best for the dance, wearing a new pair of high heels and chiffon dress she purchased for the event. Nora's children old enough to attend the dance also dressed in newly purchased finery.

The beat of music coming from the Challengers was heard a block away from the Parish Hall. Parked cars surrounded the building and filled nearby streets. Small crowds stood at their cars in conversation before going in – some smoking cigarettes and passing liquor bottles about. They were getting psyched. The entrance stairwell had a line of people waiting to get in. One by one they entered the dance hall. In the hall a traditional wedding dance commenced. The wedding march was a big part of the tradition. Mostly everyone in the hall participated in the march. The fun went on and on.

With Carole gone to live with her husband and Billy returned to California the day after the wedding, life returned to normal. July Fourth festivities were the usual hit. Cordie turned sixteen four days later.

Nora's home was modest at best, but she made comfortable accommodations for her mom. The bed was in the main hallway leading from the living room into the kitchen. Rebecca had her own space, plus was in position for easy view and access. To the left of the hallway was a large bedroom in which Nora and some of the girls slept. To the right was the other bedroom in which the boys slept. Folding beds were put to use as needed.

Rebecca appreciated her surroundings. She wanted to be around life and laughter. Here she had both. Being around family helped her forget her disabilities at times.

Summer was hot and uncomfortable for all. Nora had fans going, especially in Rebecca's space or where she was seated. Rebecca drank iced tea and water through a straw throughout the day. That seemed to help combat the heat. Having all doors and windows open also helped with the breeze sweeping through the house. Once the sun settled in the west, Rebecca sat in her wheelchair in the shade of the front porch where she had a street view. She was comfortable there. She enjoyed being out there distracted by life's activities. Occasionally those who knew her would stop and visit with her.

By August, both Rebecca and Nora's family had settled into their roles. All took part in Rebecca's care whether it'd be feeding, bathing, changing or clothing her. The girls or Nora combed and brushed her hair into place after shampooing and curling it. From humiliation, Rebecca fought her bathings, but found comfort in having a clean body and clean sheets and clothing once they were done. At times she even laughed at some of the things going on around her. The smaller children learned to keep their distance as Rebecca took her frustration out on them.

A new favorite hangout that summer was known as "Dracula's Playhouse," a large, abandoned, stone structure the kids discovered near the river on the east side of Highway 112 near the main bridge leading into town. They called it that because of the spookiness once the sunlight faded. They spent plenty of time there climbing the rafters or anything else they might get into or onto.

After sunset they wandered back to Ed's. It was never a worry for Nora as she knew they always were safe and cared for. Neighbors looked out for one another, a way of life in Del Norte as it was in South Fork. Empty stomachs ultimately drove them home in the end. Instinctively, they knew when the dinner table would be set and a hot meal waiting. The second they stepped into Nora's home the smell of fresh tortillas, beans, frying potatoes and chili or other aromas swept into their faces. They eagerly sat at the dinner table.

Rebecca's wheelchair set next to the dinner table, where her needs were seen to. A tray of food was placed at her convenience since she was able to feed herself from time to time. Most occasions she had to be fed. At times the joy of being where she was became evident in her eyes and mood. There were moments of happiness for her now that she was back in Del Norte. Through her sadness these moments would shine occasionally. At this point in her life there was nowhere she'd rather be other than being the person she once was. On August 22nd Teddy, hyper and high strung, with a head of thick, dark, unruly, curly hair, turned twelve.

On the summer evenings when it cooled, Nora sat out on the front porch with Rebecca, who would try her best to converse. Her appreciation of Nora was immeasurable. In spite of her condition, she recognized the responsibilities Nora had besides taking care of her. In her own way she marveled at Nora's strength and endurance, traits Nora inherited from her. Compassion came from Rudolf. Nora was certain she saw remorse in her mom's eyes from time to time, as though Rebecca remembered Rudolf's words from those years so very long ago.

When harvest began and the older children went to work, Nora was left at home to care for Rebecca and the younger children. She struggled with getting Rebecca in and out of bed into her wheelchair. Although Rebecca seemed to enjoy the silence in the house with several of the children gone, at times it was obvious she missed the commotion and even the chaos they brought into the home. There were always laughter and music when they were around. Things Rebecca had grown accustomed to. They were a diversion from her disabilities – a song to her heart.

She loved being on the front porch on cool evenings observing neighborhood activities. She was seldom left alone out on the porch, and the times she was, there were always children playing in the front yard. The childhood games sometimes brought a smile to her face, other times irritated her. What she took as taunting was them actually playing with her. Some made faces, and in retaliation she grabbed when they passed her wheelchair, sometimes taking a handful of hair or a pinch to whatever part of the body she was able to reach.

Many evenings Nora sat out there with her. She spoke to Rebecca as though the past they shared had been forgotten – never existed. She never brought it up to Rebecca. She wanted only peace for her mother.

With the constant needs, caring for Rebecca was almost like caring for another child. At times she leaned over into her lap, so a cloth had to be secured around her waist and tied to the back of the wheelchair. One time she tumbled onto the floor, the wheelchair on its side.

Another time she rolled the wheelchair off the porch steps, crashing it over on its side still secured with the cloth. Nora set blocks of wood against the wheels preventing Rebecca from possibly hurting herself again.

That fall, Flora and her family moved to Denver, breaking the hearts of both her children and Nora's as they would miss each other immensely. With heavy hearts, they gathered about as the truck was loaded, knowing life would never be the same. All they could do was hope that Flora and Ben would change their minds. They didn't. Nora's children were left in Del Norte, sad but with wonderful memories of laughter, fun and joy.

Nora's diversion was the same as always – nights out dancing with friends as an escape, the dancing a release of all her frustrations. Her favorite perfume, Midnight in Paris, lingered in the house long after she walked out the door for an evening of fun and laughter. On those nights she met new people, made new friends. After a night of fun and dancing, she felt renewed, once again prepared to take on the challenges in her life. As usual, those challenges awaited her the second she stepped through the door back home.

On November 22nd came the shocking news from Dallas. Schools let out early and until further notice. Del Norte, South Fork, the nation, the world were stunned that at 12:30 Central Standard Time, President Kennedy had been assassinated. Speculation and suspicions erupted immediately. Vice President Lyndon Baines Johnson was sworn in as president. Lee Harvey Oswald was arrested, and then shot and killed two days later by Dallas nightclub operator Jack Ruby as he was being led through the basement of Dallas Police Headquarters in transfer to the county jail. People in Del Norte with TVs couldn't believe their eyes as they witnessed the shooting on television as it happened.

For the kids, unable to grasp the enormity of the situation, having those days off school just meant more time for fun and games. For those who were fully aware of the circumstance it was devastating. Minorities there and across the nation grieved as they had lost a friend, a strong voice in the civil rights movement.

Although Nora was stunned as anyone by Kennedy's assassination, obligations and responsibilities kept her mind pre-occupied and distracted from the aftermath of the tragedy. She noticed a change in people when she went downtown on shopping trips, especially in the minorities. Kennedy's death was the topic for everyone she encountered both on the street and in the stores. She, too, admired Kennedy, and could only sigh in response to those who expressed their grief and frustration.

Lawrence's twenty seventh birthday on the 27th was overshadowed by JFK's death. Billy spent his twenty first in California on the 28th, where the impact of the assassination was felt even more.

Thanksgiving wasn't the same in Del Norte, or elsewhere. Although Nora cooked for her family, the atmosphere was different, somber. A sadness fell over the land. The children's laughter made up for it during dinner. Rebecca feasted on the meal as did the entire family – some taking second and third servings. They were not shy about it. Growing children meant big appetites. Nora had learned this long ago, always made more than anticipated.

With winter clouds hanging over the valley, much had to be done in preparation for the cold season and Nora and Ed began their Christmas shopping. The kids still divided their time between both households. Either way, they always had a roof over their heads and a hot meal. They were free to stay wherever they chose.

Holiday decorations went up downtown, store fronts put on displays and sales displayed in the windows in the growing commercialization of Christmas. The back of trucks and station wagons carried newly cut Christmas trees. The stars across Main Street on the east side and on D Mountain were lit, both symbolic of the season in Del Norte and visible everywhere at night.

The normal festivities resumed that Christmas, the kids played outside in the snow, carolers caroled, gifts unwrapped, families joined for dinner and joy. But for the American family, life would never be the same.

CHAPTER 36

1964. GAS GOES FOR thirty cents, a loaf of bread twenty one cents, movie tickets half a buck, and candy bars a nickel. The U.S. gets more embroiled in Vietnam. Johnson is elected president in November.

Bob Dylan's song *"The Times They Are a-Changing"* reflects a new reality across America as minorities, women and youth challenge prejudice, bigotry and old, outdated ideas. Race riots erupt in New York, Chicago and Philadelphia. Music of the Grateful Dead and Jefferson Airplane celebrate the counterculture of a new generation. The Beatles have thirteen singles including *"I Want to Hold Your Hand"* and *"All My Loving"* on Billboard's Hot 100. Their appearance on the *"Ed Sullivan Show"* drives teenage girls into hysteria. Ford Motor introduces the Mustang. Medicare is enacted.

* * * * *

THERE WERE TIMES WHEN Nora felt she just couldn't care for Rebecca much longer, but love and obligation pushed her on. Lifting Rebecca from the bed and placing her into the wheelchair was a daily challenge. She knew the consequences of leaving Rebecca in bed for long periods. She didn't want her going through that. She'd heard horror stories of these situations in her time. Rebecca's care was 24/7. Nora had to rise in the wee hours to change Rebecca and her bedding. It was all part of the responsibility. She did it with no remorse.

Nora did her best to keep both Rebecca and her family warm and comfortable. Nora had issues sending her children to school each morning in the arctic elements knowing what they were going through during their long walk. While many had the luxury of riding the bus or having a ride to school, Nora's children didn't. The second they stepped out the door the cold blast hit them in the face burning through their clothing. There was no escaping it. The cold burned through the fingertips of their gloves with no pity while they carried their school books. Still, they did what had to be done in spite of it all.

Rebecca loathed her wheelchair. On numerous occasions she struggled to free herself. It was not only a frustration for her, but also for Nora and those who watched over her. Nora understood Rebecca's frustration, remembering the person she once was and couldn't help but think of what it must be like for Rebecca under the circumstances. Her heart went out to her. She did her best to let her know she was loved and cared for her in the best way she could.

Occasionally, Rebecca's speech cleared. Unfortunately at those times, Rebecca cursed both in English and Spanish. She cursed the children as they went past her wheelchair or the girls when they came home from school or being out, using vile language so unlike the grandmother they once knew. Some viewed it as a sign that she was getting better. But to others, the woman who once used the Bible as a guide for which to live was slowly vanishing before everyone's eyes, replaced by an angry, frustrated shrew.

There was nothing Nora or anyone could do about it. It was all part of Rebecca's condition, her illness. There were times she even struck out at Nora when she tried to feed or change her. Her frustration spared no one.

Carole and her husband moved to a small community called Sergeant, northeast of Del Norte. Carole was expecting her first child. On occasion they stopped by to see Nora, Rebecca and the family.

Most of Nora's siblings had left the valley or state by now, moving to Denver, New Mexico or Texas. On rare occasion she got a note in the mail from one of them inquiring about Rebecca's welfare. Having a phone was a luxury Nora just couldn't afford. She made no apologies for it to anyone. She knew her limits and lived on a very tight budget, had learned to stretch a dollar to an art. Every cent counted.

Nora's brother Ted was far too pre-occupied with his drinking habits, more of a distraction than anything else. January became February, and Nora pushed on with her obligations. Although Nora no longer had children in diapers, she did have Rebecca in them. Her diaper days were back with her, only on a very different level this time. Rebecca's changing's were unpredictable. They could be needed at any given moment, at any hour of the day or night. Like a child, she couldn't be left in a soiled diaper and had to be changed as quickly as possible. Throughout the day she was checked and re-checked despite her objection.

The household was constantly busy. There were meals to be made, laundry to be done, with children and Rebecca to tend to. Seldom did she ever have time to even sit and enjoy a cup of coffee. She thanked the stars for having grown daughters who helped her out tremendously. Together they worked tirelessly to maintain the household.

Having Lawrence living with them was a great help. His strength came in handy when it came to maneuvering Rebecca from her bed into her wheelchair. He took on much of the responsibility for caring for Rebecca on his own. But he, too, needed his time away for himself, to be with his friends on nights out for laughter and fun.

Rebecca sighed deeply as she gazed out the window from her bed to see the first robins land on the branches of the tree next to her window. Somewhere in the back of her mind she knew what the robins meant. Lucy turned twenty six in February, Dale twenty four and the youngest seven in March.

As the days warmed, Nora wrapped a blanket around Rebecca and set her wheelchair out on the porch for fresh air and scenery. It did her heart good to see signs of life sprout about her. She had always loved flowers. Deep in her heart she missed the homestead as distant memories took her back. In those seconds, she had recollections of the trail leading down from her home to the river, lined with various flowers she planted and nurtured each season. Recollections of humming birds feeding from the succulent morning glories framing her porch also flashed before her. Briefly she was home again. Then it was all gone.

Nora knew this because at those moments Rebecca pleaded to go back home, to be freed. Neighbors heard and sympathized. They, too, kept a close eye on her when she was out on the porch as Nora warned them of Rebecca's attempts to escape. Nora's good friend across the street watched from her window when she heard Rebecca crying out or struggling to get out and came to Nora's help if needed.

Showers nourished the land. The fresh scent of rain was everywhere. Raindrops settled on leaves and petals of flowers and bushes, reflecting the sun as it peeked through the clouds. As in years past and as in years to come, children emerged to play in the puddles on dirt roads and in yards. Nature herself celebrated official arrival of spring in March.

Nora was surprised to find her brother Henry on her doorstep early in the afternoon one April day. He drove down from Denver, about three hundred miles, to visit for the afternoon. He wanted to spend as much time with Rebecca as possible. The joy of having him near was obvious in Rebecca. Tears trickled down her face. Although there were times she scarcely recognized anyone, she also had moments of clarity. Henry sparked one of those moments.

Nora wrapped Rebecca in a light blanket and set her wheelchair out on the porch. Henry sat next to Rebecca, holding her hand in his. He rubbed it gently, his heart heavy. He, too, had trouble seeing Rebecca in the condition she was in. It was though when he looked at her he could only remember the woman she once was. The frail, paralyzed person in the wheelchair was hardly that of his memories.

After a pleasant visit for several hours, he stood ready to leave. Rebecca wept as he caressed her. She watched his car move slowly down the dusty, dirt road until it was out of sight. Sadness filled her heart momentarily, vanishing as her mind was taken elsewhere.

Nora's own heart was heavy as she noticed the sadness in Rebecca, so she talked to her soothingly. It worked. Soon Rebecca was herself once again, cursing at the children as they frolicked in the sun running back and forth in front of the porch. It was though Henry's visit had never happened.

In May, Pricilla turned thirty four, Dwayne fourteen.

Rebecca's aggression accelerated. She had to be constantly watched out on the porch, either by Nora or family or friends if she was shopping or out dancing. Rebecca even found ways to remove the blocks of wood Nora set in front of her wheelchair tires, nearly tumbling off the porch. She shouted out at those going by, yelling for help.

Nora began dating a man she'd known casually for years. She liked him. And he had a car. Nora's children did not take well to this. They felt he invaded their father's space. Although she was involved with a man again, it did not stop her from enjoying nights out with her friends on the dance floor – nor would she allow it. Those nights were for her. It was on one of these night outs that she heard a song that would become her all-time favorite, *"Downtown"* by the British singer Petula Clark. She related to that song more than any other she ever heard.

As an early birthday gift for Nora, the boyfriend took her to Del Norte Airport, where a helicopter was taking guests on rides over the valley. They charged folks by the pound. Some of the children went with them to watch. With no hesitation, Nora boarded the craft. The children watched in awe as the helicopter lifted off the ground taking their mother into the sky and finally out of sight.

For forty five minutes they stood against the car waiting for the helicopter to return. They simply couldn't imagine experiencing what she had. For them it was far beyond their imaginations. Once Nora was at the car their questions began. They wanted to know exactly what it felt like. She told them with great detail of how she saw the valley through a bird's-eye view, had flown over Del Norte catching sight of their home. The children listened intently as though they had taken the ride with her. For them it was awesome. Days later, Nora turned forty eight.

During that week, Rebecca's brother Ted Allen dropped by to visit. He had a twelve year old grandson with him. Ted Allen had a thick head of snow white hair. He was a tall, slender man and dressed nicely. He favored his sister in many ways. Rebecca was delighted to see him. He did his best to converse as they sat in the living room. Nora's children were sent out in the yard to play during their visit, but his grandson stayed in the living room with the adults. For hours they visited.

Rebecca sat slumped in her chair with tears in her eyes when they left. She had another moment of clarity. Once more memories were there to haunt and torment her. Her broken heart was evident in her eyes. Nora felt helpless to her in these situations, nothing she could do or say. All she could do was let Rebecca deal with it in her own way, in her own time. With a heavy heart, Nora left her gazing out the window in deep thought. A gentle hand through the hair let Rebecca know her pain was felt. Benny turned nine on the 29th.

Early June was near perfect in the valley. Temperatures were mild, rain showers made vegetation plush. Nora sat Rebecca out on the porch to enjoy the freshness. She took it all in as though the rain brought back long, forgotten memories buried in the vastness of the past. At times she reached out with her good arm as though wanting to touch and feel the wetness, then sighed in regret.

Although having her hands full, Nora managed to get time for herself now that she was dating. In having a car, the man she dated took her wherever she wanted. Most of the time all she wanted was to drive about, enjoying the scenery. Sometimes they drove around town, at others to the country or nearby towns. Nora had found a gentle ear, someone to listen to her woes if and when she had any.

People gawked and gossiped, but she paid no mind. She never did live to please others. What she did, she did openly, driving her critics to distraction. She had learned long ago that people gossiped about her no matter what. Ridicule had become part of her life. As long as her children were strong and healthy, nothing else mattered much. In June, Pricilla moved back to California.

A few days later, Nora's heart came to a standstill when one of her daughter's friends, Manuel, pounded on her door. He found Rebecca near the dirt road in front of the house. She'd manipulated her chair, rolling it off the porch where it tumbled onto its side, somehow managing to set herself free from the cloth that bound her to it. She then dragged herself as far as she could get.

Nora ran out of the house with him and some of the girls, lifting Rebecca back into her wheelchair and bringing her back into the house. Rebecca fought them furiously, cursing and striking. She was determined to get where she wanted to go.

Rebecca had some scratches and bruises, but nothing serious. Never in the depth of Nora's imagination could she have expected Rebecca to do this. She knew then Rebecca could not be left alone for a second.

Time and time again Nora was reduced to tears at night when she laid her head to rest, thinking of Rebecca and her condition. She was angry that the strokes had robbed her of her mother, and her mother of life. She struggled to find peace with this. Yet, when the sun rose, so did strength and solace through her children. It was they who gave her the courage to face each day taking on whatever challenges it brought.

On July 4th the children did their usual to celebrate, but it just wasn't the same for Nora. Flora and her family lived in Denver, and the kids spent the majority of their time with friends at the Cement Bridge or doing other things to occupy their time and days. It took them awhile to adjust to Flora's kids being out of their lives. They missed them terribly. Ed missed them as well. Not having them next door to him was a major adjustment for him. He wasn't sure how long he'd continue to live there.

Cordie turned seventeen on July 8th. A week later Nora's brother Bill came to visit with Rebecca, who struggled with slurred words to communicate with him. His heart was heavy as he observed her. He didn't know quite how to handle her as his image and memory of her was of a strong, independent woman needing no one's help, rather being assisted by others. Through tear-filled eyes Rebecca gazed back at him, wanting so much to speak clearly. It broke her heart time and time again to have her children see her in this condition. Bill, as Nora's other siblings, came to the realization that Rebecca was where she needed to be. There was no safer place for her on the planet than where she was. As with the others, it eased whatever guilt he had.

On more than one occasion when Nora's back was turned, Rebecca manipulated herself off the porch, dragging herself out onto the street again. She learned from her first time how to do it. With each attempt she was getting better at it. It got to the point where Nora couldn't leave her alone at any cost. Someone had to be with her at all times. It became a battle of wits.

Rebecca seemed to take enjoyment in the challenges it posed for her. She had far more common sense than given credit for.

In August, Flora turned thirty three, Juanita thirty one and Teddy a teenager. He made new friends, taking up smoking on the sly, becoming rebellious – wanting to do whatever he wanted with no consequence. He skipped school and wandered around town with his new buddies, causing Nora yet another concern. A good scolding generally put him in his place thus far. Nora worried for tomorrow as he grew older.

In late August, Christine came from Albuquerque, where she lived with her family, to visit with Nora and Rebecca before winter set in and to get some of the harvest to take back with her. Nora missed Christine dearly since the day she left the valley. Nora's life was never the same without Christine in it the way she used to be. She not only lost her sister in a sense, but also the best friend she ever had.

Christine rented a cabin at Jessup's for the weekend. Nora was ever so pleased to hear that. She wanted to spend as much time with Christine as possible without taking time from Rebecca. Christine gazed about Nora's home with a lump in her throat in knowing the sacrifices Nora made in taking in their mother. She often marveled at Nora's life, even more so now that she had chosen to take on the responsibility of caring for Rebecca. She had high respect for Nora, more than she ever had.

Through the weekend Nora spent quality time with Christine. As the time came for Christine to leave, Nora's heart grew heavy. She wished Christine could stay for good. Having her near was the answer for so much of her worries. A gentle ear to listen and understand what she was going through was worth its weight in gold. As they hugged goodbye, both cried. Rebecca observed them through tear-filled eyes of her own. Having Christine near for these few days meant the world to her. Seeing Nora and Christine sparked clarity in her. She knew precisely who her daughters were. Once more, remorse touched her.

Nora and Rebecca sat on the porch watching as Christine's car drove out of sight, a cloud of dust the final reminder of their visit. Nora placed her handkerchief moistened with tears back into the pocket of her apron. Rebecca sighed, still in a locked gaze at dust going down the road. As if to escape the heartache, Nora resumed her duties.

After the emotional time of visits, Nora kept too busy to dwell on what could be but wasn't. In retrospect she sensed something about each visit – something was different. She felt it in her heart and soul, as though the inevitable was on its way.

Rebecca was more joyful. The sadness she felt in watching the visitors leave had gone, replaced by a peace with her surroundings once again. Her appetite was good, there was more laughter. Although she still feuded with the children, the fights were easily forgotten. She requested her favorite tortilla and jelly sandwiches whenever the craving struck. The children or Nora would see that she got her wish.

One consolation was that Nora got her first black-and-white television. Parking Rebecca in front of it helped a great deal in keeping her mind occupied on other things than trying to get away. It also gave Nora the opportunity to see soap operas she heard so much about, coming to find favorites that she tuned in to on a daily basis. She and Rebecca watched them together while the children were at school and there were no duties to attend to. Nora found another escape besides the dance floor.

The children rushed home to watch their favorite programs as well, sometimes arguing over what to see. On occasion the teens in the house caught glimpses of singers they so loved to listen to on the radio. They now could put faces to the voices they sang along with and danced to.

Gradually the quality of life was improving for Nora and her family. Luxuries she thought she'd never see were becoming possible and within reach. She was happy her children no longer had to be embarrassed being one of the impoverished families unable to have a TV. They could share experiences of what they watched with their friends the next day at school. For this Nora was pleased as she knew quite well the price of poverty. She'd lived with it much of her life.

The harvest left Nora with enough potatoes, peas and corn for the long winter ahead. The valley was famous for its tasty potatoes. She stored them by the hundred-pound sacks in the closet. The peas and corn she bagged and froze. Other items she still bought in bulk were flour, beans and sugar. She went through them rapidly with a hungry family to feed.

Andrew turned twelve on November 13th. In school he was heavily into sports, basketball being his favorite. He excelled in it. Lawrence's twenty eighth birthday fell on Thanksgiving that year. For him it was a double celebration to be sure.

As expected, come nightfall he and his friends were out for the evening. They piled into one car with radio going and laughter that could be heard throughout the neighborhood. Lawrence's long, black hair was tousled by the breeze of the open window as they drove away.

Nora's children munched on leftovers throughout the evening, settling in front of the television to watch whatever they wanted. With full stomachs they retreated to their beds for the night. Nora prepared Rebecca for bed before retiring herself after a long and busy day. In bed she reminisced about the day and its events. She was grateful for all life had given, and continued to give her. She thought of Billy as his birthday was the following day when he turned twenty two.

That Christmas season Rebecca was in high spirits, seemingly well aware of what was happening around her and enjoying it to the utmost. At night she sat in her wheelchair in a locked gaze at the tree, ignoring the television in front of her. Her mind was elsewhere.

Christmas morning, Nora's house was busy at sunrise as the children rose early. Rebecca's spirits remained high. She was in a good mood when she was awakened, bathed and dressed, finally placed into her wheelchair for breakfast. She teased and played with the children as they tore into their packages. She, too, ripped into hers with her good arm. It was a joyous occasion for all. This Christmas would be one that Nora would never forget. She saw happiness in her mother she'd not seen in a very long time. Her heart was content. The gifts from her children, however minuscule, were hers to treasure for a lifetime. They meant the world to her.

CHAPTER 37

1965. THE U.S. ESCALATES its role in Vietnam. By year-end, more than 186,000 troops are there with no end in sight. The anti-war movement spreads. Men's hair gets longer, women's skirts shorter. Gas is still just thirty one cents a gallon.

The dance show "Hullabaloo" debuts on TV, joining such favorites as *"My Three Sons," "The Addams Family," "Green Acres," "Bewitched," "I Dream of Jeannie"* and *"Gilligan's Island."*

For music fans there are the Beatles, Rolling Stones, Kinks, Searchers, Moody Blues, Donovan, Dusty Springfield and Tom Jones. Transistor radios are popular with America's youth. Schools ban them, to no avail to creative teens.

The arrest of a twenty one year old African-American man sparks a six-day riot in the Watts section of Los Angeles. Violence hits other cities. Minorities are angry and unwilling to cave to police. Congress passes the landmark Voting Rights Act.

$$* \quad * \quad * \quad * \quad *$$

REBECCA'S DISPOSITION IMPROVED. SHE laughed at the children, whose annoyances became entertainment. Everyone's spirits brightened as well. The morning of January 19th Nora rose early, as did Lawrence. His day usually began with making tortillas for breakfast, with hopefully enough to last for lunch. Nora made it a point of rising early to check on the children and her mom.

When Cordie got up, she walked past Rebecca, heard her take a deep breath and then nothing. Out of concern and curiosity, Cordie went to Rebecca's bedside without realizing that she'd actually heard Rebecca taking her last breath of life.

Andrew walked over, noticed no movement in the bed and called to Nora. As Rebecca lay with eyes open and staring, no sign of life, ever so gently Cordie closed them.

Nora rushed to her mother's bedside looking for signs of life. Some of the other children got up, awakened by the commotion. She did her best to calm Cordie and Andrew, along with others stood nearby. Charlotte stood by as Nora found that Rebecca was, indeed, gone. Distraught and weeping, Nora went across the street to use her friend's telephone to call the authorities. Rebecca was seventy five years old.

The friend could tell the second she opened the door that tragedy had struck. They embraced. Nora called authorities and headed back home. She didn't want the children left too long alone under the circumstances. And there was plenty that had to be done.

Nora told Teddy to bring the grim news to other family members around Del Norte. Through the bitter cold Teddy ran from one side of town to the other with the news. Meantime, Nora prepared Rebecca for the authorities, making sure she was clean and properly dressed.

Within minutes the police and medics arrived, along with the coroner. He pronounced Rebecca deceased. Nora's heart shattered as she watched them cover Rebecca's face and wheel her away. She had recollections of losing Rudolf. The pain was much the same. Her mother was gone.

It wasn't long before the house was filled with relatives and friends. Nora's hanky was soaked with tears. Everyone was sobbing. The young children observed in silence. They weren't quite sure how to handle it. They'd never lost someone this close.

To keep the children pre-occupied, Lawrence and the older girls gave them breakfast. There was silence at the table, with an occasional giggle from the smaller ones. Coffee was brewed continuously for the adults who sat in the front room with Nora or arriving. Plenty of coffee would be needed. For Nora it was going to be a very long day and week. Word of Rebecca's passing spread through town fast.

Throughout the day people came and left Nora's home with condolences. Many were there to lend a helping hand as usual. The loyalty Nora's friends had proven to her through the years was prominent again. Many arrived with dishes of food.

That evening, the last visitor left, leaving Nora and her family to grieve on their own. There was a strange silence, an absence in the house. The children felt it, too, although they didn't fully understand. The family was accustomed to having Rebecca around, hearing her voice.

As Nora sent the children off to sleep, she took notice of Rebecca's empty bed with a grieving heart. Already, she missed her deeply. As with losing Rudolf, her life would never be the same without Rebecca in it, without her to care for as she had all those past months. And yet, a part of her was relieved for Rebecca as she no longer had to suffer and struggle with her condition.

She lay in bed that night in deep thought. Tears found their way down the sides of her face onto the pillow. Although she had her children whom she adored, without Rebecca she felt somewhat alone now. She knew within her heart that she had to remain strong for the children. They would need her strength, although they didn't know it. She had to guide them through grieving as best she could.

Memories of the life she shared with Rebecca flashed before her. In spite of the rocky past they shared, she felt peace in her heart even though it was broken. Eventually she dozed off. Dreams of Rebecca invaded her sleep – dreams as close to reality as they could get. Voices in them were clear and vivid. A strange silence seemed to hiss through the house into the night.

Nora's house was continuously filled with relatives and friends over the following days. Condolences poured in. Rebecca's bed was kept for anyone who needed it.

Carole's nineteenth birthday on the 22nd was shrouded by Rebecca's passing. Funeral arrangements were set for the next day. It was a long, grueling process for Nora in making preparations.

Rebecca was laid to rest in the Del Norte Cemetery following services at the Catholic Church. It was bitter cold, the sky gray. Around her grave, people huddled as though to ward off the sting of the bitter elements. It was a sad day for Nora as she stood over Rebecca's grave reliving the life they once shared. She was ever so grateful that she took her in and cared for her the way she had. She felt privileged to have shared her last years and days with her. With a heavy, but peaceful heart she walked away. Nora's brother Ted left the valley soon after Rebecca's burial never to return again.

The following days were difficult for Nora as she mourned in silence. Cleaning out Rebecca's space was especially hard. Sorting through her belongings was painful. Each garment had a memory all its own. Rebecca's presence lingered on the bedding and clothing, as did her scent. The trunk she had given Nora those many years ago took on the most special meaning of all. Rebecca had it for years up in the homestead and kept her most precious belongings in it. The leather straps were worn from time, the metal aged. Nora swore to herself she would keep it as long as she was on the planet, and should she ever pass it on it would be to someone she solemnly trusted.

Nora tried her hardest to adjust over the following weeks. The house didn't feel the same. Passing Rebecca's bed – and the memories it held – were unavoidable in getting from one room to the next. The younger children bounced back from the ordeal; the older ones mourned in their own ways. Days dragged on.

With Rebecca gone and the children in school, Nora had more time to herself. Rides about town and into nearby communities with the man she was dating gave a change of scenery and atmosphere that did her a world of good, helped in clearing her mind. The new freedom also gave her more time and space to share with her friends out on the town dancing.

On one of these occasions she ventured into Alamosa and ran into a cousin by marriage. Rose had lived in Alamosa for years and raised her family there. She, like Nora, was a single parent raising a large family.

Lucy turned twenty seven in February and moved the following month to Denver with her family.

At times when Nora was out on her ride about town, she visited the cemetery and stood over Rudolf, Rebecca and Ernest in contemplation. She missed each one in her own ways. She missed Rudolf the most and would forever, his words of wisdom and encouragement echoing through her memory. She drew strength from him and knew she always would.

When it was sunny outside, the cemetery felt tranquil, peaceful; when it was overcast it felt dismal. Sometimes she encountered folks she knew who were also visiting the sites of loved ones. Some gawked and gossiped, others offered their peace, and she hers in return.

On one visit in spring, Nora experienced pain in her abdomen. It lasted minutes, intense enough to bend her over. After subsiding, she was left to wonder what could be wrong, then dismissed the thought. A couple of aspirin and she would be okay, she was certain. Maybe it was something she ate that hadn't agreed with her.

Nora found pleasure in the most inopportune things. One of them was taking down the clothing from the lines in April. No longer contending with Rebecca's diapers or other necessities, clothesline life was so much simpler – only the mundane basic clothing and towels. She smiled wistfully recalling those years and years with diapers and all that she learned and experienced.

Rudy turned thirty that month. Spring was in full bloom. Downtown sidewalks were busy with shoppers going from one merchant to the other. Kids walked home from school in groups, taking their time enjoying the warmer weather. The crabapple tree at Nora's exploded with color, its scent filling the front yard, as did the lilac bushes. Nora picked handfuls and placed them in jars around the house.

During this time, Nora researched the benefits of moving her family to Alamosa. Although she didn't know anybody there except Rose, she'd consider the move if it meant a better life for her and her kids and took a few trips there getting a feel for it. Rose lived on the southwest, so Nora set her sights on that part of town. If she was going to make the move, she wanted to be as close to someone she knew as possible. She kept these trips to herself. The more she went, the more she liked the place. It was certainly bigger with more to do and choose from. By comparison, Alamosa was a downright city, its population at four thousand plus, nearly triple Del Norte's. South Fork's was even less. One thing that concerned her was Alamosa's notoriety for being the coldest spot in the nation during winter.

By April 30th Charlotte and Becky's twenty first birthdays, she had made up her mind to go but still didn't tell her family. She wanted to take her time finding the right place. One thing was certain – she wanted to make the move before the beginning of the next school year.

Another reason she wanted to move was that living in the house where her mother had died became just too much. The empty feeling never went away, never left her at peace. She needed space and time to mourn and grieve without constant memories bombarding her from the moment she rose to when she laid her head to rest at night.

Moving would mean Nora's kids had to make new friends, but this was never a problem. They made new ones every time they moved and after Flora moved away. New faces were continuously being introduced into Nora's household. She totally understood the value of good friends and encouraged it to her children. She hoped her kids would have the friendship base she had throughout her life. The importance and value of friends was monumental to her. If anything in life next to family, friends were next in priority to her.

Finally in June, even though she hadn't found a place yet, Nora broke the news about the move. The children were puzzled but didn't question. Instinctively they knew Nora was doing what she felt was best. They seldom ever questioned her motives. They were psyched for the new adventure.

Nora experienced another painful attack, this time more severe. She turned pale and had no other choice but to lie across her bed until it subsided and she was left at peace. She had far too much to do in preparation of moving than to deal with health issues. She thought it also might be all the stress since Rebecca's death and now with the move.

Over the next month, on one of Nora's trips into Alamosa she made arrangements to rent a home on Edison Street four blocks from Rose. It was not too far from downtown but a long walk to school. A large tree stood proudly in the front yard of the green, stucco corner home facing north. A wooden picket fence worn by time enclosed the yard.

As days went by, excitement among the children mounted. They couldn't imagine living in a town the size of Alamosa. They were so accustomed to small communities such as Del Norte and South Fork. It would definitely be an adjustment for them in many ways. They, of course, would miss the new friends they had made. That was one of their regrets. Another was beginning a new school where they didn't know anyone.

Teddy in particular was relieved to be moving as he was having very difficult times in school. He would be fourteen in August yet still scarcely knew how to read or write. The anticipation of being called upon by the teacher to read before the class was overwhelming. At times it paralyzed him into a cold sweat.

The move was planned for early July. As it turned out, Becky, now twenty one, moved about the same time, to Denver. Nora was saddened about another of her children leaving the nest, but it also was good for her. The reality of how brief life was dawning on her, and she knew she was ready for a change of scenery and environment.

When the day came, trucks and cars were loaded up with Nora's belongings and moved into Alamosa, along with ten of her children. The kids were mesmerized by the mere size of the town. To them it was enormous. To some degree it was frightening. While the adults unpacked, the children got acquainted with the neighborhood. To the end of the block they wandered, peering down the street that seemed to go on forever. Unlike Del Norte and South Fork, they couldn't see an end to the town no matter what direction they looked. Neighbors observed curiously.

Within days Nora took some of the kids to Rose's home to get acquainted with their cousins. Rose and her children sat in the living room when Nora and her children arrived. Rose was a neat woman with a head of long, auburn hair. She was vibrant and colorful.

Introductions were made with the hopes of bonds quickly forming. Rose and Nora left that up to them. Rose had children ranging from twins, teens to toddlers. She and Nora had much in common when it came to raising a family with so many children.

As the days followed, Nora's children spent more time with Rose's. Friendships formed. Rose's children showed Nora's the town, getting them acquainted with their surroundings. Nora's kids were in awe with downtown

Alamosa. They'd never seen so many teens and young people, so many stores and traffic. The train depot was astonishing to them. Alamosa even had street lights and cabs. Alamosa's park made Del Norte's seem like a miniature. The river next to the park was swelled to its peak. A steam engine set in the park as a permanent fixture. Across the viaduct Alamosa continued. It seemed they walked for hours before coming to the edge of town.

Through July into August the children spent time together. Nora's kids got to know their way around. They found the schools they'd attend, memorizing the path to them. The high school, junior high and elementary school were all near each other on Highway 160.

On one occasion at Rose's was Bobby, thirteen, openly gay and no qualms about it. He was Rose's nephew, her sister's son. His coal, black, wavy hair went well with his hazel eyes. His laughter came from the heart and soul. He turned heads wherever he went with his androgynous looks. Bobby radiated a joy and happiness that intimidated some but was a natural draw for others. Teddy had never met such a person.

Teddy and Bobby initially didn't hit it off so well, but through time they formed a close bond. Bobby showed Teddy a world he'd never known – released and liberated him – taught him how to drive a car, a '54 Ford, stick shift. Teddy knew they would not only be cousins, but friends, forever. Nora's family grew to love Bobby as they did all of Rose's children. Nora was grateful they came into her children's lives. She felt good about the move.

Alamosa's summer weather turned out to be as hot as advertised. Nora's family made adjustments to it, just like to everything in their new home. They still missed the friends and cousins in Del Norte. Unbeknownst to Nora, Teddy and Bobby even hitch-hiked from time to time to Del Norte and back before the day ended. It took them an hour each way.

On August 21st Rose's daughter turned fourteen. She had been born the day before Teddy in the hospital room next to Nora. She, Teddy and Bobby were very close, had formed not only a strong family relationship but a hopefully lasting friendship. It did Nora's heart good to see them together. On the 22nd Teddy turned fourteen, an age when the world opened up.

Nora's children had no problems at their new schools. They enjoyed the new surroundings and faces and made new friends. Unlike Del Norte, Alamosa schools were much more liberal with fashion. Bell bottom pants were the rage. It seemed every teenager wore them. A good thing since the girls were allowed to wear them to school, which helped in keeping kids warm on brutal, cold winter days.

Nora's children spent the majority of their free time with Rose's. They walked to and from school with them each day and then hung out with them afterward once chores were done.

Rose's children were like Nora's – obedient, doing whatever their mother asked, respectful toward her and others.

In early October, Nora had another attack, this one far worse than the first two. She not only grew pale and flushed, but also the pain folded her in agony. She damned whatever it was, couldn't even begin to imagine what was going on. The thought of it being stress didn't make sense to her anymore. There was something more. After a bit it all faded, and she was back to herself. She made mental notes of each episode, sensing that information would be needed if the situation worsened. Across the bed she lay until she felt it was safe to rise.

Alamosa got its first snowfall of the season with some leaves still on the trees. A fall mist hung over the town as if to remind everyone of what was on its way. Unlike Nora and her family, the locals knew only too well what winters in Alamosa could be like. The snow and cold didn't stop the kids at Halloween. Streets and sidewalks were crowded with groups trick-or-treating. Kids in Alamosa were creative when it came to this holiday, Nora's among them.

Thanksgiving Day on the 25th was gorgeous. It was sunny but cold. To the east, Mount Blanca was snowcapped, as was the Sangre De Cristo Range surrounding the valley. This range was named after the colors it turned at sunset. The shades red and orange made it beautiful for artists on canvas and photographers on film. In Nora's and Rosa's homes, the sheer joy was overwhelming.

Lawrence turned twenty nine in Denver two days later. Nora heard from him on occasion via mail. When weather permitted he made it down on holidays, but with a demanding job that wasn't always possible. Several of Nora's children lived in Denver, and she began to wonder what the attraction to the city might be. She questioned them how they could live in such an enormous place. Billy turned twenty three the next day, another child gone from the nest living out of state.

Temperatures plunged to zero in December, but that didn't stop downtown Alamosa from decorating. Santa and Christmas trees set in storefront windows in display. Sales were advertised in every store from one end of town to the other. Snowplows cleared streets for shoppers, also making sure Highway 160 was clean for travelers. Nora's and Rose's kids loved going downtown admiring the images in the windows. Rose's daughter who was Teddy's age had a theatrical personality and stood at a lamp post for impromptu performances. She kept those around her entertained with scenes she saw in musicals on the silver screen. Her joyful heart shined through.

The holiday season in Alamosa was much different than in South Fork and Del Norte. The biggest change was there were no carolers. Nora and her family missed that. On the local radio station, nothing but holiday music was played, with the exception of K-O-M-A, which could be tuned into after sunset as it was in Del Norte. Although Alamosa was larger, K-O-M-A was the only radio station available that played rock 'n roll music.

Just before Christmas, Teddy and Bobby smoked cigarettes one evening and spied through the bushes in the back yard at a teen couple engaged in a heated argument in the car. Suddenly, the guy pulled out a gun and shot the girl in the head, killing her instantly.

Teddy and Bobby froze and dropped to the ground when the young man in the car began scanning the area frantically. The two made their way to the back door crawling into the house. In a panic they told Nora what they witnessed. She immediately locked all doors and ordered them to remain inside. Sirens and flashing lights filled the night. Afraid of walking home alone, Bobby stayed until morning. It took both of them awhile to get over the shooting.

Nora hoped against hope there would be no more abdominal attacks during the holiday season. Something deep inside told her they weren't over, so she took things one day at a time.

In early December, the pain struck again, the worst thus far. It lasted more than a half hour, folding her in agony across her bed. This time she knew something was seriously wrong but didn't want to take the time and didn't have the money to see a doctor. There was far too much to be done for Christmas. She had a family to care for. But she swore with the next episode she'd seek help.

CHAPTER 38

1966. THE VIETNAM WAR is felt everywhere in America as inflation from a disrupted economy is rising, although gas is still cheap at thirty two cents. Hundreds of thousands of U.S. troops are stationed in Vietnam, by April their death toll in the war exceeding 33,000.

Race riots increase. The National Guard is called in to restore order. Black Power becomes a significant force to be reckoned with. By law all cigarette packages have to carry the health warning "Caution! Cigarette smoking may be hazardous to your health."

"Star Trek" debuts on TV, as does Dr. Seuss' *"How the Grinch Stole Christmas."* Color television sales boom. Simon and Garfunkel sing the haunting *"Sounds of Silence,"* the Mamas and Papas *"Monday, Monday,"* the Monkees *"I'm a Believer,"* the Beach Boys *"Good Vibrations"* and the Rolling Stones *"Satisfaction"* could be heard on radios across America. The Mod Look arrives as adults take to bell bottoms, too, along with hip huggers – the bigger the bell the better, the lower the hugger the sexier. Patterned pants, flowered shirts and paisley ties replace white and gray.

* * * * *

WINTER IN ALAMOSA PROVED to be the worst Nora and her family ever experienced. Temperatures plummeted well below zero for days at a time. Children were wrapped in layers before sent off to school. There was no escaping it unless fortunate enough to have a ride. Nora's and Rose's children weren't. They had to withstand the elements each day. In spite of the bitter elements, they found time for laughter and play. Nothing would rob them of that.

In early January Nora rose for the day getting the children ready for school. Pain shot through her abdomen unlike she'd felt before. She collapsed on the bed. All color left her face. The children panicked, not knowing what to do for her. She hoped the pain would subside after a few moments, but that didn't happen. It only got worse. Barely able to speak, she asked Teddy and another to call a cab or ambulance.

They grabbed their coats and gloves and were out the door into the bitter cold. It had dropped to forty below during the night. Teddy ran out into the open with no destination in mind. He wasn't quite sure where to go for help. They ended up at Moses' Grocery Store a few blocks up. There was a pay phone he used to call for help. When they got home the cab he called was parked in front of the house waiting for Nora.

Inside, the kids got Nora's bags ready. She knew instinctively she might spend days if not a week in the hospital. The older kids would have to tend to the younger children until she got back home. Carefully, cautiously they helped Nora into the cab, watching as it drove out of sight taking their mother and one of the older daughters.

Later than morning, news came to Nora's family that she'd been diagnosed with gallbladder stones and required surgery as soon as possible. They did the surgery later that morning, taking out three gallstones the size of small marbles. They handed them to Nora in a jar when she came to. She set them on the nightstand next to the bed. The pain in her abdomen disappeared, what remained was from the surgery and stitches. Between home and hospital, doctors told her it would take a couple of weeks to recover. She was relieved that they had solved her problem. She would be able to resume her life and duties.

The stay in the hospital gave her time for much-needed recuperation. She rested peacefully, knowing the children were being cared for by their older siblings. The children who were permitted to visit stopped by, keeping her tuned in on what was going on at home. After several days in the hospital, Nora was ready to leave.

A bed was waiting in the living room. The children made her meals and saw to her every need. They waited on her hand and foot. Slowly, gradually, she rose from the bed taking small steps, moving about carefully with help, still in obvious pain. As days went by she was able to move about more. The pain from the surgery subsided substantially. She teased the children as she held the gallstones in the palm of her hand, telling them she was going to have a pair of earrings made of them. She got a kick out of grossing them out. The younger children were more in awe of the stones, asking question after question. Some even held them in their hands unable to grasp that she'd had them inside her body. They just couldn't understand that the stones were the cause of their mother's discomfort and pain.

Nora swore she'd never go through another winter like this and made up her mind to move back to Del Norte once school was out. It was just too hard on everyone.

On February 22nd Charlotte was married at the Justice of the Peace in Monte Vista. They moved in with her husband's parents in Lariat. Once more Nora was saddened to have another one of her children leave the nest. They seemed to rapidly be growing into adults and moving before her very eyes. But with the sadness came a certain satisfaction. All she wanted for her children was happiness, and if they found it with another person all the better. Nora believed firmly in the power of love.

Nora recovered from her surgery and was back to herself, feeling much better than she had in months. At least she didn't have the constant worry of another attack sneaking up on her at any given moment. She and Rose, along with friends, were out dancing in no time. Some of Nora's favorite dancing spots were in Alamosa, thus she took advantage of them when she could. Nora's Del Norte friends drove up on Saturday evenings when weather permitted for a night out with her. They danced and laughed to their hearts' content.

All in Alamosa were relieved when February came to an end. That meant spring was just around the corner. Although still cold and the winds notorious, there were signs of spring in the air. It wasn't near dark when the kids got out of school. Days got warmer. When able, Nora took trips into Del Norte looking for a home to rent. Her friends were also on the lookout.

Bobby was constantly at the house or with Teddy going into town for hours doing who knows what. Sometimes they got rides into Del Norte to Bobby's grandmother. They explored life and the world around them to the fullest.

Finally in March, the large tree in the front yard budded, robins sitting on the branches and singing away. Tulips peered through the ground, still covered in snow in patches, and reached for the sun's nourishment. People came out of their winter hibernation. Downtown was abuzz, Nora's and Rose's kids among them peering into store windows and Rose's theatrical daughter putting on a show for them as usual.

April Fool's Day always brought memories of one prank in particular. Caterpillars congregated in the tree in the front yard where Nora and the family were living. Cordie was deathly afraid of them, so Charlotte gathered a handful while she was visiting and put them on Cordie when she wasn't looking. The screams were heard a block away as Cordie ran into the house, brushing them off. Her revenge was tossing a cat onto Charlotte, who hated them as much as her sister hated caterpillars.

Nora heard of a home possibly being available to rent come June. It was about a half mile due east of Del Norte outside the city limits. The man who owned and operated Skaff's in Del Norte was proprietor. This was a somewhat larger home than she had ever lived in, set on a relatively large piece of land. A barn and corral were in back and fields to the north. Brahman bulls and cows were kept in the nearby fields along with a few horses.

Nora stopped by Skaff's on one of her trips into Del Norte to inquire. He confirmed the rumor, promising the house to her in June. She took a deep sigh of relief when she walked out of the supermarket – one less thing to stress over. On her way back to Alamosa she took notice of the property and knew her children would love living there. She would too. She loathed the thought of moving again, but the thought of going through another Alamosa winter convinced her quickly.

The kids were somewhat surprised to learn they'd move back to Del Norte, but Del Norte and South Fork were home turf to them and they looked forward to returning.

So, yet again, Nora busily gathered boxes. Some she hadn't even unpacked from her move into Alamosa. She longed for the right place where she could plant roots and settle down permanently and hoped Skaff's would be the one. She thought of the house on each trip she took into Del Norte anticipating the move. For her it was the best of both worlds as it wasn't quite within the city limits, yet not too far from town. The grocery market was a mere ten minute walk. That she would appreciate to be sure.

Little by little her family belongings went into boxes as days went by. She left the kitchen for last as supplies would be needed till the day of the move. She lined up folks with trucks in advance. Luckily, she knew several who were more than willing to help. Soon, packed boxes were stacked wherever there was space for them. Nora's family was literally living around the stacks of boxes and bags. The house was chaotic.

On Saturday May 22nd Nora's friends picked her up for a celebratory night of dancing and fun. First, they spent an hour in Del Norte, then an hour in Monte Vista, then back again to Alamosa. Music from the Challengers vibrated through the Parish Hall. You could hear it a block away.

On the 24th, Nora turned fifty. She found it hard to believe. So much of her life flashed as everyone sang "Happy Birthday." At the party, each of her children gave a present, and, as usual, she put the most special ones in her trunk. Handmade things, hankies still in their boxes, small keepsakes only a mother could love, all were neatly stacked in the trunk. She never used any of these treasures, valuable to her beyond any price.

As much as they looked forward to going back, the day of the move was disheartening for Nora's children. Their goodbyes to Rose's family were even more difficult than imagined. They drove away with heavy hearts filled with a lifetime of memories. There was an emptiness shared among them. On the drive back to Del Norte, silence dominated the space in the vehicles. Although Nora was concerned, she knew how resilient children were. She hoped the bonds they had formed with Rose's children were strong enough to hold them together for years to come.

When they finally pulled up to the property, the children became excited again. The house was one of the nicest they'd seen, and even had a barn and fields they could play and roam in.

Their instincts went on alert once they noticed the Brahman bulls in the pasture next to the property. They were well-warned of how temperamental the beasts could be. But the fields were plush, green. The Rio Grande River flowed on the other side of the fields not far from the house. There were trees to climb, and plenty of other attractions to keep them occupied and their minds busy. Nora hoped it was enough to keep them distracted from those they left behind in Alamosa.

The grueling task of unpacking trucks, cars, boxes and bags began. While the older children and adults did that, the younger kids explored and got acquainted with their new surroundings. The house was everything the children hoped it would be. It gave them both the pleasure of country living, yet not being isolated or secluded from their friends and cousins in town.

The white, three-bedroom home was more spacious than anywhere they'd lived. In the kitchen was a coal and wood cooking stove against one wall. On the other side of the wall was the boys' room where multiple beds were set up. Teddy's bed was behind the wall where the stove sat. The house was all they'd hoped for both inside and out. The surroundings they particularly enjoyed. The moment they rose in the morning they were outside exploring, venturing around with friends and cousins. Sleepovers were common. Sometimes friends stayed the night, other times Nora's kids would go. Either way they were inseparable.

With the children on summer vacation, finding them at home was rare. A short walk into town and they met up with their friends, or their friends came over for them. When the sun set, they walked one another halfway back, Skaff's being the halfway point. A count to three, and they were off running in opposite directions for home. The walk for Nora's kids between Skaff's and the house could be spooky.

The horse in the field next to the highway made it a habit of following them on the other side of the fence. Its hooves sounded in the night as though someone or something was following them. For a kid's vivid imagination, it wouldn't take long before they were at a full run for the house barging through the door out of breath – the horse running until stopped by a barrier. They repeated this the following day.

It seemed no sooner had they laid their head to sleep at night that the morning greeted a brand new day with more adventures. The smell of a cooking breakfast pulled them from their beds morning after morning. Aromas continuously filled the house as they had all through their childhood.

Having no neighbors to contend with was an added bonus for Nora. And even though she lived outside the city limits, she had no problem getting to town when needed. At times she even walked. Luckily, some of those times she got a ride back home with packages in her arms.

July 4th was awesome. With virtually no street lights, the night sky beamed with countless stars. Later was lit vividly by the fireworks the children shot into the sky. They could also see fireworks afar explode in multi-colors in various parts of town. Fireworks blasted till way past midnight until the town folded for another day.

In mid-July, not longer after Cordie's nineteenth birthday, Nora rose early to clean pinto beans for cooking in a twenty five quart pot belly pressure cooker with timers on top that she had used for years. The morning was calm.

Soon, one by one the children rose, eating their breakfast, then going outside to play. Teddy was left sleeping. Nora, the beans cooking, was in the living room watching TV. Suddenly, an explosion ripped through the house shattering every window. Smoke and ash bellowed out from the kitchen doorway. Nora's heart nearly stopped.

Teddy's bed overturned and he was tossed over onto the floor. The wall next to his bed bowed from the explosion. He heard screaming. Someone shouted, "The Vietnamese are bombing us! The Vietnamese are bombing us!"

In a panic he quickly dressed, running out into the living room where he caught sight of Nora and the chaos. She was horrified and frantic. The house was filled with smoke and ash. There were hot coals and pieces of hot metal spread across the floors. Nora made her way through to the kitchen where one of the teen girls had been sitting at the table.

Nora found her still seated but pinned against the wall. Immediately, she pulled her into her arms, hugging and kissing her, making sure she was coherent and okay. She checked for signs of injury. Frantically, she wiped her daughter's face and body clear of any liquids and food. Each wipe of the cloth exposed a pale and flushed girl. Nora's heart sank. Pieces of metal had blown past her daughter's head lodging into the wall behind her with strands of her red hair. She was drenched in liquids from the pressure cooker. Nora's heart beat harder against her chest.

The walls and ceiling were also covered in liquid. The pressure cooker and stove were blown to bits. The wall behind the stove was blown out. Every window frame in the house was bent outward, all glass shattered. Outside, the children were in a panic, not knowing what had happened. The older siblings kept them to their boundaries at a distance from the house. They weren't taking any chances.

Within minutes police arrived, as did an ambulance and fire truck. They rushed Nora's daughter to the hospital while police investigated. Nora went with her daughter in the ambulance leaving the older siblings in care of the younger ones. Her heart pounded with fear. She couldn't imagine what had caused the pressure cooker to explode. Pieces of metal were found scattered throughout the yard – some as far as the highway nearly a hundred feet from the house. The boom was heard by locals. Some drove out to see what was going on, driving by at a slow speed hoping to get a glimpse of the action. Some who knew Nora's family drove onto the premises in concern.

Two hours went by before Nora returned home. The girl only suffered minor scratches and cuts. It had been a horrific experience for her. It seemed the stars were on her side, nothing short of amazing that she hadn't been severely injured or killed. The family was grateful for this. Nora thanked whatever powers that be for the safety of her child. She never forgot the experience, the horror. The mere thought that her daughter was the only one present in the kitchen at the time of the explosion amazed her. It was though all had been meant to be. All her children were safe. That was all she cared about. For whatever reasons, she left up to the universe.

In the following days, a new stove was installed, window frames and glass replaced, the wall rebuilt. Remnants of the explosion were reminders of what might or could have been. Nora was reluctant to use a pressure cooker of any sort ever again after it was determined that a clogged valve on her old one had caused the explosion. She was told, but not reassured, that a more modern one would not pose such a threat.

Del Norte was as they left it when they moved to Alamosa. There was the Tasty Freeze on East Main. With outdoor speakers, kids could not only park and indulge in their favorite foods but also listen to their favorite tunes at the same time. Across the street was a McDonald's, owned and operated by an elderly couple. Although the hamburgers were good, with no outdoor seating the older kids weren't as interested.

As usual for any summer in Del Norte, the carnival arrived in August with all its amusement. It was set up on Highway 112 going toward Center. Once the sun began fading, kids came out in droves to participate in the fun and rides. Nora's kids were among them, joyously resuming the tradition this year. On occasion she herself ventured down to enjoy the festivities, usually riding only the Ferris Wheel. From the top of the Wheel, anyone could get a bird's-eye view of Del Norte and the carnival itself. With harvest season at its peak, there was plenty of spending money in people's pockets. Having fun was on everyone's mind.

Many times people at the carnival had to take cover from the summer thunderstorms. They huddled beneath the tents until the rain stopped. At home, moms ran to the clothes lines to remove the laundry. Thunderstorms were enjoyed, too, because they meant a cool night for sleeping and a fresh morning to awaken to.

Juanita turned thirty three on August 17th, Flora thirty five a day later. For Nora, not only days and years flew by, but now decades. It sometimes seemed as if she was watching someone else's life unfold before her. It was all just too surreal.

Teddy turned fifteen on August 22nd. He was seldom home, always on the go with Bobby or his friends. Although Nora wasn't overly concerned about him, she heard rumors of his behavior. She kept a close eye on him when he was around. She, of course, knew that like any teenage boy, where there was mischief to be found, he would find it. Her concerns like any other mother's in Del Norte with teenage children were the cigarettes and alcohol available to them. She thanked the stars there weren't worse things to be found in Del Norte. Unbeknownst to her, however, was that Teddy still had a terrible time with school, whether it be in Alamosa or now again in Del Norte. Most of the time he ditched classes, spending days with his friends who were no longer in school either.

Nora and her friends continued their nights out. Her high heels seldom rested before being on the dance floor once again. Her collection of high heels grew to a point where she hardly had storage for them. It seemed with each trip she made into town she came home with another pair, in all colors, styles and fabrics. For winter she had various styles of high-heel boots. She had something to wear for any occasion. On some Saturday nights she and her friends ventured into Alamosa where they met up with Rose for a night out.

Just after Thanksgiving, Lawrence turned the big 3-0 on November 27th. Billy's twenty fourth birthday was a day later. On occasion, Ed stopped by to give the children much-needed supplies and clothing. If Nora even suspected he'd been drinking, she'd keep her distance, allowing him to visit the children, and then be on his way.

Charlene had her eighteenth birthday on December 3rd. For Christmas in their new home, some of the children came down from Denver, Nora's heart sinking when they drove away again. She had eight left at home as 1966 came to end. Soon, she knew, others would venture away as well. It was only a matter of time until all were gone.

CHAPTER 39

1967. BY DECEMBER, U.S. troop levels in Vietnam reach half a million. Anti-war momentum and peace rallies hit fever pitch during the year. People grow concerned with the rising cost of everything. Gas costs thirty three cents a gallon. The unemployment rate is 3.8 percent.

Discos and singles bars are a huge draw. Youth groove to pot and Jefferson Airplane. Sonny and Cher make the Top Ten with *"The Beat Goes On."* The skinny, wide-eyed Twiggy is a fashion icon out of England. The world's first supermodel is on magazines, posters and storefronts around the world.

"Guess Who's Coming to Dinner" starring heavyweights Spencer Tracy, Katharine Hepburn and Sidney Poitier breaks ground on the silver screen with an interracial romance, as Hollywood steps out of the comfort zone. Not everyone is happy. Bigoted opponents call it immoral and use the Bible to back up their venom as they have for centuries.

* * * * *

FOR REASONS NORA TALKED about, she decided to move again early in the year. It was sad for her, because she really liked this home. She looked, friends kept an eye peeled for vacancies. By the time of Carole's twenty first birthday on January 22nd Nora got word of a place coming available downtown. She passed it numerous times, was familiar with it across the street from the fire station and Tasty Freeze.

As soon as possible, she headed into town to inquire and was relieved when the owner agreed to rent her the place. It would be available in early February. Nora's children were disappointed to get the news of moving yet again. They enjoyed where they lived. Nora went into no detail, just said we're moving, and that was that.

The move was made one day while the children were in school. They were given instructions of where to go when school was out. One by one they showed up at the new address, eager to look about and explore their new surroundings. Ice and snow were still on the concrete of the Bay Station, a gas and garage facility. It was a mere fifty feet from the front doorstep.

This home was long, with three bedrooms at the back. An unused one-car garage was outside the back. A gravel driveway led from one end of the property to the other. A large picture window gave a clear view of traffic moving up and down Main Street. From the sofa, anyone could get glimpses of what was happening downtown, see those cruising Main. It was a close walk to school for the kids, a mere block from the library.

It took days for Nora and the family to settle into their new environment, but it was done. With such easy access to downtown the kids were seldom home unless bad weather forced them to stay indoors. Their friends were over constantly. Some honked their cars as they pulled up. For Nora this new location was a relief as well because downtown was just a few minutes' walk away for her. Her friends had easy access to her, and it wasn't long before they were visiting.

This new home saw two major steps for Nora and her family. They had their first phone installed and got their first color television. Things were really looking up for her and her family. Instantly, the kids were on the phone giving out the number to their friends. Before long it was ringing off the hook. Nora could now also watch her favorite soaps in color, something she had wanted for a very long time. Nora told her kids all about it when she called them in Denver in February.

In March, Cordie moved to Denver, but not before pulling a stunt on her mom. She convinced Ed to go to Nora's door with a bouquet of flowers in an attempt to get them back together. When Nora opened the door to find Ed standing there, she went off on him, scolding him and running him off. Instinctively, she turned to her children for the culprit. The look on Cordie's face gave her away. Nora scolded and lectured her, demanding that she never pull something like this on her again.

When Cordie left for Denver, Nora's heart broke. She worried for her kids being out in the world on their own where she couldn't protect them from the trials and tribulations of life. She had seven children left at home now. The youngest turned ten on March 12th.

Dwayne and Teddy pressed Nora for a car, at the age where they wanted their independence. A vehicle would give them much of that. With their friends having cars, this added pressure as well. Nora was opposed to the idea as she didn't feel that they were responsible or mature enough for such a responsibility. Nonetheless, the boys kept pressuring her.

Nora relented a month later, on her terms. That they keep up the monthly payments and the insurance current, also that they'd be there at her beckon and call when she needed to get somewhere. They settled on a 1958 Oldsmobile Ninety-Eight, sporting a dusty rose color with a black top.

In having a car, the boys were seldom home unless Nora instructed them. She, too, had her needs for the car, which took priority over their fun. Word spread fast through town that the Marquez boys had wheels. What Nora didn't know was about the times drag racing went on along the cemetery road.

The Olds gained its reputation quickly among the teens around town. It not only ran smoothly and sat close to the ground but also had power behind it hard to rival. With a carload, the boys went wherever they wanted in the valley, venturing into Monte Vista, Alamosa, Center and Seven Mile Plaza. At sunset the radio was tuned into K-O-M-A blasting out their favorite tunes. The car vibrated with bass.

In mid-April, Nora's last teenage daughter at home moved to California to be married. Nora's heart sank once again. First all her grown girls had gone, now the boys as they grew up. Although the load of her responsibilities was easing, the loneliness she felt with each child leaving home was at times unbearable. In the privacy of her room and bed, she hoped the universe would shield and take care of her children no matter where they went.

Teddy, all of fifteen years and nine months, walked into the school superintendent's office that spring with an armful of books. Saying nothing, he threw them across the desk telling him where he could put them. Some bounced off the desk hitting the stunned superintendent. Teddy stormed out of the office and building, fed up with the ridicule and humiliation over his difficulties at reading and writing. He wanted to get as far away from the place as he could. He was free at last.

The second he stepped out of the building it felt like a ton of bricks off his shoulders. There would be no more moments of standing before the class with a book in his hand he couldn't read. He never could understand why the teachers would call upon him when they were fully aware of his trouble. He walked away from the school ready to take on whatever destiny had in store for him. Whenever he heard one of his favorite songs by the Beatles, *"Paperback Writer,"* he was reminded of his dreams and fantasies of becoming a novelist. The thought of holding a paperback with his name on it was the ultimate, a dream he never shared with anyone for fear of being mocked and made fun of.

Living next to the Bay Station was good for Nora. She was able to get all her shopping done without having to ask for rides and to venture into Alamosa, where shopping was even better. She planned on being in this home for a while. The six still living at home kept it buzzing. Their friends were constantly over visiting, ranging from young children to teens. Still, Nora missed having her own children running about. She always would. With her teen boys constantly on the go, it was difficult keeping tabs on them. She managed to do that through people she knew about town. Her friends knew all about the Olds and kept Nora in tuned with where the boys were sighted. They, of course, had no idea.

Tío Antonio showered Benny with gifts when her twelfth birthday came on May 29th. He was very attached to her – and she him. Antonio was a gentle man with a large growth on his forehead. He was Ed's uncle and Rose's father and lived these days with Ed near the high school football field in a large, gray stucco, two-story home. He, too, enjoyed his White Port and Tokay. Rose's daughter, who was close to Nora's daughter's age, constantly feuded over who Antonio loved more. It was a battle for his affection and attention.

Summer was on cruise control. Nora loved her new house, waved at friends as they drove by. She went shopping, danced the night away, and was at one with the universe. It had to end, and did when Teddy got into an automobile accident with one of his best friends, the son of Nora's friend Julia. The kids in town called this boy Von Zipper. This nickname was derived from him not accepting bullying from anyone. He was young, strong and prepared to take care of himself and those close to him. Teddy and Von Zipper totaled Julia and Roberto's truck while joy riding in Seven Mile Plaza.

There was a curved road leading into Seven Mile the kids called "Dead Man's Curve." They took the curve too sharply, ripping through a barbed wire fence into a field and rolling several times. The cab was flattened, the truck destroyed. Nora, Julia and Roberto were all relieved that Teddy and Von Zipper weren't badly injured. Each had a turn lecturing the two boys.

The next morning, every muscle and bone ached when Teddy got out of bed. He compared notes when Von Zipper stopped by. Boys will be boys, so they just walked off the aches in their visits into town.

Von Zipper was a real character, Del Norte's first longhaired, hippy type. Dressed in paisley clothes, knee-high moccasin boots and beads, he made a statement wherever he went. He was stocky, determined and took nothing from anyone. Von Zipper was known for taking down grown men when provoked – sometimes two or three at a time. Folks hesitated before provoking or crossing his path. He was also Teddy's protector. Von Zipper wouldn't let anyone mess with him.

The Marquez boys spent the last days of summer cruising around town with their buddies. A couple bucks worth of gas took them everywhere. By August 22nd, Teddy's sixteenth birthday, school had begun, but with him not in it. Dwayne announced his engagement to a girl he had been dating all of his school years. The wedding was set for February.

Days went by for Nora with a heavy heart, seeking consolation in her friends when they gathered and discussed life and motherhood. Their children were leaving and beginning lives of their own as well. All agreed that although being a mother was their most rewarding experience, the heartaches that came with it were equally as challenging.

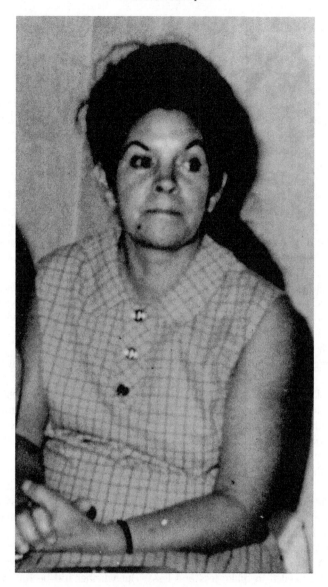

Nora

IN THE POOL HALL, Ed told of his own sadness at seeing the kids grow up, marry and move. His marriage might have ended for all intents and purposes, but Ed remained a loyal and loving father living up to his responsibilities to them.

With all of the children in school come the fall, this gave Nora freedom to do what she wanted. She could spend hours upon hour's downtown visiting with merchants she befriended or sharing coffee or a meal with her friends in local cafes. Nora had always dreamed of the time she'd be free to do the things she enjoyed. She relished every free moment she had nowadays. Many days she simply stayed at home engrossed in her favorite soaps on television. She reflected many times on her favorite song "Downtown".

She also could finally take her time on those monthly get-togethers with other mothers and wives to chat and shared baked goodies. Nora through the years referred to their group as *El Asociar*. After a meeting, Nora always returned home with bagsful of cookies, cakes and breads for her family. Most of the time baking was done in whoever's home hosted the meeting. Only rarely did they meet at Nora's since the others were well aware of her family size and keen responsibilities there.

Nora didn't have to do much for Halloween. For the first time she could remember she wasn't bombarded with costume ideas and wishes. This year it was only the three younger ones out trick-or-treating – but they were mighty excited. The Marquez boys spent the night cruising Main Street, car loaded with friends, radio blasting.

At long last, the Olds pulled up home. The boys made their way through the dark, calling it a night.

The following day Ed showed up, liquor on his breath. Nora was busy cooking dinner over the stove when he sneaked up behind her with a grin. Gently he kissed her on the neck. The kids found it humorous. When Nora turned to see who it was, she grew livid, cursed and ordered him to leave immediately.

With the grin still on his face he left. His love for Nora had never diminished. This was obvious to all who knew him. She reflected on the stunt Cordie pulled on her, wondered what Ed could be up to. Nonetheless, it wasn't going to work. There was no going back. She was a free woman who relished her freedom and was going to keep it that way.

When she cooked the big Thanksgiving dinner over the years, Nora was reminded of how much of her family had gone. She always made plenty, and now she needed to make less and less. But whether it'd be for two dozen or for two, she was determined to put as much love into it as always. The aromas she created in the house always teased the palates.

On Thanksgiving Day, Nora prepared her usual feast for the children and guests. With no grown daughters in the household, what children she did have there were put to work. Nora embedded her cooking skills into her children from the time they could walk. She didn't want them going through life not knowing how to fend for themselves. Anything she knew how to cook and bake she passed on to them, most of it from scratch. Gender was not an issue. Boy or girl. In her opinion they all needed to know the art of survival and that included how to cook.

Lawrence turned thirty one on November 27th in Denver. He called mom that day and generally checked in with her on a regular basis. At times he made the trip down into the valley to visit. With a full-time job in the city, his visits were not as frequent as Nora would have preferred. But now that there was a telephone in the house, at least she could hear from him and most of her children. That phone was the best thing she ever got, and the kids felt the same. The phone constantly rang throughout the day and evening. Sometimes it rang during the night when the boys' friends wanted to talk, and often was a battle as to whose turn it was to use the phone.

Billy called on the 28th, his twenty fifth birthday. He lived in Idaho. By now, Nora and Ed had lost count of how many grandchildren there were. They had never even met some of them. Remembering names was second nature to her, but the birthdays were another matter. Keeping track of her own children's was enough, and she would always remember each and every day that they were born. That was a given.

With no harvest season work or school to keep him occupied, Teddy was a concern. He spent his time with a group of friends he made through the years, and Nora heard rumors that he drank and smoked heavily. She worried for him. He was seldom home, and when he did come home it was late at night only to sleep. Come morning he was up and gone once again.

The Olds was a thing of the past as the boys did not fulfill their promise and agreement with Nora. Thus, she returned the car to the dealer. The boys' hearts were broken. It was a lesson they couldn't grasp at the time, but she hoped in time they would learn the lesson of responsibility. To keep a promise was priority for Nora. For her, a person's word and dignity was all they had. Her heart was heavy in having to make that decision as she knew what the car meant to the boys, but a life lesson was more important and far more valuable. A car could always be replaced.

It took a long time for the boys to come to terms and peace with Nora's decision, but eventually they did. With their friends having cars of their own, they had no trouble getting about town. Besides, the February wedding took priority. There was much to be done. The closer it came, the heavier Nora's heart grew as she knew she say farewell to another of her children. Her son's plan after the wedding was to join the Navy. For that she was grateful as it would give him a foundation for the rest of his life. She'd seen what the military forces had done for Rudy, thus was at peace with it. Her concern was having any of her boys sent into the Vietnam War. It was every mother's concern who had grown sons.

Lawrence and his friend Mack came down from Denver for Christmas. Teddy's wish for more black clothing was satisfied. He'd taken to dressing in all black for quite a while. He always wore a long, black trench coat like his friends. It was the fashion for teens then, along with Beatle Boots and skintight black jeans and black turtle necks. He would throw on a pair of bell bottoms when the mood was there.

Bobby was visiting regularly as the year came to a close. He left his family in Alamosa after not getting along with his stepfather and was living with his grandma in Del Norte. He was far happier now that he was with her. He and Teddy were on the go constantly, had become very close. Bobby was extremely protective of Teddy, to the point if he found a bottle of liquor in his hand he tossed it to the ground shattering it. He didn't like the idea of Teddy drowning his problems in liquor. He had seen enough of what it could do to a person. The love he now had for Teddy wouldn't allow for that. He had not only found a cousin in Teddy, but also a friend for life. He wasn't about to let anything or anyone destroy or hurt that.

Nora was pleased with their relationship. She knew in her heart that he'd take care of Teddy. That was a Christmas gift for her in itself. She had learned long ago the value of having people like Bobby as her friends represented exactly that. She welcomed Bobby with an open heart in their home as well as in their lives.

CHAPTER 40

1968. PRESIDENT JOHNSON STUNS the nation and world with his announcement that he will not run for president again, in a way making himself a political casualty of the war he waged on the battlefield. The Democratic National Convention's attempt to select a candidate erupts in chaos when Chicago police clash with anti-war demonstrators.

Two U.S. athletes make the Black Power salute during ceremonies at the Olympics in Mexico City. The Big Mac goes on sale at McDonald's for 49 cents. The Zodiac serial killer begins his reign of terror in California.

Burning up the airwaves are the Beatles' *"Hey Jude,"* Simon and Garfunkel's *"Mrs. Robinson,"* the Doors' *"Hello, I Love You"* and Marvin Gaye's *"I Heard It Through The Grapevine."* *"Planet of the Apes"* is on the silver screen, the controversial musical *"Hair"* on Broadway.

* * * * *

As HARSH AS WINTER might get, it wasn't Alamosa. Nora was happy for that and for all the conveniences she had. The house was kept cozy with the exception of the back bedroom, which was Teddy's. He made up for it with plenty of thick blankets. When he was home, music poured from a phonograph. His bedroom walls were decorated with 45s he hung on nails for easy access. The albums he stored in a box next to the phonograph. On occasion Nora heard her favorite song *"Downtown"* coming from his room and pause from whatever she was doing to listen and sing along.

Dwayne left for the naval base in San Diego shortly after the wedding. Ed took it particularly hard. He was very close to this son. He, too, was feeling the emptiness as more of his children left the valley. He spent much of his time at the pool hall playing cards, keeping his mind occupied. His group of friends met at the pool hall on a frequent basis. Ed had many friends in Del Norte as he'd lived in the valley all his life, was born and raised there. Although he and Nora were no longer together, having her nearby brought a certain comfort to him. In his heart, he would love Nora forever. That he made clear to several people who knew him. Nora's home seemed unusually quiet after Dwayne left. With five left, she could only wonder who was to be next to leave the nest.

What happened to Nora and Ed was happening all over Del Norte as teens, as soon as they came of age, married and left, replaced on the streets by the elementary kids of yesteryear. Nora, her own youngest girl now eleven, marveled at how quickly some of her friends' children had grown too.

Nora planned a short trip to Denver in May. She not only wanted to see the children but she also what the attraction was. Her children constantly spoke of the many conveniences of living in a large city.

May arrived with Pricilla's thirty eighth birthday on the 8th. Nora's trip to Denver was rapidly coming upon them. She planned to take her two youngest girls and Jimmy along. Andrew still had school, and Teddy was Teddy.

On an early evening in mid-May, Bobby darted into Teddy's bedroom and told him to pack his bags.

Hesitantly, Teddy asked "Why?"

"Because we're going to Los Angeles," Bobby answered.

Teddy was reluctant. He didn't want to leave his mom.

"I've taken care of things with my *Tia* Nora," Bobby said. "And she said it's okay with her."

Teddy couldn't believe it. He went to Nora. Cup of coffee in hand, she told her son, "I want you to leave Del Norte, to get as far away from the valley as possible and make something of yourself."

What Teddy didn't know was that Nora had heard more rumors of his behavior. Her heart broke at the thought of losing another child to the waves of life. But in her heart she knew it was best and that Teddy could be no safer than with Bobby.

On the day he left, Teddy embraced Nora and made a promise – that a day would not begin or end without her hearing the words "I love you" from him. To himself, he vowed in his heart and soul to keep that promise. Nora wept after he left.

As if to delay the inevitable, Teddy asked Junior and Annie, a couple Bobby had befriended and who were making the drive to California with them, to cruise around one last time. On their way out of town Teddy noticed his best friend's black '58 Thunderbird parked at McDonald's and asked to pull over so he could say his goodbyes. When Teddy told his friend he was leaving town and would probably not return, both had tears in their eyes. His friend challenged Teddy on his words, insisting he'd be back within days. He peered over his shoulder as the car drove out of sight.

For forty five minutes Bobby did his best to comfort Teddy, who wept in the back seat – his heart broken for having left Nora, his siblings and his friends behind. He knew deep in his heart that it would be a very long time before he returned. Into the darkness they drove toward Albuquerque bound for L.A. At last, Teddy found sleep through his tears and slept through the night. The humming of the motor and music from the radio were his lullabies.

The next morning, the telephone rang at Nora's.

"I love you," Teddy told her, keeping his promise.

They were in San Bernardino. Teddy had insisted that Junior pull over so he could call. With a lump in his throat Teddy hung up. Tears filled Nora's eyes as she, too, hung up the phone. Not only did the house seem emptier with Teddy gone but also her life did. She had four children left with her. That night, the phone rang.

"I love you." It was Teddy, again. He and Bobby were at the home of a friend of Junior and Annie's. They would be there at least several days, Teddy assured her, and would keep her informed of where they'd be at all times. Teddy assured her he was safe although he missed her and his siblings terribly. She consoled him, telling him to be strong. In heavy thought, Nora laid her head against her pillow and drifted off to sleep.

* * * * *

THE DAY OF THE TRIP to Denver arrived. She and the three youngest boarded a Continental Trailways bus. Reluctantly she sat watching out the window as the bus made its way out of the valley. The kids were too excited to be distracted by anything else but the trip. They chatted among each other while Nora pondered with her thoughts on why she was doing this and hoped she would find all was well in Denver.

Hours later after stopping in nearly every town and city along the way, they pulled into the Denver Bus Depot on Broadway. There to greet them was Becky. Nora and the kids were to stay with her family, returning to Del Norte on Sunday. The kids were in awe as they looked about the city. For them it was enormous. The buildings towered high into the sky unlike they'd ever seen before. People and cars were everywhere. The roar of the city was loud. They drove down streets and avenues finally getting to Becky's place. Excitement filled them.

While in Denver, Nora got to see firsthand what the attraction was for her children living there. She was amazed the first time she went downtown. She, too, was taken by the multitude of conveniences available. She'd never seen so many stores of every variety before. On storefront windows she saw the most beautiful clothing ever. There were even stores that sold just shoes! Every style of shoe was on display. Downtown Woolworths on 16th Street was her favorite. Instinctively she knew she could spend hours upon hours there. Constantly she related to her favorite song. The next two days were an experience for her as well as the children.

Nora, Jimmy and the girls were on a bus bound back for the San Luis Valley before they knew it. Nora was anxious to get back to Del Norte after leaving Andrew on his own for these few days and also wanted to begin the process of a decision she made. The bus ride home was long. The children were tired, weary. They, too, had a very busy weekend enjoying their brief visit to the city. They slept most of the way home.

That evening the bus stopped in front of the Bay Station letting Nora and the kids out. Nora was relieved to step into the house finding Andrew and their home intact. He was glad to see her back because it had been spooky at night for him staying home alone. An active imagination could make nights seem to last forever.

Days later, Nora marked birthday number fifty two. Her mind was occupied with the decision she made in Denver. She hadn't announced it to the kids yet and waited for the right time and place. She did, however, talk to her closest friends about it. It seemed Nora's decision echoed many who lived in Del Norte. Some of her friends felt the same way. Nora's heart was heavy.

The rain showers of June brought lilac bushes exploding with fragrance and color. Nora's friends who knew lilac was one of her favorites brought her bouquets of blossoms to place about her home. Nora missed having lilac bushes in her yard like she once had. Her lilac perfumes made up for it.

Teddy kept calling Nora as promised, also informing her that he and Bobby moved to Duarte, a suburb of Los Angeles. There they found jobs in a place called Chef Raymond's Show House. It was a restaurant-lounge establishment. Bobby was a busboy and Teddy a kitchen helper. Along with the job came the one-bedroom cottage in back of the restaurant. Nora was content in knowing Teddy was doing okay for himself, that he was safe. He gave her telephone numbers to the cottage and restaurant. With the job and cottage came responsibility for the owner's cat. It was a wild, temperamental creature that attacked at the slightest movement.

When Teddy and Bobby were home in the cottage, the cat would sit in a corner and growl, daring either one to make a sudden move. Many a times Teddy was awakened with the ruckus of Bobby in battle in the wee hours of the morning after the cat attacked him while he was asleep. Nora found humor with the situation when Teddy told her about it. Her solution was simple – place the cat outdoors at night, but that was strictly forbidden by Chef Raymond. Chef Raymond found humor in what they were experiencing as though he'd known. Teddy also informed Nora that he and Bobby purchased a 1957 tan Ford Retractable Convertible. They came to know the city in that car, putting the top down and cruising the streets of Los Angeles on their days off.

Nora's kids were shocked when she informed them of her decision – she was moving to Denver herself. While there she got a strong sense of the many opportunities for both her and the kids. Not to mention the conveniences she didn't have in the valley. Although somewhat delighted of the move, the four kids at home were also saddened they'd be leaving their best friends and cousins behind once again. They also couldn't imagine living in a city the size of Denver, much less going to schools there. Denver schools made Del Norte's seem tiny in size and attendance. In many ways that was very scary for them.

While the three younger children were okay with it after awhile, Andrew resisted as he didn't want to leave his sports behind and begin in a whole new school environment. Three of his coaches went to Nora's home and made a proposition that Andrew stay in Del Norte with one of the coaches and his wife while pursuing his promising career in sports. They would cover all expenses and felt with Andrew's participation Del Norte stood the chance of taking first place in the state in basketball and football. He excelled in track as well. Time and time again Andrew had this conversation with Nora trying to convince her otherwise, but to no avail. Nora was not about to leave him behind at age fourteen. She did agree, however, to wait for Andrew's football season to end before making the move.

Cordie turned twenty one on July 8th. For Nora, days were crawling by, but for the children they flew. They couldn't seem to get enough time with their cousins and friends. Nora's friends were also saddened with the news that she was to leave the valley. They would miss her terribly. Nora had been a major part of their lives, throughout their lives. They couldn't imagine the valley without Nora and her family in it. They would miss their nights out dancing around the valley. They would miss their monthly gatherings and visits.

Ed was particularly saddened with the news as he would be virtually alone in Del Norte without his kids. He also knew there was no changing Nora's mind. Once she made a decision it was done. There was no going back. In this respect Nora was much like Rebecca. Nora inherited many of Rebecca's characteristics. Being strong and stubborn was two of them. She would always be in his heart. Although there were other women in his life, none would or could ever compare to Nora.

In the hot days of August, Nora began gathering boxes and packing. This would be the biggest move ever for them. At times she had second thoughts but then realized it was for the better for all her family. She missed her kids who lived in Denver, and if moving there was the only way to be near them, so be it. For them she would do anything. Keeping her family together was top priority. She not only needed them, but they needed her as well.

Nora sorted and packed, donating many of her things to friends. The less she had to pack and take with her the better. With a heavy heart she did all this. She couldn't get the fact that she'd be hundreds of miles from the valley out of her head. She'd never lived far away from what she knew as home. Rudolf's and Rebecca's resting places were in Del Norte, something that weighed on her. She would miss her visits to the graveyard and her private conversations with Rudolf. She couldn't help but feel she was leaving her mom and dad behind. A part of her would always be in the valley, in Del Norte and South Fork. Juanita turned thirty five, Flora thirty seven and the days flew by the closer their move came.

In California, Bobby helped Teddy celebrate his seventeenth birthday on the 22nd with wine coolers, which Junior and Annie introduced them to. They were hooked on them in a flash. The coolers were refreshing for the summer heat. Junior and Annie returned to Colorado a few days later. They tried talking Teddy and Bobby into going back, but the two were having far too much fun to leave. They enjoyed being on their own, responsible for their own lives and decisions. As always, Teddy spoke to Nora on his birthday.

Teddy and Bobby could only watch as their two friends drove down the street out of sight, never to be heard from again. Meantime, life in the cottage and in the Show House went on. They started a savings for whatever they wanted in the future. Being underage limited what they could spend their money on. Movies and eating out were the highlights. Most of their meals were at the restaurant as Chef Raymond had given them a key for access to whatever they needed. He was very good to them.

By September, Nora was nearly finished with all her sorting and packing. In the midst of it all, she still took time for her nights out of dancing with friends. Her high heels and favorite dresses seldom got rest. Whatever opportunity she had to go out dancing she took. It seemed the older she got; the more she enjoyed the dance floor. Music and dancing always took her far from her problems, gave her space to think out solutions for whatever troubled her. In her heart she knew dancing and music would always be a part of her life.

She found comfort in the excitement the children had for the move. She knew for them the change would be difficult, especially changing schools and being around unfamiliar faces. She also knew it wouldn't take them long to make new friends in the city. Hopefully, Andrew would have his fill of sports there as well. This she could only hope for.

Nora made arrangements for Becky and her husband to drive down to move her. They would rent a U-Haul for the purpose. Nora scheduled the move for early October. She wanted to move before winter and the cold set in. She also wanted to keep her promise to Andrew. In her heart that was the least she could have done. His disappointment was obvious. It broke her heart to see it, but she couldn't as a mother leave him behind. She could not find peace with that.

Moving day neared. The kids spent as many hours with their friends and cousins as possible. They were constantly at Nora's house visiting. Nora, too, spent much time with her friends and relatives. The move weighed heavily on the whole family. This time they all sensed it was for good, a reality they all had to face. In solitude Nora would weep, hope that she made the right decision. She often thought of Rudolf and Rebecca, of how she'd miss her visits to them. A new chapter in her life was about to begin.

Finally the day of the move arrived. Becky and her family pulled into the yard as scheduled. Without delay the loading commenced. Box after box and bag after bag were loaded into the U-Haul, along with beds and mattresses, dressers and other belongings. Nora's most treasured item was loaded as well, the trunk from Rebecca. After one last night in Del Norte with friends, Nora and her family were ready.

The following morning they set out for Denver, the U-Haul carrying their lives with them. At times there was silence. Nora as well as the kids felt the emptiness. Already they missed those they had left behind. The kids would watch the scenery as they drove. Denver seemed so very far for them. It seemed they were on the road for hours before they stopped for lunch.

Fall colors speckled the mountains around them. Snowcaps reflected the sunlight, sparkling like a treasure chest of diamonds. The air was much cooler in the higher elevations than it was in the valley. They caught catch sight of deer and other wildlife wandering through meadows, dashing from the sound of traffic. They were beautiful – awesome.

Eventually, they drove over the final hill that led them into the city limits of Denver. Nora sighed as she gazed over the vast community. She could only wonder what her life would be like living here. There was so much to do and see, so many people to meet so many places to dance. Some of her daughters had spoken to her of places she'd probably enjoy. But Nora's main objective was getting her family into their home and settled. They were to stay with Becky and her family for a short period until suitable housing was found.

Nora's belongings were put into storage while she looked. For two weeks she searched until she found temporary housing on the west side of Denver on 6th and Osceola. They quickly moved in. Nora knew within herself it was temporary as it was not what she truly wanted for her family. Her next task was getting the kids enrolled into schools and back on schedule. Once their schools were situated, Nora began unpacking what she'd need in the short time they'd be there. Her eyes were set on a place closer to downtown. If she was going to live in the city, she wanted to be as close to its heart as possible. Osceola not only didn't feel right, it was also too inconvenient for what she needed.

Halloween was spent on Osceola. Andrew had his sixteenth birthday there on November 13th. The kids did well in their new schools, also making new friends. Gradually all were adjusting to their new environment. City living was totally new to them. They dared not venture far from home in the beginning. Little by little the kids got acquainted with their neighborhood one block at a time.

On Thanksgiving, Becky came over, as did Lawrence, who turned thirty two on the 27th. Billy turned twenty six a day later. Nora's home was abuzz with activity for dinner. The kids ate to their heart's content, their adrenaline still going high from their recent move. They just couldn't get over that they were actually living in Denver. Life was good for all.

Nora came across a home on Court Place on the East Side. The moment she set foot in the neighborhood she sensed it was the right place. She couldn't wait to get into the house. This, of course, meant the kids changing schools again, but that was the least of her worries. She was more concerned about getting them into a permanent housing situation than anything else.

So by the end of November, just a month after taking the house on Osceola, they moved again. The house on Court Place was a little smaller than she wanted, but it would serve its purpose – for now. Nora had her eye on a house down the street that would be available before long. Nora knew in her heart that it was the home for them. It was merely a matter of time. Meantime, Nora made do. She was close to downtown, within walking distance if she chose. Otherwise, there were city buses to use.

Nora's daughters were right – they introduced her to places she totally enjoyed for dancing and nights out. The music suited her well. In some places bands came from all over to play for the weekend. Most of these establishments were jam packed Friday and Saturday nights. Nora began making friends of her own and spent hours dancing her heart away.

The Christmas season was unlike anything Nora had ever seen. Signs of the holidays were everywhere. Storefront displays caught every person's attention walking by. The skating rink at the May D&F was a popular place; the music could be heard a block from it. Many stood around the rink enjoying the view. While downtown, Nora would often pause to take a look herself. There were so many things to see on 16th Street downtown. The traffic was unbelievable. She'd never seen so many vehicles and people. There were theaters, cafés and restaurants by the dozen. For her it was pure excitement.

For hours she walked up and down 16th Street going in and out of stores. She usually ended up at Woolworths in the café downstairs, where she met folks to sit and chat with. Woolworths was a favorite for many – it was always packed. Christmas music pumped throughout the store was soothing for her, got her in the spirit. She browsed up and down aisles for gifts for the children and others in the family. There was so much to choose from. In her heart she knew moving to Denver was the right thing to do. She was at peace with her decision.

Nora spent many hours on many days downtown shopping for Christmas. In her home they set up the tree, decorating it with familiar decorations from the valley. It made them homesick just seeing the pieces and recalling memories of Christmases past. Nora recalled her last Christmas with Rebecca as she sat at the tree in her quiet moments.

Teddy lost contact with Nora during this time. He didn't have a new phone number for her, and in not having sibling telephone numbers was left to wonder and worry. Common sense told him she was okay, that she was capable of taking care of herself and his siblings. Still, he worried. Nora didn't call and let him know her new number because she had misplaced his. They were nowhere to be found.

Bobby kept him busy cruising L.A., going into Hollywood on numerous occasions. They discovered the Golden Cup on Hollywood Boulevard, a hamburger stand where youths from every walk of life hung out. There they met runaways as young as fourteen living on the streets. For them Hollywood Boulevard was a circus. They saw everything imaginable – sometimes stopping in their tracks in sheer amazement.

A week before Christmas, Teddy and Bobby were at work. It was a typical day for them. Teddy worked hard in the kitchen trying to keep up with dirty dishes, while helping the cook whenever he had time. Bobby made his way in and out of the kitchen waiting on diners, carrying trays of glasses filled with water or coffee pots for refills. Regardless of how busy they were they always found time for humor. Their laughter could always be heard in the kitchen or dining room, wherever they were. Bobby's sense of humor was enjoyed by all who met him.

On this particular day while Teddy was carrying a large tray of clean glasses, he suddenly lost his balance, the glasses crashing to the floor. The building shifted, shook and swayed. From the dining room, Bobby screamed and ran into the kitchen. All they could do was hold on to each other, unable to comprehend what was happening. They ran for the door.

Just then Chef Raymond grabbed both by the arms, pulled them back and warned that going outside was the wrong thing. They were in an earthquake! He made them stand in a doorway instead, a safe place. Teddy and Bobby panicked but stayed. They had heard of earthquakes but never imagined being in one. It took Chef Raymond quite some time to calm them down.

They retreated into the cottage after work. Still shaken, they couldn't stop talking about what they'd been through. There were traces of damage down the street. The two couldn't sleep at all that night, tossing and turning, wondering when it would happen again. By morning they came to a decision: They were heading back to Colorado. There was no way they wanted to experience another earthquake like they had. Their minds were made up.

The first thing they did when they walked into the restaurant was tell Chef Raymond they were leaving as soon as possible. Chef Raymond was very disappointed as he valued them and the work they did for him. They were hard working and dependable. But he also understood. He recalled his first experience in a quake. He could relate only too well, although he wasn't nearly as young as Teddy and Bobby at the time.

For the following days, Teddy and Bobby explored ways to get back to Colorado. They thought of flying, but both had terrible fears of that. They thought of the bus, but the idea of sitting on one for two days didn't appeal to them either. They finally settled on Amtrak. A train ride would be a totally new experience for them. Besides, they wouldn't be confined to their seats. They were pumped, excited for their new adventure.

First thing they had to do was dispose of what their belongings. All they were taking was their clothes. The rest they gave to people walking by the restaurant. Their '57 Ford, that, too, they gave to a stranger walking by, signing over the title to him. The stranger was dumbfounded. They were not taking chances on driving it to Colorado and perhaps getting stranded on the way. They were both sorry to let the car go, but the only thing on their minds was getting as far from L.A. as possible.

The following day they were at the train station, debating. Bobby was afraid the train might derail. It took Teddy forever it seemed before he could talk Bobby into boarding the train before it left them behind. Once on, Bobby walked from one car to the other. In no time he befriended two youths on their way cross country. That helped ease his fears and concerns.

After a sunset and sunrise, they arrived in Trinidad, Colorado, where they changed into an older train. That, too, was an experience for them. Being grateful that they were now in Colorado, they eagerly gazed out the window watching as the train made its way toward Denver. All the while they laughed and joked. The snow was a change. It seemed very strange to see homes in L.A. decorated with Christmas decorations and no snow. Santa and his reindeer on plush, green lawns were very unusual for them. They were happy to see snow again.

Finally the train pulled into the station in Denver. A blast of cold air hit them when they stepped out of the building. They had to pull out clothes from their suitcases. They were not prepared for the cold, had forgotten what Colorado winters were like. Still, they were pleased to be home.

On city buses they made their way to the last known address Teddy had for Nora, the home on Osceola. After changing buses they finally found the address. To their surprise the house was empty. They were at a loss. It was Bobby who called information at a phone booth, finding one of Teddy's siblings' telephone number. They called, got Nora's new address and headed to the East Side. It was Christmas Eve. Darkness began to cover the city.

Through the cold they found Nora's home, paused in front to make sure it was the right address. They knocked. When the door opened and Andrew stood there, they knew they were home for sure. Familiar aromas poured from the kitchen. The table was set for dinner. They walked into the dining room. There stood Nora. The delighted look on her face when she saw Teddy was worth all he'd been through. Instantly he embraced her. She'd been so worried about him since they hadn't been in touch and was grateful that he was safe and home, where he belonged.

Without delay a place was set for Teddy and Bobby. Happiness surrounded the table as they all sat to eat. Nora's heart was fulfilled on this night. All her worries were at ease. It wasn't long before other members of the family stopped by, bringing bags and boxes of gifts for the family. They, too, sat at the dinner table to enjoy the meal Nora lovingly prepared. Nora couldn't think of a better Christmas than this. It was going to be a wonderful holiday. In her heart she thanked whatever powers that be for bringing her family together on this night. The stars were on her side. She was more content than she'd been in a very long time. The smile on her face spoke for itself.

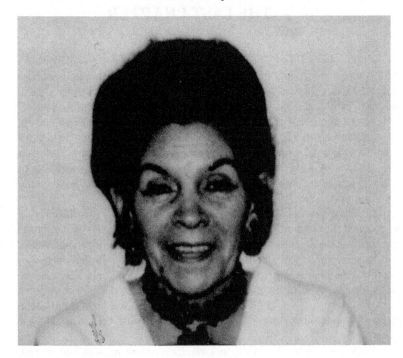

Nora

THE LAST CHAPTER

NORA LIVED ON COURT Place into the 1970s. Early in that decade, both Andrew and Jimmy married and left home. Nora's wish for the house down the block came to be. She and her two remaining children lived there happily. Teddy on occasion stayed with her while going to the Hollywood School of Beauty and other academies working on a cosmetologist license. He shared an apartment with friends on Capitol Hill off and on. He kept his promise to Nora, calling her every morning as she rose and every night before she went to bed, and throughout the day. He did this regardless of what he was doing and where he was. Friends who knew him were totally aware of this.

In July 1973, Bobby was found dead in the Del Norte jail. Speculation surrounded his death as many who knew Bobby were aware of the threats the cops gave him upon sight with a simple wave of the finger pointing at him in warning. It was said he committed suicide, but folks had their own interpretation of what had truly happened. He was found on the floor of the cell with the sleeve of his windbreaker tied around his neck. The attorney working on the case vanished without a word, never to be heard from again. Bobby's grandmother cursed the cops, taking his demise very hard. He was her world.

Days after Bobby's funeral in Del Norte where he was laid to rest, Teddy left for Las Vegas with friends Emil and Dan. He had to get way to grieve. Losing Bobby was the most devastating thing he'd ever been through. He was lost without him. They stayed in Las Vegas for a month before driving across country, landing in Atlantic City, New Jersey, where they stayed for several more weeks before Teddy returned to Colorado. Eventually he finished school after completing a nine-month course in three years. His difficulty in reading and writing was a hindrance. To pass his tests, he memorized what he needed to know.

Nora lived contentedly on Court Place having no more to contend with than the average mother. With teenage daughters in the household she was kept on her toes. Living on Court Place was everything Nora had hoped it'd be. She was very close to downtown, which she took full advantage of. She was down there nearly every day meeting up with friends at Woolworths. She related more to her favorite song "Downtown" now than ever.

She met a man and had a close relationship until he left the country. That was hard on Nora as she cared for him dearly. She also became a grandmother to her first racially mixed grandchild, whom she adored. Although all her grandchildren were special to her in every way, this grandchild was immediately attached to Nora in ways the others weren't. The bond was tight.

In 1976, Nora moved to the Stapleton Projects on 52nd and Broadway in Globeville, a suburb in northeast Denver. It was further from town than Nora wanted, but the bus stop was just outside her doorstep, very easy access for her. Nora's brother Henry lived in Globeville just a short distance from her. That was a plus for her as well.

Fabián came into Nora's life during this time. He was a gentle and compassionate man from Mexico who loved her immensely. There was nothing he wouldn't do for Nora. He was hard working and devoted. He spoke no English. When all the children were on their own, Nora and Fabián lived a content, quiet and happy life. Even when health issues arose from the onset of kidney failure, he worked religiously on a daily basis and made sure Nora had all she needed. His attentiveness was almost to a fault.

On holidays Nora's home was packed with family visiting. She was surrounded by grandchildren of every age. They loved and cherished her. She also became a great-grandmother. She was radiant.

With Teddy a licensed cosmetologist, Nora had a new hairdo whenever she needed or wanted. It was during those occasions that she opened up to Teddy telling him stories of her past. She shared many of her precious memories with him. Stories he took to heart, would become a major part of his future and life. Because of that bond, she passed to him the treasured trunk Rebecca gave her so many years ago.

In Globeville, like in all the places before that, Nora was notorious for her sense of style and grace. She took pride in her appearance from the time of her youth. Growing older only enhanced this quality. The first thing she did each day was put her make-up on, comb her hair and pick out an outfit. Jewelry was her trademark. Her collection grew hugely through the years. She filled a new and bigger trunk with it, acquiring yet another for the overflow.

So very often she thought back on her life and all its changes. She'd been through the Great Depression, World War II, the Korean War and Vietnam War. She'd seen dance crazes of all types – the Charleston and Swing, Twist, Mash Potato, Locomotion, Jerk and Saturday Night Fever disco. She couldn't help but wonder what tomorrow would bring. She'd seen fashion go through dramatic changes over the decades, sometimes shocking the older generations. She found beauty in all of this, taken pleasure in youths expressing themselves through music, dance and fashion as she once did.

Nora, nearing seventy, moved in the early 1980s with Fabián to West Denver to rent the basement in Lawrence's home. Fabián needed dialysis three times a week. Nora still made daily trips downtown to Woolworths to meet with friends for lunch, many times taking a grandchild along. She had small grandchildren who adored her, wanted to spend as much time with her as possible. Thus, she took them on shopping expeditions' whenever possible. She loved the time spent with them. For the grandchildren it was a joy just being with her where they felt safe. Nora's bond with many of her grandchildren was very close. Her granddaughters in particular looked up at her through eyes of admiration. The bonds she formed with them would last a lifetime.

During this time, Nora was diagnosed with diabetes. It came as a shock. She thought feeling tired, dozing off wherever she sat, was just a sign of old age. She eventually was placed on insulin. Giving herself injections was difficult in the beginning, but like anything that must be done she dealt with it. Diabetes introduced her to a whole new world of challenges. She had to give up many of her favorite foods, some she ate in strict moderation. Changing her diet was a challenge of its own. As always, she did what had to be done.

On sunny days, Nora and Fabián sat in Lawrence's back yard among the aspen and pine. Lawrence's love for nature and plants reflected in his home. It was filled with plants of various sorts. The back yard was his pride and glory. He spent many hours there. For the most part, Nora and Fabián were content living with Lawrence. She was surrounded by loved ones.

Nora

Theodore Marquez

CHRISTINE DIED ON AUGUST 5, 1984. A brokenhearted Nora gazed into the coffin and wept at the funeral in Albuquerque, reliving all they had been through. She had lost her only sister – and also her first and dearest friend. Nora's heart and soul ached.

Nora left Albuquerque with emptiness much like she felt when she lost Rudolf and Rebecca. She knew her life had changed once more forever. Not to have Christine on the planet available to her by a mere phone call would take some getting used to. The family she grew up with was dwindling before her very eyes. It was the thought of her own children that pulled her through these difficult times. It was through her children that she drew strength – and they drew strength from her as well.

Nora's family held their first family reunion in the San Luis Valley in August of 1986. It was a four day weekend of joyous times and reflection. Nora made connection with many of her grandchildren and great-grandchildren. Family members from everywhere joined in the festivities. Ed, too, took part in it all. As Nora sat in the midst of it all, she was amazed at the legacy she and Ed had created. Literally there were hundreds present at the reunion, all of their seed. The pride she felt was only rivaled by the love she held for her family.

Nora and Fabián lived with Lawrence for a few years, then moved to a duplex next door to one of Nora's daughters. Nora was pleased with her move and living next door to her girl. She spent some wonderful birthdays and holidays there surrounded by her loved ones. It seemed at all times family was over to visit. She was seldom left alone. Her diabetes, although in control, was taking its toll. She struggled with complications and doubted there would ever be peace and harmony with the disease. Although she learned the art of cooking accordingly for herself, there were times that even that wasn't enough to keep the illness in check. The periods she was free from effects of the diabetes were times she relished.

In January 1988, she suddenly collapsed and fell to the floor unconscious while cooking lunch with a young granddaughter. The distraught girl ran next door for help. Within minutes the paramedics were there. They found her on the floor, skin blue from lack of oxygen. Her heart had stopped.

She was administered CPR and rushed to the hospital. It was chaos to say the least. Word spread. It wasn't long before the halls of the hospital were filled with Nora's family awaiting the verdict of her condition. News came that Nora had had a heart attack and was in a coma. All that could be done was being done. Meantime, the family could only wait and worry. They were devastated. No one was allowed to see Nora until further notice. The stress for the family was immeasurable, the worst thing they'd ever been through. It was a nightmare.

Outside, a blizzard hit the Denver area causing major difficulties for those coming to town. Flights were canceled by most airlines. Streets were impassable, leaving some to walk to the hospital through the intense elements.

Days went by. Nora's family remained in the hallways and lobbies of the hospital awaiting news. Until Nora came out of the coma, no one could be say for sure of the damage done from the attack. Finally those from out of town or state were able to make it in. They, too, could only wait and worry. Days were long, nights longer for those sleeping on hospital sofas and chairs. The hospital cafeteria made a small fortune from Nora's family during this time. For many, having lunch was an escape from the stress and worry if even for a short time. In groups they ventured into the cafeteria, and then returned to the floor to wait and worry more. Emotions ran high, sometimes conflicting.

Days turned into a week. Still Nora was not out of the coma. That week turned into two, then three, and then at long last she came out of it. Rejoicing swept through the family at the news. Nora was dazed and confused, could only gaze about the room wondering where she was and what had happened. The family was relieved when they were finally able to see her. Hugs and kisses were bountiful, as were tears of joy.

When Nora's bed was adjusted to a sitting position, the first thing she asked for were her dentures. When she was told that her daughter had them at her house and would bring them back soon, Nora disputed that. She insisted she saw the paramedic who administered CPR pull them from her mouth and place them into his coat pocket. No matter how the children tried to reason with her, Nora was adamant.

Nora's children could only look at each other wondering how it was possible that she knew this. And she turned out to be right. The paramedic had put the dentures right where she said. What puzzled Nora's children was that she was unconscious and her heart had stopped.

Overjoyed with having Nora safe and with them, they dismissed the incident. They were far too pre-occupied in having their mother, grandmother and great-grandmother back. Everyone breathed a sigh of relief. The incredible stress the family had been under was finally lifted. Joy was in its place.

Their confusion turned to new worry when she asked for Rudolf and other deceased people. When questioned why, she stated Rudolf had been in her room visiting shortly before the family arrived, as did the others she asked for. No matter how Nora's kids tried to reason with her, she insisted Rudolf and the others had visited. Nora said she had a good visit with her father, and he stepped down the hall prior to her kids arriving. Doubt and speculation filled the room. Some actually were led to believe in what Nora had told them. After all, who were they to say it never happened just because it had never happened to them? Nora stood firmly to her words, was not budging.

The following days Nora continued to recover, although her short-term memory was affected. Doctors said that would change with time. The doctors also said Nora's life expectancy would be five years give or take, which put a thorn in the good news they had been celebrating but wasn't enough to keep them from just being grateful at having her back.

As Nora rested and recovered, she complained that little people went to her room at all hours of the night. The kids dismissed this as nurses making their rounds, but Nora had her own theories. She denied the little people visiting her were nurses or orderlies. This left much to speculate and ponder. What Nora experienced was only for her to know. She left it up to each of her kids to believe her or not. Within her own heart she knew the truth. Since that day Nora always said her fears of leaving the planet had vanished. She was at total peace with it.

Nora

NOT LONG AFTER NORA recovered, she and Fabián moved to another duplex on Grove Street. The two of them lived there happily. But her trips downtown came to a halt. She just wasn't the same after the heart attack, nor did she trust going to and from town on her own. That didn't stop her from doing things that needed to get done. Fabián drove them about town at will. They were constantly on the go. She was living life to its fullest, spending as much time with her family as possible. Although she didn't see all her children as much as she wanted, those who were there showered her with affection and attention. Each holiday was celebrated as though it were the last. Nothing was to stand in the way. Most of her kids saw to that. There were those few who missed out on special moments, never to be recaptured.

At Grove Street, Teddy gave Nora a phonograph stereo with a 45 record of *"Downtown"* on it. Nora played the record over and over. She would never get enough of the song. On quiet days when she was alone she played the record, singing along with it. She had other records and albums she played as well, many of which were her old favorites from way back when. Her love for music would never diminish.

She and Fabián danced to those favorites in private sometimes. In knowing her love for dancing he wasn't about to deny her of those moments. He fulfilled them himself. Other times they would merely sit in front of the television holding hands. She was an avid wrestling fan. Her excitement when she watched the matches was uncanny. She was more excited than anyone else in the room.

With the onset of spring came news that Ed, seriously ill, was in a nursing home in Del Norte. Much of the family drove to the valley and was able to see him. On March 22, 1989, shortly after he was admitted, Ed died. He was eighty three. It sent shock waves through the family. Nora relived all the years she spent with him upon getting the news. She was concerned about her children and what this would do to them. One by one the family departed to Del Norte for the services being held in the Catholic Church.

Ed

IN HER OWN WAY, Nora was devastated as well. After all, she and Ed did have an incredible past they shared. Sorrow filled her heart not only for those years she spent with him, but for the pain in her children's hearts. Life seemed brief to her as she gazed down into his casket. She recalled so much – the good, the bad and the in-between. She was grateful for all he had given her – her kids.

After the funeral at the dinner, Hueso approached Nora and said it was time to bury the hatchet. Nora informed Hueso she had buried the hatchet in her back years ago. That it was because of her that Nora's kids grew up without a daddy. It was because of her that her marriage had so much turbulence. As Hueso placed her hand on Nora's shoulder, Nora warned her to move it immediately or get smacked. She told Hueso she would never forgive her for the harm she brought to her and her family. She would never forget the hardships she caused.

Hueso walked away, remorse across her face. It was as though she finally realized all she did to Nora. Her heart was heavy.

Ed was laid to rest in the Del Norte Cemetery.

This was a solemn day for Nora's kids. Losing their father devastated many of them. They were left to wonder what life would be like without him. He would be missed dearly. The hall was crowded with those who went by to pay their respects as Ed was well known in the community. Many were stunned to see Nora there in all her radiance. Some gawked, only to find something for which to gossip. To Nora it didn't matter. She was there for her kids, not to please anyone else. She held her head high, dressed in her best as usual.

Nora left Ed's funeral with heavy thoughts. She worried for her kids as she knew what it was like losing a parent. Reflections of her life with Ed flashed before her often. His passing was like an awakening, making her realize even more just how precious life was. And how precious all her children were to her regardless. Nothing would ever change that. Nothing could or would ever destroy the love she carried for each of her children. That love was part of her soul, the very core of her being. No sacrifice she ever made was too small or great for them. She'd do it all over again.

As time progressed, so did Nora's diabetes. Her struggles with it became an everyday challenge. Although it didn't keep her from living her life to its fullest, it was bothersome. Doctors told her in having so many children her body had been depleted. That in itself had been a sacrifice. She never gave it a second thought as her children were priority over all else. She would have sacrificed anything for them.

Christmas Eve 1992 Nora was admitted to the hospital with complications from the diabetes. In a matter of minutes family members were at her side. It was a solemn time. Christmas was Nora's favorite holiday since childhood, even more so when she had children of her own. Although all her children were grown and gone, Christmas remained her favorite. The worried look on her children's faces at the hospital concerned her. She didn't want to worry them or cause them grief of any sort.

On Christmas Day, Teddy arrived at the hospital with gift in hand. As he greeted her with a kiss and an "I love you," he handed her the package. She tore away the wrapping to find a blue sequined dress. She spread it across her lap, running her hands over the fine fabrics. It was beautiful. Something he knew Nora would look sensational in. She held it up to her body, carefully placing it back into the box, and then said, "I wonder if I'll ever get to wear it?"

Those words burned into Teddy's heart. It was though Nora knew or sensed something he and the family didn't. He assured her she would not only wear it but also look beautiful in doing so.

Two days later Nora was released. The family was relieved. It was quite a scare for them all. They were grateful she was home in her own environment where she wanted to be. Nora's family was constantly at her house visiting and checking in on her. All wanted these holidays to be especially special for her. A Christmas tree was set up in the front room and her home decorated as she loved seeing it. The doctors' orders were for her to get plenty of rest. The family planned a New Year's Eve party in Lakewood. They wanted desperately to put the latest incident behind them, needed a time of joy and laughter.

Many of the children stopped by Nora's on their way to the party. Nora was joyful, although tired, weary. They attributed it to her stay in the hospital and what she'd been through. Nora wanted them to stay longer, but they thought it best to let her get the rest required. Their joy and laughter at the party felt tainted. There was a shadow of despair over the evening. Although the family tried to enjoy themselves, they couldn't get into the swing of things. Something just wasn't right.

The following morning, the telephone rang at Teddy's downtown high-rise apartment, rousing him out of sleep. It was Fabián. He told Teddy he couldn't get Nora out of bed, that she was unresponsive. Within minutes Teddy was up and out the door and down the elevator on his way to Nora's home – his heart heavy with foreboding. Tears filled his eyes, some streaking down the sides of his face.

When he arrived with his friend Randy, Fabián escorted Teddy to Nora. She was lying on her side. Nora did her best to sit up when she noticed him. She was weak, her skin discolored. Teddy's heart sank as it sensed the inevitable. He motioned Randy to dial 911. With her hand in his, Teddy spoke.

"Mom, I don't know what I'd ever do if anything happened to you." Tears rolled down his face.

"You cry too much," she said. "Why do you have to cry so much? Be happy."

"What am I going to do if anything happens to you? How can I ever be happy without you?"

"You'll be okay. This is what you do. You go to your brothers and sisters and tell them to be kind and good to each other. Not to fight. Take care of each other. That's all I want."

Within minutes the paramedics arrived. Teddy stood aside while they placed her on a gurney for departure to the hospital emergency. Teddy was distraught with grief. He watched over the paramedics' shoulders as they loaded Nora into the back of the ambulance.

"Where are my children?" Nora cried out. "I need my children. I want my children."

The words echoed in Teddy's mind as they drove her away. He sobbed uncontrollably, as though the tears would never cease. It wasn't long before the hospital waiting rooms and hallways were crowded with Nora's enormous family. The news was Nora had lapsed into a coma after a massive heart attack. Her organs began to fail. Crying was everywhere as the family stood in shock. Not being allowed to see her during this crucial time was the most difficult part of it all, everyone knowing she was somewhere in the hospital and not being able to be at her side when she needed them most. A thickness of sorrow and sadness filled the air.

Throughout the day Nora's children and family waited, some pacing the hallways waiting desperately for positive news. Nora remained comatose. The kids were frustrated, hurt beyond measure. They wanted only to be at her side. Still, doctors would not allow Nora visitors. By evening the family was told to go home and try getting rest. They'd be notified if any changes occurred. The anxiety and stress were overwhelming.

That night at Nora's home, her kids gathered in prayer. They planned to stay there, close to the hospital, also close to Nora's belongings. Their mother's presence filled the house. Her jewelry displayed on the dresser took on new meaning. The scent of her perfume lingered in her bedroom, on her bedding. Her robe hung on the closet door. Her bedroom slippers set below it. It was heartbreaking for all.

They finally settled in for the night wherever they found place. Some slept on chairs Nora had in her room and in the living room. The girls rested next to each other in Nora's bed. All were trying hard to make sense of what was going on, yet nothing made sense no matter which way they looked at it. It was an emotional roller coaster ride, with an unpredictable end in sight. Finally, an eerie quiet filled the house. Some drifted off to sleep. Others laid or sat in the darkness in heavy thought.

Early on the first day of 1993, while breakfast plans were being made, a call came through. Everyone was requested at the hospital as soon as possible. Nora's condition had declined through the night. The kids piled into vehicles and headed for the hospital. The silence was deafening.

Chaos met them at the hospital. Other family members had already arrived, filling the waiting areas and hallways once again. Doctors were still not allowing visitors. Breakfast was at the hospital cafeteria that morning. With nothing to do but wait, all everyone could do was visit and hope for the best. After breakfast it was back to the waiting area to wait and pace more. It was tormenting.

Occasionally, Nora's doctors updated the family, bringing no good news. The only thing they wanted the doctors to say was that Nora had made it through and was going to be okay. It was a hope all of Nora's family clung to. Hope was all they had at this point. As if to escape the heaviness, some family members roamed the hospital looking desperately for diversions. There were none. There was no escaping the pain and sorrow all were enveloped in. All they could do was lean on each other, comfort one another when needed.

As the day lingered on, more and more family members arrived at the hospital. People who observed were amazed at the size of Nora's family, could only wonder and guess how many were present. More than one waiting area was used.

In the background, Fabián stood in silence, his heart shattered beyond anything he'd ever experienced. He, too, only wanted to be at Nora's side. He knew the words that might bring some comfort to her. Doctors only said that Nora would or could not understand anything in her current condition. She was heavily sedated, in a deepened coma.

As the long and heavy day drew to a close, some family members retrieved to their homes for rest or to attend to their own family needs. Many remained in waiting areas refusing to leave. If anything they wanted Nora to feel their energy, to know she was not alone. It was going to be a very long night for all. Some found sleep on sofas and chairs, while others paced the hallways unable to catch a moment's peace. Minutes seemed to crawl by, lasting forever.

When the sun dawned on January 2nd Nora's doctors came out. The children were directed into a private room to discuss the circumstance. A decision had to be made. The silent atmosphere spoke for itself. The doctors told the children that Nora's organs were failing and that they had to decide whether to disconnect the machines that were keeping her alive. Down the line the daunting question was posed to each one. However difficult, it was a unanimous decision to unplug the machines and set their mother free. Her suffering had lasted long enough.

Once the machines were unplugged the family would be able to see her. Due to the size of Nora's family, two at a time were to be allowed into the room for their goodbyes. A silence swept over the family when they heard this. Many broke down into tears. Two by two they entered the room. It took hours for all the dozens of family members to go through.

Incredibly, Nora had nineteen living children and nearly three hundred fifty grand, great-grand children, and great-great grand children.

Teddy was the last to enter Nora's room. Hand in hand he walked down the hallway with one of his sisters. His heart pounded with each step. It was the longest walk of his life. He feared what he'd find the second he stepped into her room and wondered if he were strong enough to withstand the shock and trauma. He squeezed his sister's hand tightly.

A nurse stood next to the monitors beside Nora's bed as Teddy and his sister entered. Teddy's heart broke when he saw his mother. He lost his breath, hurried to her bedside to take her hand in his. Nora's hand twitched. He glanced up. Releasing Nora's hand, he stepped up to the nurse with a questioning look. The nurse knew what he meant.

"She's just hanging on. She won't let go for some reason."

Teddy knew what the nurse meant. He went back to Nora's side, taking her hand back in his. He whispered into Nora's ear.

"Mom. We love you. We're all here. Try to relax. Don't be afraid to let go. It's okay. We'll all be fine. We love you and always will. You'll never be forgotten. I'll tell the rest what you want me to. But for now, try to relax. Don't be afraid to cross over. There are people waiting for you on the other side. I promise, I'll tell the others what you want them to know. We'll be good and kind to each other. We love you, Mom. We always will."

Nora's eyes opened. She gazed deeply into Teddy's. He was stunned. Her gaze seared into his memory forever. Seconds later, she closed her eyes again and faded away. Teddy glanced up to the nurse. She nodded as though to confirm Nora had, indeed, left the planet. She was seventy six years old.

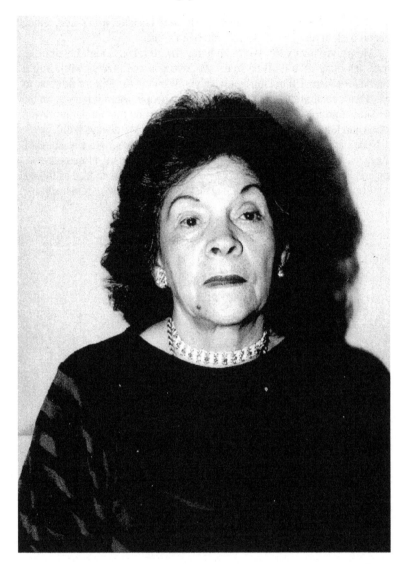

Nora

IT WAS THE SADDEST moment in Teddy's life, but also one of his happiest. Nora would suffer no longer. Her days of Insulin, needles and struggles were over. He drew a deep breath, kissing her on the forehead. He and his sister walked out of the room, down the hallway. The second the family was in sight, he threw his arms in the air letting them know it was over. Although Teddy's heart was shattered, there was a smile on his face.

Nora's body would be moved into a private area for viewing. Meantime, the family did their best to comfort each other through their tears. Many embraced. They had lost a mother, grandmother, great-grandmother, great-great grandmother, and most of all a best friend. Without Nora, life would never be the same. The sadness was overwhelming.

Once Nora's body had been moved, all the siblings were notified and led into the room first. Their mom lay covered with a sheet. She looked at peace, as though she were sleeping. While the doctors spoke, Teddy stood at Nora's feet, caressing them gently, lovingly. Her body was still warm. Voices around him became echoes as he delved into his deepest thoughts of how life without Nora would be for him. She was his world, his everything. Still, he was so very grateful that she was no longer suffering.

For the family, Nora's passing was emotional and at times confrontational. Under tremendous stress and grief, the children struggled to keep their composure. That night several daughters spent the night at Nora's home. The family was exhausted, needed rest more than anything. Although sleep was shallow, some managed it. Others tossed and turned, awakening during all hours. It was beyond belief that Nora was gone forever. It just wouldn't sink in. A haunting stillness went over the city that Nora loved so dearly. It was bitter cold out. City lights twinkled through the frozen air in multi-colors like so many diamonds, rubies and emeralds. The night skyline was one of Nora's favorite scenes.

The following days were spent at Nora's home sorting through her belongings. With hearts filled with grief, the children did it. Going through her closets sorting through her favorite dresses and clothing was especially painful. Each garment had its own special memories. Nora's scent lingered on each one. Her presence was felt. She seemed to be everywhere.

All of Nora's precious items were divided among her family. The collection of jewelry in the trunk and elsewhere was passed on to Teddy, along with other pieces of jewelry. He took them to his apartment. Her collection of beautiful dresses and high heels was divided among the women. Each pair of heels held special memories of Nora's dancing at points of her life. The children broke down into tears while sorting through Nora's things. It was heartbreaking for them all. On the door of Nora's closet hung the blue, sequined dress Teddy gave her for Christmas. It tore into those who saw it, especially him.

Days later, some of Nora's daughters and Teddy were at the mortuary preparing Nora. Her hair had to be just right, along with the make-up and dressing. Teddy did her hair while the girls did her make-up. Next, the blue dress was slipped onto her. She looked beautiful. Nora had always specified to her children that when this day came, under no circumstances were they to spend outlandish amounts on a casket. They were to purchase the least costly one available, which was what was done. But Nora's daughters dressed the casket with satin and silks, personalizing it and making it look like a million dollars. Doing Nora's hair, make-up and dress helped with the grieving. Tears were shed, but so was laughter found in the midst of sorrow. When all was done, Nora and her casket looked incredible – just as she would have wanted it.

Leaving the mortuary was saddening for Nora's children. Leaving Nora behind was daunting for them all. Nora had a unique and special relationship with each of her children. As with any family there were rocky times, but Nora found forgiveness for all her children as any mother would. Regardless of what may have ever transpired, she always found the peace and forgiveness. The intense love she had for all her children was a testimony of her life. Nothing ever changed that through the decades of high heels and diapers. Her memories, her legacy would be shared among her loved ones for all time.

Arrangements were made for Nora's children to transport her body to Del Norte, where she would be laid to rest next to Rudolf. Days later, a caravan of mourners followed Jimmy's truck as it transported their mother on Highway 285 to Del Norte. It was a gray day, the trip dismal, the sadness haunting.

For hours they traveled down the highway reliving the past they shared with her. Nora had left the planet far too soon for them. They still had so much to share with her. The trip was surreal, like a dream they wished never would come, and from which there was no awakening. At times the silence in the vehicles was deafening. Thoughts were heavy.

Finally they drove into Del Norte, pulling into the chapel where Nora's body would lie for those who wished to see her. It was on Main Street, not far from the Bay Station where Nora last lived in Del Norte. Memories filled everyone's minds as Nora's casket was carried into the quaint, quiet chapel.

Late that afternoon the chapel doors opened. Locals who knew Nora stepped in to pay their respects. Memories of the life Nora lived in Del Norte danced about. The town she left behind was where she had chosen for final resting. The San Luis Valley, South Fork and Del Norte would always be a huge part of Nora's life and history. For those who knew and loved Nora, the valley would always speak of her.

At one point the chapel was quiet when Teddy walked in to find a lone man standing at the casket. Unbeknownst to the man, Teddy sat curiously, quietly, and observed for several minutes. The man finally spoke.

"If this woman doesn't open the gates to heaven, I don't know what will!" he said, throwing his arms in the air and walking away not saying another word.

Teddy didn't recognize the man, but obviously he had known Nora and her life. He observed as the gentleman left the chapel. After the man left, Teddy sat with a pad in his hand writing. There he sat for an hour or so, alone with Nora and his pad in the chapel. His heart was shattered beyond repair, but there was a contentedness about him as well. In the soft glow around the casket adorned with photographs and mementos from loved ones,

Nora looked as beautiful as ever. The soft light glimmered off the sequins of her dress. The vision froze forever in Teddy's mind.

That night, family members stood one by one to speak of Nora as they gathered in the chapel. Crowded with family and friends, there was standing room only. Emotions were aired, many tears shed. What Teddy had written while sitting with Nora was read by his friend Randy. He couldn't compose himself well enough to do it.

The next morning at Nora's services, a female pastor spoke of Nora and her legacy. Granddaughter Becky, a gifted musician and writer, sang Nora's favorite song *"Downtown"* that day and forever brought to life memories of Nora. For many in Nora's family, *"Downtown"* would always be reminiscence of her. Wherever they heard the song Nora would be vividly remembered.

Following the services, family and friends gathered at the grave site. It was cold as usual – the air frozen in an arctic mist. The lead singer in the Challengers, a good friend of Nora's, along with some of his family members played guitars and sang. He shed tears at singing the emotional *"Madre Querida."* He, too, took Nora's passing hard. He had known her for decades and formed a lasting friendship.

Following the music and ceremony, Nora's body was lowered into the ground for final resting. Teddy applauded her trials and tribulations, joys and sorrows, her achievements and most of all for being simply Nora.

Nora's family left the graveyard, the void in their lives overwhelming. Life would never be the same. For them, Del Norte and South Fork always held special memories of her. For many of Nora's children, the San Luis Valley, especially Del Norte and South Fork, were home, no matter where they lived.

In the years and decades that followed, Nora's family legacy grew even more, to nearly five hundred grandchildren, great-grandchildren, great-great-grandchildren and great-great-great grandchildren. It continues to grow.

Teddy took time to pair up all of his mother's jewelry, matching the earrings with necklaces and bracelets and placing them in baggies. He ended up with a collection of more than five hundred sets, and then distributed them among his sisters as Nora wanted.

And Nora's treasured trunk he once boyishly painted and later was bequeathed to him by his mom? He has it to this day. It is the most prized and special of his possessions.

Made in the
USA
Middletown, DE